HOW NOT TO GROW UP!

A Coming of Age Memoir. Sort of.

RICHARD HERRING

EBURY
PRESS

3 5 7 9 10 8 6 4

First published in 2011 by Ebury Press, an imprint of Ebury Publishing
A Random House Group company
First published in the UK by Ebury Press in 2010
This edition published 2011

The Random House Group Limited Reg. No. 954009

Addresses for companies within the Random House Group can be found
at www.randomhouse.co.uk

A CIP catalogue record for this book is available from the British Library

Penguin Random House is committed to a sustainable future for
our business, our readers and our planet. This book is made from
Forest Stewardship Council® certified paper.

Printed and bound in Great Britain by Clays Ltd, St Ives plc

Designed and set by seagulls.net

ISBN 9780091932091

To buy books by your favourite authors and register for offers visit
www.rbooks.co.uk

For Catherine,
Hope you build your pyramid.

INTRODUCTION

My name's Richard and I am immature.

I have been ever since I was a small child.

And that's fine when you're four – the world expects puerility in children, even if it still seems wearily disappointed when it occurs. But when you're almost ten times that age you're not supposed to spend your time, as I seemed to be doing, playing video games, eating Monster Munch, giggling at farts and drawing ejaculating penises in the condensation on windows.

When you're 40, you're supposed to be responsible, capable, sensible and married with kids.

Yet here I was, about to reach the age where life supposedly begins and I was irresponsible, incapable and insensible. I was single and the only thing that depended on me was my rubber plant.

Which had died.

The last proper office job I had had was nearly eighteen years ago in 1989 when I had helped compile the west London phone book. Although I did spend most of my time there looking up people with rude names on the ex-directory list on the computer. My favourites were the entirely genuine Mr Cunto and Dr Wank. Why wouldn't they want to be in the phone book like everyone else? My greatest achievement was to successfully change the listing for my flatmate at the time from 'Stewart Lee' to 'Stewart Wee'. I was and still am genuinely proud of that. I can't imagine why I only lasted three weeks in the position.

So how had I survived the intervening two decades, with such a juvenile attitude and the lack of income that must surely inevitably follow?

I was a stand-up comedian.

I made a living writing cock jokes and saying them in front of drunk and braying crowds, appearing on TV sketch shows, which amounts to basically playing with the dressing-up box, and writing the occasional expletive-filled sitcom script.

And it was, on the whole, a good living. I had a house in an unfashionable part of west London, though in the five years I had lived there had been too lethargic and incompetent to decorate or improve it. Takeaway and microwave meal cartons littered the floor (I didn't know how to cook), a big damp patch on the wall of my kitchen got damper and remained untreated (I didn't have any DIY skills), the stairs up to my bedroom were in total darkness. Ironically, for a comedian fond of asking how many people it took to change a light bulb, I scarcely knew how to do so myself. Or was at least too lazy to bother. I could feel my way up in the gloom.

My job gave me the freedom and the licence, and possibly the actual necessity, to behave like a child, allowing me to travel the world, sleep in, sleep around, never settle down. I was like Tom Hanks in the film *Big* in every aspect except that there was no way or imperative for me to physically return to my thirteen-year-old form.

If I stopped and thought about it, my life seemed pathetic, so generally I didn't stop and think about it.

But there was an iceberg on the horizon and the pleasure cruiser that was my charmed and ludicrous life was heading right for it. I was making no attempt to change course. If I ignored it, it would surely go away.

We were about to find out what happened when an immature force meets an immovable object.

So this is the story of the year I turned 40.

It was a year of turmoil, of changes, of madness and of magic, a year in which I tried to ignore my troubles and my solipsism, like an ostrich with its head up its own arse, then to deny my problems, then run away from them and ultimately to face them. It was a year I had to decide what it meant to be grown up and then to decide if I wanted to bother. I had to think about who I was, what I was doing and whether I could and should keep on doing it.

It was a year where my life impacted on the lives of a lot of other people, many of whom would not want their part in my sordid antics to be made public, so I have changed names and some details in order to protect the innocent (and the guilty). Some of the people I met briefly and when drunk and can't actually remember what they were called, so I've just made up names for them anyway. There's a chance that I might accidentally have chosen their actual names. But what better alias could there be in the circumstances?

I apologise to those who might not have wanted their stories told, but feel that more likely I will need to apologise to those who played a part in the year but are not mentioned in the book. It was, as you'll now see, a very busy and confusing time for me.

It was the best of times, it was the worst of times, but it was ultimately the most ridiculous of times. And it's that which makes it such a good story. Dickens didn't know squat.

CONVERSATION 1

I love kids.

That's a sentence that an unmarried, childless, middle-aged man isn't really allowed to utter in this day and age for fear of being chased out of his home by an angry mob of idiots who've already banished the local paediatrician. But I don't care. I do love kids and I don't think there's anything wrong with that and so believe we should come up with some harmless Greek word to describe this innocent affection. Paedo means child and phile is the suffix generally used to indicate love of something and so if we put that together...

Let's start again. I think kids are great and I seem to generally get on well with them. They nearly always make a beeline for me when I am around them and force me to get involved in whatever they're doing. It's probably because they instantly spot that, despite my adult appearance, I am a child like them. Just like a dog will always recognise another dog, no matter how disparate the breed, a kid will know a kid in whatever body he's hiding. Sometimes I feel that it's only the children who really understand me. I am like Michael Jackson in that respect... Oh dear, this is getting worse.

Just as the momentous year in which I would turn 40 was beginning I went round to my new girlfriend Sarah-Jane's house to meet her two-and-a-half-year-old son, Buster, for the first time. It was a big moment. Sarah-Jane and I had only been dating for a couple of weeks and this was a massive test. What would I make of him? What would he make of me?

'When you get here just ignore Buster,' Sarah-Jane had warned me. 'He isn't really good with new people and you don't want to overwhelm him. Let him come to you when he's ready.'

'Honestly, you don't have to worry,' I told her, hubristically tempting fate. 'Kids love me. Pretty much all of them. The

occasional Damien will treat me with scorn, but I am like the Pied Piper, but without a pipe or, you know, the unfortunate consequences for the children...'

Sarah-Jane looked at me for a second with a slight trace of worry on her face. She didn't always seem to understand when I was joking.

'Look, it'll probably take at least a couple of visits for him to get used to you. So don't take it personally.'

It went against all my instincts. I like to clown and gurn and charm kids with my stupidity. Children are the purest comedy audience. If they find you funny they will laugh, but if they don't they will stare at you like you are the most miserable and pathetic wretch on earth. Polite laughter is not something that they are capable of.

But I respected Sarah-Jane's wishes and after the briefest of hellos I sat quietly on the sofa while she went into the kitchen to make a cup of tea. Buster got on with playing with his toys as I tried my utmost not to draw attention to myself or pull even a slightly amusing grimace or smirk. I wasn't entirely successful and Buster spotted the child within me struggling to escape the confines of adult society and looked at me quizzically.

He wasn't yet sure about me. He was sizing me up. Working out if I was someone worthy of being his friend. Or just a gigantic idiot. Or maybe both.

And I wasn't being needy. I had lots of friends already. I wasn't going to beg.

After a few more moments of considered silence, he approached me with a chunky yellow toy digger with a cartoon face and said, 'Look at this!'

Puffing his chest up with pride, he pressed a button and the digger spoke. 'I can dig it!' it exclaimed.

'Ah, very impressive,' I commented. 'I particularly enjoy the double meaning of the word dig, indicating both the function of the vehicle, but also that the vehicle is capable of enjoying that function.'

Buster stared at me for a second: it wasn't quite the full disdainful dismissal, but the comedy jury in his brain was certainly still out.

'He's called Scoop!' he deadpanned with innate comic timing.

'Very apt,' I replied. 'Hello, Scoooop!' I enjoyed elongating the name and alternating my pitch as the suddenly silly-sounding word whistled from my mouth.

Buster let out a little shriek of delight – I had found his comedic level. He pressed the button again.

'Can we fix it?' asked Scoop.

'Yes we can!' said Buster and me together.

Although I have no kids, I often wake up at 6.30am with a hangover and the only way to get myself back to sleep is to watch children's television for a couple of hours. Bob the Builder is not my favourite – his antics can be a little childish for my liking – but I am aware of his oeuvre.

Buster was impressed and delighted. The coincidence that we both knew the catchphrase was enough for him. We could be friends.

He now wanted to show me his remote-control Thomas the Tank Engine. I sensed that Scoop was for everyone, out there in the shop window – a tester – but Thomas, he was only for the elite inner circle.

'That is completely brilliant,' I told him. But he didn't need telling. He gave me a nod that said he knew. I knew enough not to even ask if I could have a go. Thomas was Buster's and Buster's alone. To be an observer of his awesome ability to move across the carpet, apparently unaided, was enough for me.

Sarah-Jane returned to find Buster leaning against me as we laughed together. She gave me a surprised and impressed look. I returned with one that clearly said, 'You doubted my powers?'

Sarah-Jane found a plastic spider in Buster's toy basket and put it on his head. He threw up his hands in mock panic and ran away screaming. We all laughed. I picked up the spider and got into a play struggle with it. It was making for my face, I was trying to push it away, but the spider was too strong.

'He's biting me in the face! Aaargh!' I shouted.

Buster laughed, a full and joyful guffaw.

'Don't just laugh at me. He'll eat me alive. Help me!'

But now Buster wasn't quite sure if the spider was dangerous or not. It had, after all, overpowered me.

'Be careful,' I warned him. 'I think this is one of those South American leaping spiders. There's no way of knowing where he'll go next... BOIING!'

The spider leapt away from my neck towards Buster. Buster laughed and screamed. We were having fun. We made the spider leap back and forth between us, boiinging for all we were worth. We'd throw it up in the air and then Buster would have to find it wherever it landed.

'Where's it gone?' I'd ask and Buster would search.

The expensive toys had occupied the lad's attention for maybe three minutes, but the tiny plastic spider, that must have cost at most 20p, kept him entertained for approaching an hour. Even after he had gone off for a bath, when he came back he still wanted to play with the spider. The fun had no sign of abating and the only way to stop this exhausting cycle of spider throwing and searching was for me to surreptitiously hide the toy. The child continued his search in vain, not knowing the fake arachnid was up my shirt.

But he was so desperate to see his friend again that I couldn't keep it from him for ever. 'Maybe he has crept into your belly button,' I suggested. And bless him, he had a little check to see.

I too checked my own belly button and indeed the spider had made my navel his residence and so the relentless game continued again and our fledgling friendship was sealed.

I liked his commitment and his joie de vivre. Throwing a plastic spider around a room for an hour or so is what life is all about. At least being able to enjoy such an activity without qualification and without becoming bored is what makes kids great. And that's why I love them.

And if that makes you want to rip me limb from limb then that's your problem.

More importantly I had passed the test. My girlfriend's son liked me. My girlfriend seemed to like me even more. As I sat cuddling them both on the sofa, I felt like part of a family. And I felt happy. At the age of 39 and a half, maybe at last I was growing up.

Act your age, not your shoe size...
That means something different on the continent.

CHAPTER 1
FIIIGHT!

11 June 2007 – 31 days to 40

What the fuck was I doing?

This wasn't like me.

Some feral force had taken over my body and filled with indignant fury I was heading with unbreakable resolve towards the object of my rage. All reason had been paralysed by a potent fog of adrenalin mixed with alcohol. Pure animal instinct was controlling my actions now; I was a cougar about to pounce on my prey; I was a Viking berserker screeching into battle; I was a mindless zombie infected with a monkey virus about to chase down my latest victim, rip off his limbs and then gnaw on the bones with my unfocused red eyes staring off into the middle distance as his blood spurted all over my face.

With no thought for the consequences, I was intent on the destruction of a man I barely knew.

His friends tried to block my path.

'No!' I screamed, as I pushed them aside. 'He hit me in the fucking head, I'm going to hit him in the fucking head as well!'

This wasn't like me at all.

It was only when I got to where he was standing that some remote portion of my brain still connected to reality remembered that I don't really have any idea how to fight. I'm a lover, not a fighter. And I have to be honest with you, I'm not much of a lover.

But I'm an even worse fighter.

However, it was just a feeble voice trying to make itself heard over a crowd of furiously firing neurons urging me onwards. Subconscious intuition had got me this far. Surely it would carry me through?

Why was I behaving in this awful way? I don't get into fights. I flee from the merest whiff of trouble. I am an expert in the studious examination of my shoes at times of even mild peril. Why was I voluntarily embroiling myself in this unnecessary contretemps?

All that was certain was that I wasn't myself. This wasn't the kind of thing I'd usually do.

In fact, I could count the number of fights I've had in my 39 years and eleven months on this planet (excluding the regular drubbings from my older brother – domestics don't count) on the fingers of one of my weakly clenched fists – though whether any of them really qualify as 'fights' is possibly open to question.

Fight 1 – 1977. Jackie Nixon. Lost.

Yeah, OK, Jackie is a girl's name. My first fight was against a girl. And I lost. But I was ten and she was twelve and a good foot taller than me and fierce and wiry while I was soft and podgy. I can't remember what precipitated her assault on my person, during lunch break, but I seem to recall her fists descending, the sweat flying off her furrowed brow, her long hair swinging with her punches. Or maybe I'm confusing the incident with a scene from *Raging Bull*. The other kids barely had time to gather round and chant, 'Fight! Fight! Fight!' before a hard blow on the nose incapacitated me. A Jasper arrived – this is the name that Somerset schoolchildren used to give to both wasps and dinner ladies. In this case it was the latter. Don't you love that imagery? Those occasionally mean-spirited, spiky denizens of the playground do indeed seem to swarm around in random swirls, before spotting their target and swooping in for the kill. She broke up the one-sided battle and grabbed me by my collar and escorted me to the boys' toilets. I could feel something warm and sticky dribbling from my nose, and the kids we passed were frozen where they stood, mouths agape with horror. I assumed that Jackie had bloodied my nose and felt strangely proud and manly. I was displaying a battle scar, a badge of bravery. It was only when I got to the sink and looked in the mirror that I realised that the substance emanating from my nasal passage was a long string of viscous snot.

My humiliation was complete.

Fight 2 – 1978. Kevin Nixon. Moral victory. Actual loss.

Kevin Nixon was Jackie's younger brother. I don't know what their family had against mine, perhaps some ancient vendetta stretching back through generations, of which no one could any longer recall the provenance. Yet pride and unjustified anger still fanned the flames of a forgotten blood feud. Or maybe the Nixons just liked beating the snot out of anything that chanced across their path.

Who am I kidding? I was a swotty, clever-clever little creep with shiny shoes and my tie done up properly from a respectable middle-class family who loved me. If there had been any tracks in Cheddar in the 1970s then the Nixons would have been from the wrong side of them. I don't know what their exact circumstances were, but it's clear that they had none of the advantages that I had been lucky enough to acquire simply by having plopped out of the right vagina. Our lives were mapped out and it was clear to the Nixon siblings in which direction we were separately heading.

As with Jackie, I failed to land a single punch, but this time that was a deliberate choice.

I was enjoying the summer sunshine on the school fields and minding my own business, when apropos of nothing, Kevin Nixon ran at me from behind, then jumped up and gave me a tremendous flying kick in the back.

This time I retained my dignity and my bodily fluids and simply carried on walking, trying to pretend that nothing had happened. This behaviour aggravated Nixon even more. He executed another run-up, leapt and kung-fu kicked me in the spine. I can't say this didn't hurt, because it really did. But I wasn't going to be beaten by him. 'What was that?' I asked in a loud voice, so that Kevin and his gawping cronies could all hear. 'Did a fly land on my back?'

I have to say I am pretty impressed with my coolness even today. Kevin wasn't though. He was enraged. He took a longer run-up and again lunged at me, even harder than before.

Still I retained my composure, despite the pain of the assault. 'There he is again, I think. I'm not sure if I felt anything or not.'

This violent pantomime continued for maybe five or six more kicks. But I refused to rise to his bait. I didn't turn and fight, I didn't fall down and cry. I just carried on walking around in a strange figure-of-eight pattern.

I don't think it would be hyperbole to say that what I was doing was more impressive than anything Gandhi ever achieved with similar tactics.

Kevin Nixon was trying to provoke me to turn and fight, but I did not rise to the bait. Eventually, I like to imagine, exhausted from the Herculean exertion, he gave up. Despite all his efforts I had remained totally unaffected. He left with his gang to find someone else to torment. Someone who would give him the satisfaction of trying to defend themselves or squealing like a baby. He had been defeated. I had won.

Or I would have done had the shock of what had happened not then hit me. I went over to a grassy bank and sat down and cried the tears that I had manfully been holding back.

Later, Dave 'Tom' Shrewsbury, who was the hard boy in our tutor group, came up to me and said, 'The lads were very impressed with the way you stood up to Nixon today. That was very brave. You did well... but you still went off and blubbed afterwards, didn't you? We all saw.' He pulled a face that indicated that all their admiration had evaporated along with my first tear.

---

1. Interestingly, all the bad lads followed the convention of being addressed by their father's first name – thank God I was one of the goody-goodies or I'd have been known as Keith.

So my moral victory morphed into defeat. And Kevin Nixon got the chance to feel superior to me for a few minutes, which is all that this was about, and in a childhood where I had been dealt all the aces and he'd got the jokers and the instructions for playing bridge, I can't begrudge him that.

Fight 3 – 1991. Unnamed assailant. Total defeat.

After a hard day of work writing at Broadcasting House for some long-forgotten radio show, I was enjoying an alfresco pint with my work colleagues. A woman I was hoping to have sex with made a crap joke about René Descartes, and I pretended to find it amusing – as I say, I was hoping to have sex with her. As I laughed I threw back my head in what I took to be an alluring manner. I happened to catch the eye of a gigantic drunk man, some ten feet away, who was in the process of slamming his fist into the face of his smaller, but equally drunk, companion.

'What are you fucking looking at?' he slurred as his 'friend' slid down the wall.

There is no way to answer this question and remain undamaged, but I was young and so stupidly gave the worst wrong answer: 'Nothing.'

'You think it's funny, me hitting my pal?' he continued, walking towards me, leaving this person that he was so friendly with slumped unconscious on the floor.

'No, I was laughing at something my friend said,' I replied, the register of my voice rising from baritone to falsetto in the space of nine words. Was it worth trying to explain the unfunny gag about a dead French philosopher or my base motivations for pretending to enjoy it?

'Because I don't think it's funny,' he growled, ignoring my protests which were, in any case, now in so high a voice that they could only be heard by bats.

I would have run, but I was sitting on one of those picnic tables where the seat is fixed and your legs are penned in, making it impossible to extricate yourself in an emergency situation.

Unless there is a gigantic, furious alcoholic on hand to grab you by the hair and pull you to the floor. Before I understood what was happening, I was supine on the dirty, cigarette-butt-strewn paving stones, with a large boot crashing into my temple – the head's Achilles heel (I am more or less a reverse Achilles and will crumple wherever I am struck, although my heel is impervious).

The man picked up an empty glass and raised it above his head with the clear intention to bring it smashing down on my blubbering face, when a brave and diminutive PA called Ellie jumped to her feet and held on to his arm and somehow prevented him from leaving me scarred or blind or worse. Even more impressively, despite being approximately two feet shorter than him, using nothing but the power of shouting she managed to convince him to stop attacking me and leave. If I am not being beaten up by a girl, then they are coming to my defence.

On the bright side, the woman who told the rubbish joke felt so guilty that we ended up having sex that very night, though I don't remember much about it and my head was aching and I was worried that if I fell asleep I would never wake up. But the point is that laughing at ineffectual, intellectual jokes does indirectly get you laid. If you are prepared to risk death to achieve your goal.

Fight 4 – 1994. Drunk fan'. Victory!

Pretty much every August since the late 1980s I have made the annual pilgrimage to the greatest arts festival in the world, the Edinburgh Fringe, where every church hall, gymnasium and broom cupboard becomes a venue. It's a vital shop window for the comedy industry, but more importantly, from my point of view, it is a month-long party, where there are plenty of opportunities to drink into the early hours and meet women, with the occasional inconvenience of having to perform a show.

One of the major venues, the Pleasance Theatre, has a large courtyard, which on those rare days when it isn't raining is the ideal alfresco congregation point for punters and performers alike. This night I was there with some friends from my schooldays who had come up to see me perform. We were talking with some young women that we had just met and having quite a jolly time. Things were looking promising. Then a fairly drunk, smiling man swaggered up to me.

'Hello,' he interrupted. 'I have to apologise to you.'

'Why's that?' I asked.

'I met you here last year and I called you a cunt! Sorry, I was drunk.'

'Oh right,' I said, mildly surprised yet amused. 'Don't worry, I don't remember!'

'Well, just wanted to say sorry,' he replied, although that was a lie as he then hung around to chat some more. I didn't particularly mind though. I am usually up for chatting with strangers. Even if they have compared me to female genitalia for unspecified reasons in the last twelve months.

So the bloke joined in with our conversation, which may seem weird, but it was the Edinburgh Fringe, where much stranger things happen and I felt I was being magnanimous by allowing the man who had insulted me back into the fold. Sort of like Jesus. Only less show-offy about it.

However, after an hour had passed, in which he had drunk more and more on top of the skinful he had had already and then begun making inappropriate and lewd remarks to the girls, I thought it was time to bring things to a conclusion. 'Look, mate,' I said in as friendly a manner as I could muster, 'it's been lovely to meet you, but I am here with some mates from school that I haven't seen for a long time and we don't know you. Maybe it's time for you to go back to your own friends now.'

All right, I'll admit it, perhaps there was a little bit of edge in my voice and an awareness that the man was almost certainly here on his own, hence his latching on to us. He stared back at me, dumb-struck, but instantaneously seething. He didn't leave.

'It's just I think you're a bit drunker than us and I've talked to you for over an hour and I'd like to talk to my friends now, so…'

He carried on staring, fury visibly boiling up in his alcohol-addled head.

'I was right about you last year,' he said, breaking his silence. 'You *are* a cunt!'

'I'm not a cunt,' I countered. 'I don't know you at all and yet I have talked to you for a long time, which most people wouldn't have done, especially after you admitted having been rude to them before, but now you're being rude to my friends and I think it's time for you to go.'

The girls we were with were already freaking out a bit at this stand-off. There was clearly violence in the air and they had assumed that this bloke was a friend of mine. Suddenly a gay evening was turning sour. The staring continued and I was steeling myself for worse to come, but the man then walked away.

Everyone breathed a sigh of relief and I explained to the confused women that I did not know the man and apologised for both the things he had been saying and the situation that had developed. Maybe the evening hadn't been derailed after all.

But about ten minutes later the man came back, holding a pint glass. He circled the group, saying his goodbyes and remarking on how nice it had been to meet each person. Finally he got to me and said, 'And as for you…' before pouring the contents of the glass all over my head.

The liquid was warm and within a nano-second I arrived at the obvious conclusion that the glass contained urine. That would explain the luke-warm temperature, as well as the time it had taken him to fill the receptacle. Also fresh in my mind was a story of how fellow comedian Arthur Smith had had piss thrown at him by an aggrieved punter. Uric-acid-based vengeance seemed the obvious explanation.

I don't know what he expected to happen next. Sometimes in films a bad man gets a bucket of something wet thrown over him and he just stands there, dripping, making funny kind of spluttering, surprised noises, holding out his arms in disbelief. But in reality if you assault someone, especially with your own bodily fluids, they are much more likely to attack you.

Which is what I did.

I don't remember much about it. The red mist descended. And the next thing I knew I was about twenty feet away with this sozzled scumbug in a headlock aiming weak punches at his head. Most of which were still missing despite the proximity of the target.

'Stop it!' whined the piss-flinger, still holding the empty pint pot, not having the wits of the assailant from Fight 3 to think of smashing it into my skull.

'You poured piss over my head!' I bellowed.

'It wasn't piss, it was water!' he shrieked pathetically. He must have filled it up from the sink in the toilets. The cold tap there is never cold, just as the hot tap is rarely hot.

Although this made a difference, it didn't make that much of a difference. It was still extremely annoying and inconvenient and wet and my only real crime had been to be hospitable to someone who had done nothing to deserve hospitality and done everything to deserve hospitalisation.

There was no danger of that. The few punches that had landed on his now pathetic visage were ineffectual and my oldest friend Phil Fry managed to drag us apart within seconds. My thwarted nemesis skulked off into the night, while we returned to our drinks.

Any atmosphere of fun or romance that had once existed had dissipated and the girls, appalled, no doubt, at the Jekyll and Hyde style transformation that they had just witnessed, quickly made their excuses and left.

At least when I lost the previous fight I ended up with the girl. This was a victory that would leave Pyrrhus quite smug about the way things had turned out for him.

Fight 5 – 1996. Stewart Lee. Lost.

I met Stewart Lee (future co-author of *Jerry Springer the Opera*, world-class stand-up comedian and west London phone book 1990's 'Stewart Wee') at university in 1986 and we quickly formed a friendship and began writing and performing comedy together. It was a partnership that would last until 1999, by which time we were a cult double act with four BBC2 series under our belts. But it took a lot of work to get there. We spent practically the entire 1990s together, six days a week for up to sixteen hours a day, most of the time caged up in cramped offices and claustrophobic tour vans. However much we liked each other, this was bound to lead to tension.

If you put Jesus and Mother Teresa in a similar situation then there would come a point where he was punching her in her walnut face and she was pulling down on his crown of thorns or gouging her fingers into his stigmata.

Thinking about it, it seems remarkable that we only came to blows once in all that time. Although we shared a sense of humour, we were very different personality types: him cool, aloof, serious with an impatient inability to suffer fools, me socially awkward, loquacious, needy, annoying and, pertinently, a fool.

Plus we were in our twenties and still both similarly sure of ourselves, equally convinced that any issue, however trivial, was worth arguing to the death until we were proven right, as yet unable to understand that our every word and action was not, as we believed then, of the utmost significance and importance to the world. Healthily we were also too repressed and childish to openly discuss any of the problems that there might have been between us, preferring to bottle them up and leave them to fester and ferment in the basement, next to those powder kegs we were storing. What could possibly go wrong?

But we weren't brutes. We didn't *fight*. The way we got through it was to argue and bicker, badger and psychologically torture each other, and to use it to fuel our on-stage dynamic. Much more civilised. I admit I would sometimes have wonderful dreams where I was punching him in his smug, leonine face, my fists like steaming jackhammers, over and over again, but I never imagined that we would actually come to blows.

Instead we'd spend half a day vociferously debating whether the word 'a' or 'the' would be funnier in the sentence we were working on, which I now realise was our repressed way of letting off steam. Subconsciously we must surely have known it wouldn't make a blind bit of difference to the joke. Or should that be *the* blindest bit of difference? Which would you say was funnier? Come on, it's *important*!

On the day of the melee, we were in our office doing some separate writing work before heading out to do a gig somewhere out of town that night. Stewart was at the time trying to lose weight and had been prescribed some diet pills by a doctor who specialised in such murky areas of medicine. I'm not sure he lost any weight, but it did temporarily shave off the sparse amount of forbearance that he was naturally blessed with. I think to be fair, the drugs must take responsibility for thawing what would always otherwise have been a constant cold war. Or maybe they were just a convenient excuse for Lee to make his own dreams come true.

Prosaically enough, Stewart was struggling on his computer, having a formatting problem with an article he needed to finish within the hour and was getting frustrated and angry. I offered to help him sort it out, but when I wasn't immediately able to rectify the problem he grouchily told me to get away and leave his computer alone. I said, 'Oh, fuck off, I was just trying to help,' and petulantly kicked his chair. In normal circumstances he'd have shouted swear words back at me and that would have been the end of it.

But this time Stewart got up, his eyes unfocused and blazing with fury, his head buzzing, his reason clouded, his stomach growling from hunger. He strode purposefully towards me. Confused by this unexpected reaction, I backed away, holding up my palms. I didn't want any trouble. But Stewart would, it seemed from his countenance, only be appeased by my death.

Luckily he was only a little better at fighting than I was and as he tried to punch me I grabbed hold of his hands and we pushed at each other so we resembled crap and crapulous dancers rather than street fighters. When the one opportunity came to make my dreams come true, my jackhammers were nowhere to be seen. My hands were sponges, intent on defence.

Despite my attempts to placate him, Stewart was a man on a mission and managed to overpower me, pushing me to the floor.

As I fell, the back of my head caught the edge of a desk and I felt the sting of an abrasion. Lee was on top of me.

A woman rushed in from the next office down the hall and pulled us apart. For a moment I was stunned by what had just happened, doubted it was even real, then I put my fingers in my wounds, felt my own sticky blood and, like Thomas, I believed. Unlike Thomas, my next action was to attempt to kick the man in front of me in the balls.

True to form I completely missed my target and with my sponge-handed guard down, Stewart got in a couple of proper punches before the perky PA managed to get between us again.

I stormed out of the office, having resolved that the partnership was over: we would never work together again. But that night, tempers having cooled and things back in perspective, we found ourselves waiting in the wings at the gig. After an uncomfortable, embarrassed silence, Stewart apologised for what had happened. 'I think we're allowed one fight every ten years,' I said, smiling.

Beneath it all we were and still are great friends, who had been through a lot together and who actually had, I hope, a great deal of respect for each other. And we got on very well most of the time. I don't think I have ever laughed as much with any other human being.

It would still have been satisfying to have got one good punch in, though.

So after five fights I had won one and lost four. Not an impressive record by any standards. In 20 per cent of these encounters my opponent was female and in an embarrassing 60 per cent a woman came to my rescue.

And while I had been on the ground at least twice, been bruised, suffered mild concussion and been drenched in water, blood and my own nasal effluent, I had never once executed a punch or a kick that had done another human being any harm whatsoever. Even when I won, the defeated party had walked away without a scratch on him, while I was soaked to the skin.

All this does make me feel like rather an ineffectual example of manhood. Surely I have harmed someone or something at some time in my life.

Oh yes! I did once smash Steven West's front teeth out when I was playing hockey at school. But this was an accident, caused by sporting incompetence, and I sensibly spent the rest of my schooldays hiding from him. Because tellingly, even though he was only fourteen, the teeth I knocked out were false. He'd had his real front teeth knocked out already. Plus he had once inadvertently set himself on fire when he'd thrown paraffin on a bonfire. You probably couldn't think of a worse person to smack in the mouth.

And the fact that my weapon was a hockey stick – the plaything of a schoolgirl – pretty much says it all.

Surely, if life had taught me anything, it was that I shouldn't get into any more fights. Indeed, I had got through almost my entire thirties without confrontation, using a blend of cowardice and simpering, blubbering apology.

So given this history, why was I now striding towards a man who was fifteen years my junior and a good six inches taller than me, my hand already clenched into a fist, intent on pummelling his face until it was just a bloody mass of sinew and broken bone? What on earth had motivated this unlikely and (if the form book was anything to go by) inadvisable aggression?

I get knocked down, but I get up again, you're never going to keep me down! I get knocked down, but I get up again, you're never going to keep me down! I get knocked down, but I get up again, you're never going to keep me down! I get knocked down, but this time I stay down. I'm clearly losing here and am in danger of getting a head injury. No need to be a dick about it.

CHAPTER 2
FIGHT 6

11 June 2007 – 31 days to 40

'How's the tour been going?' my mum had asked during our weekly phone conversation that morning.

'Good,' I told her. 'The show's been going really well.'

'Where are you tonight?'

'Liverpool! Last night of the tour.'

'Oh, you'll be glad of that, won't you? How many jigs have you done on this one?'

'They're called gigs, Mum. It's been about 50 nights.'

'Goodness! Fifty?' But her mind was elsewhere. 'You're not driving home tonight, are you?'

'No, I'm staying in a hotel.'

'Good, I worry about you driving around in the middle of the night.'

'I'm 39 years old.'

'Don't go out and get drunk, either.'

'I'll do what I want. I'm 39 years old!'

'Not that anyone would know from the way you carry on.'

'Muu-um,' I said, very much like a petulant teenager would have done, as if to prove her point.

'I just worry about you,' she said with the unique warmth that only a mother can radiate. There was the slightest pause and then with just the tiniest weight behind the question she asked, 'Are you happy?'

How was I meant to answer that question? What could I say to a mother who already worried that I was about to drive over a cliff every time I got into a car? If I was honest I'd say, 'No, Mum, I'm not. I'm pretty unhappy just now. I've been out on the road for the last two months, playing the country's most medium-sized theatres, with a schedule that seems to have been organised by someone who has no map or sense of geography. So I've been in Aberdeen on Monday, then Derby on Tuesday, then back up to Edinburgh for Wednesday. I'm driving myself and have no tour manager or support act or any meaningful company. It's as lonely as hell and I am exhausted. I broke up with Sarah-Jane just before the tour began, even though we both still really care about each other, because we knew we were too different to make it work. And I've been missing her and Buster and they're missing me. Sarah-Jane told me on the phone that he was holding up his toy spider and plaintively asking, "Where's Rich?", and it made me openly and uncontrollably weep in a service station restaurant. I've had one or two drunken sexual encounters with strangers in strange towns, in the hope that that might make me less depressed, but it just makes things worse. And I'm a month off my 40th fucking birthday, which frankly speaking sucks a big dog's cock.'

But instead I said, 'Yes, yes, I'm fine.'

'Are you sure?'

Luckily I was rescued from further interrogation because at that point my buffoon of a dad came into the kitchen, where Mum was busily making his tea.

'Who's that?' he asked.

'It's your youngest son,' my mum replied.

'Ah, Richard! Richy-boy! Ricardo! How you doing, old boy?' he bellowed from a distance and I could imagine the way he was clowning around and gurning as he did so (partly because it was exactly the way that I would clown around and gurn myself, much as I hate to acknowledge that). He then cried, 'So... are you famous yet?'

This was my dad's little joke. He had been asking this pretty much every week for the last two decades. My parents have always been very supportive of my unusual career choice, but that does not mean that they don't take every opportunity possible to point out that I wasn't as successful as I might have hoped or, if I am being fairer to them, as they, as doting parents, believed I should be.

'No, not yet,' I said wearily and Mum relayed the usual message.

'You need me as your manager,' he chirruped. Again, this was part of the weekly script, but it wasn't exactly a joke. He genuinely felt that he, a 70-year-old retired headmaster with no experience of the entertainment industry, would be better able to guide my career than the hugely successful professional agency I currently employed.

My parents had been to see the Taunton show (the nearest gig to Cheddar in Somerset where I had grown up and they still lived) and Dad had been a bit dismayed about how few people had turned up to see me. He had then been doubly perplexed when I told him how much I had been paid.

'Oh dear,' he had said, his natural sense of decency and fairness coming to life. 'The theatre will have made a terrible loss tonight. You shouldn't charge so much. You should give some of that money back.'

Call me crazy, but I didn't really want to employ a manager who was trying to get me less cash.

'Shut up, Keith,' my mum said, with her hand inexpertly over the receiver. 'I think he's a bit down.'

Should I tell her how I was really feeling?

'Anyway, look,' I told my mum on the phone, 'I've got to go. It's a long drive.'

'Oh, do drive carefully,' she fussed, filled with palpable dread.

'Oh, thanks for that advice. I was going to drive really dangerously, but you've made me reconsider my insane plan.'

'Yes, yes... Ha ha,' she said mirthlessly. 'You should be a comedian... I love you.'

'Bye, Mum. Say bye to the old duffer for me.'

The tour had been more fun than I had perhaps suggested in that emotional moment on the phone, but I was still very glad that the end was nigh. Life on the road is intense and sometimes it gets to you.

I think people must imagine that stand-ups have the most wonderful and gregarious of lives: working for an hour a day, then getting pissed, taking the finest drugs and sleeping with a string of nubile groupies. But in reality this kind of thing only happens about 97 per cent of the time. And it doesn't make up for that yawning three per cent chasm in which we are a secluded breed of unloved outcasts. If a gig goes badly, there is the mortifying walk of shame, through the throng of disappointed punters, before you are swallowed by the night and make your way anonymously back to your hotel, where you sit alone in your room attempting to pleasure yourself to the poor-quality soft pornography laid on for sexually unambitious businessmen.

If the gig goes brilliantly, it is even worse. You have wowed a room of people; you are literally a god to them. But when you return to their earthly realm, real life seems monochrome by comparison. The company of such tedious mortals is not something that you crave. So you head to your hotel alone again, contemplating the fact that the fleeting adoration of a room of drunken idiots is probably no substitute for the true love of a faithful wife or the unconditional devotion of a tiny child. So you drink yourself into oblivion before inevitably tuning into *Lusty Asians VIII*, even though you haven't seen *Lusty Asians VII* and are worried you might have missed some important plot developments.

I was mainly just very tired and was looking forward to celebrating having finally finished this, as it turned out, aptly titled show, *ménage à un*.

The show in part dealt with my failure to procure a threesome in my four decades of life (though to be honest I hadn't really been trying that hard for the first seven years). I had assumed that if I went round the country essentially using my time on stage to beg women in the audience to go along with it, then statistically speaking one time in 50 times there'd be a couple of slags who would make my dream come true.

I would claim in the show that I had deliberately asked that we put Liverpool at the end of the tour as a kind of safety net, just in case the threesome hadn't happened anywhere else, which of course it hadn't.

I must have been stressed because within ten minutes of arriving at the lovely Unity Theatre, I was throwing a strop. I am the least diva-ish of performers and hate to give theatre staff a hard time, but one of them had just told me that my slot tonight was 60 minutes maximum.

'What do you mean 60 minutes?' I moaned. 'This show is over 90 minutes long. Plus an interval. I need a slot of closer to two hours.'

'I'm sorry,' said the reasonable and, unlike me, unflustered theatre manager, 'but whoever booked you in only asked for a 60-minute slot and the staff aren't contracted to stay beyond 9.30.'

'This is the last time I do this show,' I whined. 'I was looking forward to doing the routines for the last time and now I am going to have to drop half of them...'

'Well, I'll have a word and see what I can do.'

'Honestly, this is just the living end,' I said, storming off to brood in my dressing room, and wondering where the phrase 'the living end' had come from. It wasn't the kind of thing I'd usually say. This wasn't the kind of thing I'd usually do. That would keep happening tonight.

Eventually we effected a compromise where I could do pretty much the whole show, but without a break. It wasn't ideal. I was a little unsettled and conscious that the staff at the theatre (correctly) thought I was a prick. It had stirred up my emotions, making me feel a little belligerent and antsy – it was the first spark smouldering in the dry moss of the conflagration that was to occur.

Despite my concerns, the gig turned out to be one of the best of the entire run. The venue was sold out and the audience were up for it from the start. There was even an actress from *Hollyoaks* on the front row. It was like all my dreams come true. I gave the swansong my best shot and was filled with confidence and swagger: this was all kindling being thrown on to the fire. If some idiot tried chucking petrol on me now, we were going to end up like Steven West.

After the show I headed to the bar to sign autographs and to celebrate the culmination of all this graft with a few well-earned drinks. Quite a few people were waiting to meet me, including three attractive young women. One of them immediately made for me. 'Hi there, I'm Sarah,' she said with brazen assurance. 'That was a brilliant show. Me and my friends Suze and Jenny –' Suze and Jenny were shyer than Sarah, but waved as they were introduced '– are going off for a drink at a bar round the corner. D'ya wanna come?'

She smiled at me seductively, giving off an air of absolute certainty that I would want to do exactly that. She was right to be certain. This might be the kind of thing that Russell Brand experiences on an hourly basis, but it doesn't happen to me very often. Usually, post-gig, I end up talking to a 35-year-old man with a beard in an anorak about a sketch that I have forgotten writing from some 1992 radio show that I have forgotten I appeared in.

Given my other hotel-based *Lusty Asians* option, I didn't have to think twice. 'That'd be great! I just need to hang around here for a bit in case anyone else wants to say hi.'

'Oh.' She pouted, disappointed that I wasn't prepared to drop everything that instant. 'Don't leave it *too* long.' The implication that I might lose the initiative was clear.

But we chatted as I signed some programmes and I drank a couple of large glasses of wine. I was trying to be healthy and avoid beer, but I was drinking the wine as quickly as I would beer, which must surely have cancelled out whatever tiny health benefits I had imagined I was getting.

'So what do you all do?' I asked Sarah.

'We're students at the university.'

'Really? So how old are you? Twenty?'

'We're 21.'

'Oh, well, that one year makes all the difference!' I laughed mournfully.

'You're only as old as the woman you feel,' said Sarah, smiling. The night felt full of possibility.

There was, I admit, a tiny, if unrealistic, part of my brain that was projecting forwards and making the mental calculations: 'Is this it? Maybe if I play my cards right it's finally going to happen? A threesome! On the last day of the tour! In fact, there's three of them. This could be a foursome! I have a spare!'

I was already weaving from the booze and fatigue as we headed round the corner to the drinking hole that the girls had selected. Two or three other audience members had tagged along, but it was very much the more the merrier. I wanted this difficult tour to end on a high and it seemed to be doing just that.

It was a Monday night, but things were quite busy in this trendy, dimly lit establishment. We got some drinks and headed down some sticky stairs and found a small table surrounded by sofas and sat down. Sarah purposefully sat on my immediate left, so close that our legs were already pressing together. It was at least looking positive for a *ménage à deux*, which was 100 per cent better than most nights on tour.

'So has that begging for a threesome thing ever worked?' asked Sarah as Suze and Jenny coyly giggled.

'Of course not,' I replied. 'It's way too desperate and brazen. My problem is that whatever the real me might actually want, the stage me only wants to go for the laugh.' Did that make me sound mentally ill?

'Well, it was very funny,' she agreed cheekily.

Usually I am a bit shy and introverted after gigs, but I was in party mode and found myself very much the centre of attention, holding court to this table of strangers, like an extra exclusive bit of the show. The drinks were coming thick and fast and the laughter came just as easily. As the girl next to me enjoyed a joke, she surreptitiously brought her hand down on mine, our palms briefly locked, her fingers furtively circling in my palm. I allowed myself a sly and drunken smile.

As midnight approached, the bar got more packed. Soon a group of young men arrived, looking for somewhere to sit. One of the sofas at our table was empty and they asked if it was taken. Magnanimous and full of love for humanity, I allowed these interlopers into this sycophantic court where I was king, though of course they hadn't seen my show and had no idea who I was and an *Emperor's New Clothes*-style situation might not be far away. But I didn't anticipate a problem. They certainly looked harmless enough: they were in their early twenties and pretty weedy, most of them had glasses, sweatshirts, jeans and non-brand white trainers. They looked like and quite probably were a group of maths students. Some of them might possibly still live with their mums.

But there was one guy with them who was slightly cooler and better-looking than the others, but only in the way that food poisoning is slightly cooler than dysentery. If you'd seen him on his own, you would have thought he was a massive geek, but because he was hanging around with a load of blokes who were more dweeby than him, in comparison he looked pretty good. Because of the company, he might be able to fool a woman into thinking he was an attractive proposition. Now I finally understood why The Fonz socialised so much with Richie Cunningham and Ralph Malph.

'You don't mind if I sit here, do you, ladies?' said this skinny wannabe Fonz, as he perched himself on the arm of the sofa opposite, where Suze and Jenny were meekly sitting. It was a *fait accompli* in any case. He then immediately started chatting them up. I was actually quite impressed with his bravado. I could never do something like that. Not only am I shy outside the glare of the spotlight, I am also conscious of not imposing my company on strangers – possibly because of the bad, head-wetting experiences I have had when strangers have imposed themselves on me.

The girls, however, were not that interested in the guy; every time he leaned in to try and get a bit closer to them, they would lean away at an exact parallel angle – which must have delighted the maths students on the sofa.

I turned to Sarah and said, 'He's getting on pretty well with your mates. Maybe it's him who's going to end up with the three-some. Ha ha ha… Ha!' The laughter caught in my throat.

'No,' she replied, surprisingly aggressively, 'they're just humouring him. He's an idiot!' She'd taken an immediate dislike to him and fairly enough. He was a bit drunk and pushy and had broken up our cosy fun. His motives were breathtakingly obvious. Which might seem a bit rich coming from me, but at least I'd put in the groundwork here!

On a positive note, the distraction gave me and my prospective lover the opportunity to talk on a one-to-one level. 'I love the bit you did in the show about the BNP,' she told me, referring to a routine in which I had called for anyone who voted for the right-wing political group to be disenfranchised for their blatant stupidity, arguing that we should 'Fight fascism with fascism!'

'I hate racism,' she told me, as if she might have been the first to come up with such a ground-breaking perspective on the subject. 'For me, racism is so ridiculous, I think it's funny! I'd say the idea of hating anyone based on the colour of their skin or where they come from is so ludicrous and wrong that I think racism is hilarious!'

'Yeah,' I agreed, not wanting to sour this sure thing, 'I understand what you're saying there, but it's probably best that you never say that out loud to another human being. There is room for misunderstanding in your theorem.'

'No,' she slurred, 'racism is funny. It just is!' I was relieved that no one else was listening in.

On the sofa opposite, the comparatively attractive geek was making some headway with Jenny.

Clearly fancying his chances, the garrulous nerd made his move and gave her his business card. She proudly, though possibly sarcastically, handed it round the table for her friends to look at. Sarah took the gift and apropos of nothing started ripping off the corners and then flicking them back into the bloke's smug face. Admittedly this was quite a provocative thing to do. But it was only a business card: it wasn't the end of the world. Presumably he had another one! Unless he was like Top Cat and just has one on a piece of elastic – though that would seem to counter the whole point of having a business card.

The previously affable, if slightly lubricated, man's demeanour changed within a heartbeat. He was instantly, furiously angry. 'You stupid bitch!' he snarled at the woman that I loved (if only on a quite temporary basis). 'You moron! Why are you such a bitch? Why are you such a fucking moron!'

I was too aghast at this transmogrification to even point out its inappropriateness.

But the forthright Sarah would not be intimidated. Off the back of the conversation that only I had been privy to, she responded to his aggressive entreaty in what must have seemed quite an unusual way by matter-of-factly replying, 'It's because I am a racist!'

A confused silence descended on the table. This made no sense, even to me. All of us were white. Momentarily the furious interloper was bamboozled by this non sequitur but then he became more enraged, fuming as he spat out, 'How dare you? How dare you say you're a racist? My wife is black!'

By now the man was up on his feet and preparing to physically assault this seated 21-year-old girl. Everything was happening at breathtaking speed, but despite being slightly addled by booze, I recognised that as the only man in our group, it was my duty to stand up and protect the honour of this admittedly quite stupid and annoying woman... who I was still hoping to have sex with. So I got to my feet and held up my hands and said, 'All right, mate, calm down. It was just a joke. It was a bad joke, but it was just a joke. In any case, if you're married, surely it's not relevant what race your wife is – maybe you shouldn't be out at a bar at midnight giving your business card to a 21-year-old girl. Just a thought.'

But he was too befuddled with rage to pay attention and before anyone could stop him he stepped forward and attempted to kick Sarah in the head. Fortunately he was so pissed that his foot merely flailed in the air, missing its target, but his intention had been more than clear. His nerdy friends, realising he had gone way too far and was in danger of doing something truly reprehensible, grabbed hold of him and pulled him, literally kicking and screaming, up the stairs and out of the pub.

Astonishment enveloped us all as we sat there with mouths agape. What on earth had happened there? I looked around me. Everyone was relieved it was over.

Except for me.

Weirdly, I felt cheated that he had gone.

I had been ready to fight him and had adrenalin rushing through my veins and now no way of channelling out the aggression.

Jenny looked shell-shocked as she commented, 'He was so nice to begin with. And you know what he does for a living? He's a university lecturer!' How would his superiors react if they found out he'd attempted to kick a 21-year-old woman in the head?

About ten minutes later the bar closed and we had to leave. Where are we going now? I wondered. What wonderful treats are awaiting me? Are my dreams coming true? But outside the lads were waiting. The idiotic lecturer saw us coming out and aimed a lunging punch at Sarah. Again he missed, but then he saw me and screamed, 'And you're a fucking cunt as well!' and punched me in the head.

I might end up getting a complex about this – all these belligerent strangers convinced of my cuntdom and trying to harm me. But I don't think I'd really done anything to deserve this attack. *Ménage à un* had some controversial moments and when I headed off on tour I did think I might get physically assaulted at some point, but not by someone who hadn't even seen the show! But the punch was ineffectual and normally I'd have just sneered at him and walked away, aware of my pugilistic limitations, but now petrol was splashing on to the gently glowing kindling and the whole thing exploded into violence.

The fight itself is little more than a blur to me now. I started by wildly windmilling my fists in the vague direction of the rat-face of this lubricated and lecherous lecturer. But with embarrassing haste I realised that I was incapable of hitting a moving target so high above my head and decided my best course of action was to punch him as hard as I could in the testicles. Alas, these would be the only genitals I would be making contact with tonight.

Fortunately he was pretty much as useless and clueless as me. We were both just flailing around, failing to connect. It must have been quite a surreal sight, a middle-class comedian and a university lecturer brawling on the streets of Liverpool.

At one point I accidentally managed to crack him quite hard in the side of the head. It felt amazing. Honestly, if you've never hit anyone go out and do it now. It's better than sex. It gave me the most amazing, life-affirming high. For a few seconds of my miserable existence I knew what it was to be a real man.

He responded by kicking me in the balls – there's just no call for those kind of low and unsportsmanlike tactics. But he couldn't even do that properly and only scored a glancing blow. It stung, but as anyone with testicles reading this will know, it could have been a lot worse.

It felt like the whole gladiatorial combat lasted about six minutes, but I was later told that from start to finish it was approximately 35 seconds. By which time, from the foggy images that remain in my memory, he had me in a headlock and I could hear the rending of garments. The girls came to my aid, if not quite directly, by persuading the reluctant bouncers to intervene.

'All right, that's enough,' said the one who latched on to me, 'we don't have to do this. You're outside the club. It's not our responsibility.' I think they were more embarrassed by the poor standard of our fighting rather than actually concerned for our welfare. I wasn't too badly hurt. Apart from slightly achy balls and a couple of scratches that had probably been inflicted by the doorman's rescue, there was no real damage. Except that the T-shirt I had been wearing had been badly ripped in the melee.

I was standing on the cold streets of Liverpool with my chest hanging out, like some kind of Incredible Hulk that had failed at any point to transform from a weak-looking bloke, but his clothes had ripped off anyway.

With impressive haste, two young policemen arrived on the scene, ascertained what had occurred and asked me if I wanted to press charges (he had hit me first and was thus criminally speaking in the wrong). But they were laughing as they asked that, because I am guessing that the police in Liverpool have seen worse things than a ripped T-shirt. I said to let it go. The lecturer had in any case skulked off into the night, but I was cooling down and was embarrassed and ashamed about having lost control and humiliated myself in this manner.

The girls were very apologetic. They couldn't believe things had escalated like this and realised that a lot of this was their fault. Of course at this point I should have said, 'Yes, it is your fault and as a result all three of you have to come back to my hotel room now and lick my damaged testicles until they are repaired.' But I was embarrassed and deflated and cold and my balls were aching so I just got in the cab and shooed them away when they tried to get in.

They *wanted* to come to the hotel with me and I said no. What a tragic culmination to the evening.

The cab driver had been on his rank and seen the whole thing. As he pulled away he said, 'That was the funniest fight I have ever seen.'

The first rule of Fight Club is you do not talk about Fight Club.

The second rule of Fight Club is you do not talk about Fight Club...

Hold on, I've just noticed rule one and rule two are word for word the same. When I was copying up the rules I must accidentally have copied the first one out twice. We don't need rule two. It's covered in rule one.

And thinking about it, just by reading out rule one you do immediately break it.

I think we'd better start again with the whole rules for Fight Club...

CHAPTER 3
POST-TRAUMATIC EUPHORIA

12 June 2007 – 30 days to 40

'All right, pal? What was that all about? Why the handbags at dawn? Well, six hours before dawn, ha ha ha... You know, I like to wake up at the crack of dawn. She's a lovely girl that Dawn. Ha ha ha. You get it? Crack of Dawn. I mean her crack... You all right, pal?'

The taxi driver was jabbering at me, but I was too distressed to give any meaningful answers. Only minutes had passed since my descent into animalistic madness and I was still struggling to come to terms with what had happened. The adrenalin, though diminished, was still running through my veins; the red mist was lifting but my mind was fugged by this unfamiliar combination of hormones, slowly intermingling with indignity and contrition and the dawning of familiar, ignominious defeat. Another ingredient in this potent cocktail of metabolism-altering chemicals was that just twenty minutes before I had been anticipating what seemed like a certain sexual encounter, so thwarted lust was swirling in the mix. By the time the still-smirking cab driver had dropped me back at my hotel, I was finding it hard to believe that any of it had really happened. Surely it had just been a terrible dream.

But the cold air pricking through the holes in my shredded shirt and chilling fresh wounds plus my now gently throbbing testicles reminded me that this had all been horribly real. The hotel door was locked and I faced the shameful additional humiliation of ringing the bell for the night porter to let me in.

'I've just been in a fight.' I jabbered at him, mortified but suddenly babbling. 'This guy just attacked me and I hadn't done anything wrong. Look at my shirt. I'm so embarrassed. The police came, but I didn't press charges. I'm really sorry about all this.'

'Oh dear,' stated this uninterested man who was itching to get back to watching TV. I realised that as much as I wanted to skulk away and hide, I really needed to talk to someone about what had just happened.

'Is the bar open?' I asked.

'No, sorry, sir,' came the curt reply, and he was already halfway through the door behind reception with his back towards me. 'Mini bar in your room.'

The door slammed.

I didn't want to drink, I wanted to unburden my soul but it was too late into the night to ring any of my friends. I headed to my room, alone with my jumbled thoughts.

After throwing my ragged garments on the floor and checking out my frankly unimpressive battle scars in the mirror, I lay in the dark on my bed, sobering up, unable to sleep because of my whirring brain and aching body. So much had happened so fast that it was hard to process. I was feeling both exhilarated and ashamed in a hotel room. Not for the first time, but for once I hadn't just had sex with a stranger. The same question was coming round again and again. Why had I done this stupid thing?

Certainly provocation and moral indignation had played their part, as had booze, exhaustion and sexual competition. But I had been provoked and drunk and sexually competitive on other occasions and still known that violence was not the answer. So what had been the real root cause of this preposterous slapfest?

I didn't want to acknowledge the obvious truth, even though it was staring me in the face. It was now the early hours of 12 June 2007. I was exactly one month away from my 40th birthday. And the closer that milestone was getting, the more my life was heading for meltdown.

I couldn't be nearly 40, I still felt like I was twenty... unless I was walking up some stairs. I couldn't be that old. My calendar must be malfunctioning. Surely it was just a couple of months ago that I left university to start my journey into the adult world. Twenty years couldn't have flown by without me even noticing. I felt like one of those unfortunate people who fall into a coma as a teenager and wake up to find that while they feel the same they have missed two decades of their life, their bodies have aged and the world has moved on without them. Except I hadn't fallen into a coma. I'd been awake for at least six hours a day, every day, for the last two decades. How hadn't I noticed the sands of time swirling away? Or that Margaret Thatcher was no longer prime minister?

In my head I was a teenager, but when I looked in the mirror I saw a wrinkled, grey-haired, toad-faced old gonk staring back at me. Either I was older than I imagined or I was a teenager suffering from one of those terrible premature ageing diseases. The fact that I was hoping it would turn out to be the latter said a lot about my state of mind.

Just a week earlier I had been sitting in a dressing room in one of the theatres (and I'd already forgotten which one as each town and each performance had blended into the others), the bright bulbs around the mirror shining harshly in my face, giving me an all-too-accurate reflection of my no longer youthful appearance.

I'd been astonished to notice how white my hair was. I had imagined that I just had a few distinguished flecks of grey, but now I studied myself I couldn't quite believe how predominant the encroaching snow on my peak had become.

When I was younger I had one grey hair in my fringe, which I first noticed at university. In those days I thought it was funny to have this one stalwart wayward and maverick follicle, which was perhaps trying to let me know that it was time for me to start acting with more maturity. I ignored this rooftop protest and dealt with the subversion with brutal hubris, by pulling it out and throwing it to the ground. Undeterred and faithful to its cause, it grew back, only to be discarded again and again. But its persistence and the injustice of my heavy-handed methods perhaps inspired others because it began to be slowly but steadily joined by other literal turncoats. Who would have thought that one angry hair could convince hundreds of others to change allegiance? For a while I continued to remove the rebellious greys, but recently that had become too time-consuming and if I had attempted it I would have been left with strange bald patches, like a doll whose owner has given it an inadvisable haircut.

An uneasy truce was declared. The apartheid was ended and brown and white lived together side by side.

In that dressing room I stared at what, in my mind at least, was the Reflection of Dorian Gray. It struck me with sudden horror that I had in all likelihood lived half of my life. I winced as I tried to make sense of that fact. Worse still, it was the good half that had gone. If my life was a sandwich, I had eaten half of it. And the half I'd consumed had contained most of the filling and all the meat, so I was left with the half that was dried up, curling at the edges and just has a bit of lettuce inside and a big dollop of way too much mayonnaise in the corner.

I tried to be positive. People have been known to live to 120, in which case I was only a third of the way through. But even a third seemed depressing.

Maybe scientists would come up with some medical advance which would extend human life to 160 years. If I still had three-quarters of my life to go, that might give me the chance to make up for lost time and to do all the things that I regretted never doing.

Who was I kidding? With my unhealthy and stressful lifestyle, it was more likely that I was already three-quarters of the way through. I might even be forty forty-oneths in. Or even less. No guarantees.

At that moment I had decided to put the whole thing to the back of my mind, to try and forget about it. I resolved to live the next five weeks as if I was still twenty. At the next opportunity I would be down at my local roller-blading rink, wearing my Sony Walkman, wired for sound like some kind of Cliff Richards. I would drink beer, eat chips and kiss girls as if there was no tomorrow.

Then on my 40th birthday I would accept defeat, dig myself a grave and lie in it and wait for sweet death to claim me. Or better, maybe I'd do this on 11 July, so that I might die while still in my thirties, which at least would be slightly cool and elicit some sympathy. Hopefully the effort of digging a six-foot hole, wide enough to accommodate me and my ever-expanding belly, would be enough to finish me off. I was perilously unfit.

The escalating events of my Liverpudlian escapade certainly suggested that my decision to pretend to be 21 until I was 40 was setting me on a course to self-destruction.

As I tried to shift my body into a position where my wounds didn't ache quite so much, it became increasingly obvious that it hadn't been that scrawny drunk academic that I had been fighting. I'd been fighting to recapture the youth that I was just, too late, beginning to realise I had squandered. My fading juvenescence was like a flask of water left open in the hottest desert sun, with only the merest vapour remaining. And like a man dying of thirst, driven to the point of insanity, I was going to hold that vessel to my mouth and furiously shake it and suck it and slap it to try and capture those last precious molecules, even if they gave me just a few more milliseconds of life.

All the elements of my denial of the cold hard fact that I was no longer young were combined in this extraordinary night. On pretty much every evening for months I had been drinking like I was a student. Trying to blot out not only my ageing process, but also avoiding having to go back to my home or hotel room alone and face the fact that I had nothing and no one important in my life.

I had also been hanging around with girls young enough to be my daughters (if only I'd had sex before I was twenty), partly because I hoped on some subconscious level that I could feed off their youth like a social vampire, but also because most of my friends my own age, unlike me, had spouses and children who kept them in at night. Or at least proper jobs, which meant they had to get up early. In the last couple of years I had dated several women who weren't alive when I was doing my O levels. Or in some cases my A levels. Part of me felt this made me a Superman, part of me worried I was just a dirty old man.

The ripped T-shirt on the floor was a fitting symbol of both my attempts to defy unstoppable time, like the massive Cnut I was, and of the ultimate futility of doing so. Just recently I had begun dressing in the clothes of a much younger man, and he was furious about it, because I was really stretching them out – they were useless to him when I gave them back.

The sad truth was that I had begun to wear tight, figure-hugging trendy garb because I reasoned that if I was going to deny I was old, I might as well deny the fact I am fat as well. Two for the price of one.

The shirt was one of many that I had recently bought from a shop frequented by surfer dudes. I am not a surfer dude. I have never even been on a surfboard. In fact, the last time I had been paddling in the sea I'd been knocked over by a medium-sized wave, hit my head on the sand and as a consequence, somehow, inexplicably one of my testicles had swollen up to three times its normal size. I found out on the flight home that my knackered knacker had become a very sensitive gauge of shifting atmospheric pressure.

Testicular injury is not as common an occurrence for me as this book might be suggesting. Although I wasn't making life any easier on my maltreated marshmallows by squeezing myself back into my 34-inch jeans that I hadn't worn for ten years – as if wearing trousers that were a decade old would somehow make me ten years younger, like a denim time machine. Of course they didn't anywhere near fit me, and my balls were so crushed up they were turning into coal.

My newfound need to appear cool and fashionable (I had certainly not been interested in such matters when I was really a teenager) had already started getting me into embarrassing situations.

Recently I had been in a rush to get to a gig at the Battersea Arts Centre, near Clapham Junction. It had been a blistering hot summer day and the train had been packed and I came out of the station drenched in sweat. There was only 30 minutes until the show began and I didn't want to go on stage in a clammy T-shirt, so I quickly dashed into Debenhams to buy a fresh one.

But even though I was already late and supposed to be in a hurry, I couldn't just grab the first top I saw. Of course not. I had to get one that was trendy and cool enough for a 21-year-old surfer dude to wear. So even though time was ticking away, even though I would only have to wear it for one gig, I was being select-ive. I had to look good for my audience. I didn't want them judg-ing me. I was rejecting shirt after shirt for being too dowdy or plain or just not quite expensive enough.

After five flustered minutes I thought I'd found something suitable. It was a cool chocolate brown colour, with what seemed to be a swirling retro seventies logo on it. There was a bit of pink in there, showing I was in touch with my feminine side. Oh yes, I thought, I'll look quite the bomb in that.

And even though I'd only said that in my head, I still felt immediately sheepishly embarrassed.

There was no more time for prevarication. I grabbed it, took it to the till, paid and then ran up the hill to the venue, arriving to find some anxious-looking theatre staff who were somewhat relieved to see me.

It was only when I got to the dressing room and put my new show shirt on that I looked at it properly.

My mouth fell agape.

That wasn't just a swirling logo, it was actually a humorous motif. The pink area, in the shape of a sausage, had the phrase 'Free Hot Dog' within it. Then underneath there was a large arrow pointing down towards my groinal area, which contained the words 'Bring Your Own Buns!'.

Far from picking up a cool designer T-shirt, I had in fact chosen a crude comedy garment with a laddish double entendre implying that I was willing to give my penis, for no money, to anyone who was prepared to provide me in return with their buttocks.

That was going to send out a very different message to the audience. They wouldn't be thinking, wow, there's a cool 39-year-old man who is trying to pretend he's still 21, they'd be thinking, wow, there's a 39-year-old man who thinks that it is clever to refer to his penis as a hot dog.

Furthermore, anyone who considered the epithet more closely would conclude that I was announcing my desire for anal sex with anyone who happened to read the legend on my chest. I was giving away my hot dog (penis) for free, but in return I required buns (buttocks). The clear implication is that I wanted to place my hot dog between those buns in an unnatural sex act, which, if that's your bag, it's probably not the best course of action to advertise it in T-shirt form. It's the kind of thing you want to build up to slowly, rather than blurting out in this clumsy manner.

And you're unlikely to get any takers. I think the Venn diagram of 'People who are amused by double-entendre T-shirts' and 'People who want to have anal sex with someone they have just met' probably has no intersection whatsoever.

I walked out on stage and was forced to shamefacedly admit my error and discuss the pickle that my vanity had landed me in.

Suddenly, in the darkness of that Liverpudlian hotel room, I finally understood the phrase 'over the hill'. Because getting to 40 is very much like reaching the top of a hill. For the first 39 years of your life, you're rushing, struggling to climb the hill, you're not even looking around you, just desperate to get to the summit and see what's on the other side. Finally at 40 you reach the peak and you get a clear view both ahead and behind.

You look back and you see a lush, fecund valley, full of wines and fruits and cavorting young people who want to make love to you and be your friend... You've left that behind. You rushed to get away from that.

You look forward for the first time and see what had been hidden from view and it's an icy, rocky crevasse, basically a sheer cliff falling away into nothing, littered with the bodies of the dead and dying. So inevitably you ask if you can go back down the way you came and come up a bit more slowly and enjoy the stuff you missed out on, but you get pushed into a toboggan and are sent hurtling towards icy oblivion.

You'll probably get thrown off straight away and die. You might manage to hang on until you get to the bottom, where you will die. The only certainty is that you are going to die... very soon... along with all the other idiots who rushed to climb the hill, not realising that it was the climb that it was all about.

So perhaps it's no wonder that so many of us try to grab on to that last tuft of grass at the top of the hill, refusing to let go, holding on to our fading youth.

Because I had realised I was not alone. I am just one of the millions of people born in the sixties, seventies and eighties, who unlike their parents were not expected to find a career and get married the second they were out of school and have been able to extend their adolescence into their twenties and thirties. Possibly even their forties?

It's true that in recent years some of the soldiers in my battalion of kidults had fallen by the wayside. Nearly all the friends who had left university in a similar state of arrested development were now married and every year saw another of them spawn progeny. A few of them had even got a 'proper' job. But I hadn't sold out or compromised. I was still fighting the fight. I was a hero. Right?

But as one of the pioneers of adultlescence, I would be among the first to reach the apex of that cruelly two-sided hill and to find out how I would respond to the blast of icy reality that was about to hit me in the face.

The phone rang. Who could be calling at this time? Who even knew I was here? Had the police come to arrest me? Was it the belligerent lecturer, having followed me to my hotel, waiting outside to resume hostilities? Did the night porter now fancy a chat or had he realised I was a soft touch and was going to beat me up himself? The world was suddenly a terrifying place.

I fumbled for the receiver. 'Hello?' I fearfully enquired.

'Oh my God, I am so sorry about all that. I can't believe that happened,' came the gushing response. It was Sarah. I must have told her the name of the hotel. 'Are you OK?'

My replies were monosyllabic: I suppose I blamed her for much of what had just occurred, though I knew in my heart that I was denying my own culpability.

'What are you doing now?' she asked. Given it was 2am, the subtext of the question hung heavily in the air. She was asking if she could come and spend the night. Desperately alone as I was feeling and as much as just two hours earlier I would have jumped at the chance, now I couldn't be less interested.

'I'm going to sleep,' I blankly told her.

'Oh... right... but...'

'Goodbye,' I tetchily interjected and hung up before she could respond.

Immediately I regretted my grouchiness and felt even more isolated than before. Much as it would have been comforting to have a soft, warm body beside me, I had to get through this night alone.

Finally I discovered a vaguely comfortable position and somehow quelled the questions flying around in my head and fell into an uneasy, unhappy sleep.

The next morning, I woke up... and I felt fantastic. Yes, my wounds still ached a little, but aside from that I felt practically euphoric. Somehow in my sleep, shame had transmuted into masculine pride. No longer was I feeling abashed and humiliated. Instead I felt invigorated, alive; my senses seemed keener than before. I was conscious of every breath and was savouring the sweetness of the air that I usually took for granted. It was like that bit in *An American Werewolf in London* (not the bit with Jenny Agutter in the shower, alas, worn out to a fog of static on the VHS tape I had had as an adolescent boy), when the day after committing his atrocities the American Werewolf feels full of life and vigour and is ravenously hungry. I had been in a fight, I had lived, I had released my inner caveman and the non-intellectualised part of myself felt fulfilled. Regardless of the result, I felt like a real man and it felt amazing.

The intellectualised part of myself still felt bad and was trying to make itself heard, but the non-intellectualised part had its fingers in its ears and was chanting, 'Nyah, Nyah, Nyah.'

I found myself unable to fight the compunction to tell people about what had happened. Far from trying to pretend the previous night had never happened – and so far from home it would have been easy to let the incident be forgotten – I began texting friends to tell them of my daring deeds. They were just texts so I couldn't go into too much detail: 'In fight last night – protecting girl – I am awesome!'

The pretty receptionist at the hotel who had checked me in the day before and knew I had been doing a gig asked how it had gone.

'Good,' I replied, before adding without missing a beat, 'though I was in a fight afterwards.' Her shocked reaction made me feel even better about myself. What strange and primeval forces were at work here? Why was I being such an arse? Why did I like being such an arse?

'Did you win?' she asked. Was that a slight hint of excitement in her voice? Perhaps I wasn't the only one turned on by this Neanderthal activity. Maybe my being a fighter made me more attractive to women – at least women who weren't there to see how bad I was at fighting and how quickly I resorted to below-the-belt tactics.

'It's hard to say really,' I replied. Even though I knew I had lost.

I travelled back to London on the train, feeling that my fellow passengers could somehow sense my newly acquired machismo. Was I imagining it or did they quickly avert their eyes every time I looked up and caught them staring at me? Were they whispering to each other, 'That's him. Don't do anything to upset him. We'll all be in for a pasting'?

I arrived back at Euston station and as I went down the escalators to the tube I saw a friend of mine, Lucy, also a stand-up comedian and an Edinburgh Fringe flatmate, coming up the other way. 'Ooooh, hello,' I said, surprised, though she realised immediately it wasn't quite such a big coincidence.

'On your way back from Liverpool?' she asked. Obviously she was heading out to perform at the festival too.

'Yeah. Be careful up there. I was in a fight last night!' But it wasn't a warning, it was a boast.

Lucy gave me the reaction of shock and concern that I had been coveting and then she was gone. Maybe if I had had time I would have gone into detail and told her that the fight was an embarrassing shambles. Maybe.

Why this need to spread the news? Why not just not mention it at all? What was I becoming?

That night I was doing a charity gig in a big theatre in Clapham. The dressing room was full of comedians and I couldn't wait to tell them about my exploits. 'I'm a bit pumped up,' I told TV's David Baddiel. 'I was in a fight yesterday.'

'Wow, you've come out of it pretty well,' he replied. 'Not a scratch on you.'

'Yeah,' I bragged, 'and you should have seen the other guy.'

After the minutest of pauses, David asked, 'Was he totally unscathed as well?'

I sheepishly responded, 'Yeah… Pretty much.'

But for the next few days I was still in a heightened state of emotion. I was almost seeking out confrontation, hoping to experience that high again. I had been to the supermarket and as I left I attempted to hold the door open for a man coming the other way.

But I misjudged it slightly – he was moving slower than I had reckoned on and I released my grasp a bit too early – and the door swung shut faster than I had anticipated, slamming in his face.

'Oh, thanks very much,' he said sarcastically, but without aggression, which is exactly the kind of comment I would have made in the circumstances. But I was annoyed that he hadn't appreciated my efforts and although usually I would have walked away, not wanting to make a scene, today I turned and said, 'Oh, don't worry, any time,' with a real threatening edge to my voice, staring him confrontationally in the eye. I think I wanted the chance to experience the high of post-battle adrenalin again. I was willing him to fight me. Flustered and frightened, the man averted his eyes and scurried off without further comment. I had intimidated him and I liked it. I was becoming a real man.

I headed home to eat the Dairylea Dunkers, fishfingers and Cheestrings I had in my carrier bag.

With Angel Delight for pudding.

When I was a child, I spake as a child, I understood as a child, I thought as a child: but when I became a man, I put away childish things...

But as I was putting them away I thought, hey, some of these childish things are pretty good. There's KerPlunk in here and Buckaroo and some Space Dust... And then I realised that now I'm a man I can afford those expensive, electronic childish things that my mum and dad wouldn't let me have. Result!

CHAPTER 4
IT'S MY PARTY AND I'LL SULK IF I WANT TO

22 June 2007 – 20 days to 40

'So I suppose, when you think about it, this is our engagement party,' said Emma peskily, as she rang the bell at the closed door of one of the West End's most fashionable private members' clubs.

'What are you talking about?' I asked, squinting in the warm evening summer sun, waiting for the woman at reception to buzz us in.

'I mean we've told everyone it's a joint 40th do, but, in reality, you and me know this is just a preamble to our forthcoming nuptials.'

'Have you been drinking already?'

'Jiminy Crickets, you must remember!' she squawked with mock incredulity. 'When we were about 25, we made a solemn vow that if we got to 40 and both of us were spinsters...'

'I'm not a spinster. I'm a man. I'm a bachelor.'

'In your dreams. You so are a spinster. You're the most spinstery person I've ever met. You know what your friends all call you behind your back? Spinsty McSpinster.'

'They do not. They call me Batchy McBachelor!'

'All right, if that's what you prefer, Batchy. Stop trying to change the subject. We vowed that if we were single at 40, we would get married to each other.'

I screwed up my nose as I wondered if I could deny it. But it had definitely happened. Back then that had seemed like a safe and empty promise. Forty seemed a lifetime away and there was absolutely no doubt in my mind that I would have a wife and kids by then. I was pretty sure I'd be on my second wife by that time.

'I don't think it was exactly a vow,' I weaseled.

'It was,' barked Emma. 'It was a solemn vow. Made on our most sacred book – the *Beano* annual.'

'No it wasn't.'

'Don't contradict me. You'll learn the foolishness of that once we're hitched...'

'We're not getting –'

'And here we are, neither of us spoken for. Neither of us even dating anyone else, by criminy. I have saved my maidenhood for you and I expect you to make good on your promise, mister man.'

'Why aren't they opening the door?' I asked, pressing the doorbell with an increased sense of urgency.

'Never mind that, fiancé of mine. Where's my ring? When's the big day?'

'Wait a minute. I'm not 40 yet. Not like you. It's only you that's in your forties.'

'I'm three weeks into my forties...'

'You're still in your forties, you dried-up, mawkish old harridan. I'm comfortably in my thirties...'

'For three more weeks...'

'Now you're just showing your jealousy. I pity you, I really do.'

'All right, that's true. You're off the hook. For now. You've got three weeks to find someone to marry you but if you don't find anyone, which you obviously won't, then YOU'RE MINE!'

She pushed her face close to mine as she yelled this and then laughed like she was the merriest hobbit in Hobbiton.

'It's like some kind of rubbish Hollywood film and I'm Matthew McConaughey,' I observed.

'Yeah, after he's been hit 500 times in the face with a cricket bat,' added Emma slyly.

'Which really he should be. If there was any justice in the world.'

We laughed as we had laughed together so many times and at last the buzzer sounded and Emma pushed the door open.

'Well, all right. I'll marry you in three weeks. As long as we never, ever have to have sex.'

'Oh my giddy aunt, I should coco,' said my bride-to-be, pretending to vomit as she entered the building and shocking the rather demure lady on reception.

I had known Emma for over half my life. We'd met at college more than twenty years before, performing in comedy shows and plays together. Initially we hadn't really liked each other, though neither of us can quite remember why, but over time we had realised we were essentially identical aside from our gender and had literally forgotten our imagined differences. We had the same sense of humour, the same spirit of childishness, were both hopeless kidults. We even look quite similar, both short and mousy with cheeky grins made for comedy. If someone informed me that we were twins who had been separated at birth like in some convoluted and rubbish Shakespeare comedy, I would be utterly unsurprised.

In the last few years we had spent a lot of time together, as we'd ended up working on the same TV and radio comedy shows, and had also run the London Marathon in the same year. Coincidentally we had both been asked to take part in a TV reality show in which we were taught to row by Olympic heroes, in order to compete in a ridiculous version of the Oxford/Cambridge Boat Race. The show had the word celebrity in the title, even though it had none in the actual boats (Grub Smith, anyone?). But as underdogs in the contest, our crew – under the inspirational Olympic gold-medal-winning coach Martin Cross – had bonded into a fanatical unit, prepared to die for each other and victory. Astonishingly, against all the odds, we defeated the stronger, taller and altogether superior opposing crew. It was one of the most amazing experiences of my life and it had brought Emma and me closer together than ever.

But not *that* close.

At no point in our twenty-year friendship had we ever been romantically involved. Once, early on, when we were 21 and on a miserable student comedy tour, we had shared a bed in some digs or other and in the middle of the night I had reached out a hopeful and exploratory hand. It was quickly rebuffed by Emma and I unconvincingly pretended that I was asleep as she laughed at my inappropriate and incompetent attempt at seduction as well as my pathetic pantomime of feigned slumber.

She was right to mock. The idea of us ever getting together was ludicrous and slightly unsettling. We had to kiss in one play we were in at university and it was (I imagine) like having to snog my sister. While I have entertained ideas of making out with most of my female friends (and indeed have done so with many of them), I couldn't imagine a situation where Emma and I could be naked together and have anything approaching lustful feelings. She could pump me full of Viagra and I could pump her full of Rohypnol and make her wear a mask of Natalie Imbruglia's face and we'd still not be able to get through it.

We were, I hoped, only joshing about taking the marriage proposal seriously, but maybe there was an argument for going through with it. Sure, there were no sexual feelings between us (or did we protest too much? Maybe we should think about it… oh dear, I just thought about it), but apart from that we were perfect companions. We could share a house like strange spinster siblings, playing poker and Scrabble and Hungry Hippos and watching *The Simpsons* and eating Smarties. And maybe with the aid of a turkey baster and some entirely separate cubicle arrangement we might even have a child. Oh, but pity the issue of such an unholy union. Kidults must never marry each other. They need to find a responsible adult if they're ever going to reproduce.

I couldn't believe I was even thinking such a thing. Who'd want to marry someone in their forties? The idea was too disgusting for words.

Having said that, Emma did look pretty foxy tonight. She had dressed up in vintage 1967 clothing in honour of the year of our birth and as we climbed the stairs to the room we'd hired, I was behind her and could see more of her legs than I was used to seeing. And I have to say they looked pretty good. For a second my brain forgot who it was looking at and almost began to appreciate the sight in a sexual way. But I quickly snapped my brain out of that. It must have been the alcohol… Oh but hang on a second, I hadn't had a drink by then. Let's just forget the whole thing.

'The problem is, Em,' I said as we entered the room, 'you didn't get anything in writing. There's no proof that that conversation even happened.'

'Curse you, Herring, you're too sly for me!'

'But I tell you what, I like you, you're all right, in a limited sense, so if we both get to 80 and we're single, I will definitely marry you.'

'You promise.'

'I absolutely guarantee it.'

I chuckled to myself like a James Bond villain as I said in a quiet voice, 'Ha ha, you fool, I'll have been dead for decades by that time! I win again!'

'Right, let's get this party started,' announced Emma. 'It's our job to test the mojito and rossini cocktails and check they're suitable for our guests. I think we should check a lot of them! Just to be sure.'

'Agreed!' I said and we walked to the bar where a ridiculously handsome barman was already mixing the drinks.

We grabbed a glass each from the counter and held them up, looking each other in the eye.

'Hang on just a cotton-picking minute here,' said Emma. 'Look at you, Richard Keith, in your suit and your fancy swanky-wanky shoes. Why don't you dress up smart more often? You look blooming lovely.'

She put her finger against my arm and made a hissing sound,

like bacon frying. 'You hot!' she growled. 'You are looking swit and furthermore might I say you're looking fairly swoo as well.'

'I was just thinking the same about you.'

'If we drink enough of these, you never know what might happen tonight.'

But I'm not going to keep you in suspense. If you think the book is going to end with me and Emma realising we were made for each other all along and getting together, you are 100 per cent wrong. I know we seem like a perfect couple (of idiots), but believe me, there aren't enough mojitos in the world.

For either of us.

'Happy birthday!' said Emma as we clinked glasses.

'Is it?' I replied morosely and drained my glass in one.

And then spent the next two minutes picking sprigs of mint out of my mouth.

What kind of a drink is a mojito? Drinks are supposed to be liquid!

God, I wasn't in the mood for a party. I didn't feel I had anything to celebrate. Firstly I wasn't yet 40 and secondly even if I had been then that was still no cause for merriment. Emma had done most of the preparations for the night and it already felt to me more like her thing than mine.

I was feeling distracted and detached, but I was, apparently, looking good and hoped I might get a snog out of all this. The room hire and catering had cost a lot, so it would be good to get a bit more than a kiss and a fumble. It was churlish and disingenuous of me to care about how much I'd spent. I should just try and enjoy myself, but I was in a churlish and disingenuous mood.

So I got stuck into as many cocktails as I could get down me before anyone had arrived. I'd bloody paid for them. The barman, knowing I was the birthday boy, made them extra strong. This probably wasn't going to help things. Alcohol, I discovered later, is apparently a depressant. Who knew?

One of the first guests to arrive was another friend from my university days, Ewan. This was a bit of a celebration for him too as he'd met his wife at my 30th birthday party. Ten years on and they had recently had a baby, all thanks to me. Me, sad, childless and alone – merely a facilitator of love. Or so it seemed on this miserable evening. Gazing at my navel, finding it filled with terrifying, imaginary spiders.

Ewan's present was a good one and the perfect gift for a Kidult with a midlife crisis. He'd got me a skateboard. I don't think I'd ever been on one before, but I fancied having a go. Or maybe just heading down to the shopping centre with it casually slung over my shoulder, nodding my head at all the other sk8erbois that I happened to encounter, as if to say, 'Yes, I am the same as you. Fourteen years old.'

I had a little try out, as the room was still empty, though we were two floors up, all the windows were open and I was already drunk. Ewan asked me to take care, adding, 'I hope I don't regret getting you this.' Luckily I was so incompetent I fell off pretty much straight away. It was much harder than it looked.

The party quickly got into full swing, but I found the whole experience overwhelming for many reasons. In my drunkenness I was conscious that Emma seemed to have more friends there and was having a better time than I was. Furthermore I was a bit pissed off that she was getting more presents than me, her half of the table conspicuously overloaded with gifts. I was also slightly offended that the few gifts I got seemed to be kitsch and childish. I was nearly 40 years old, for fuck's sake. As usual I was unable to see the irony that I was reacting to this slight with a sulky, juvenile huff.

But I was also mentally calculating the cost of all the tat I'd received and the drinks and the canapés I'd consumed and comparing it to the cost of the venue hire and realising that I was over £1000 in the red.

I was becoming increasingly desperate to pull someone tonight to give the evening some kind of positive spin, but I was preoccupied with meeting and greeting every new guest, getting no more than a few seconds with each person before someone else arrived demanding my attention and handing me some Top Trumps or a whoopee cushion.

A guy that I barely knew, who had come up from the bar

downstairs and was gate-crashing, had, just an hour into the proceedings, his tongue down the throat of one of my official guests. That wasn't fair. That should be my tongue in her throat. Yet if I'd punched him and pulled him aside and forced my tongue in there, then it would be *me* who was in the wrong!

To make it worse, in whichever direction I looked an ex-girlfriend would loom into vision. I am fortunate in that I have managed to remain friends with most of my exes once we've broken up (though there are a handful of notable exceptions) and so should have been glad to see them. But in the state of mind I was slipping into, the preponderance of failed or lost love on view just added to the feeling that I had wasted the first 40 years of my life.

Not that everyone would see it like that. I knew that some of my married male friends envied my noncommittal, irresponsible lifestyle. And sure, it seems like fun to begin with, for a middle-aged man to be dating a string of women in their early twenties, but once you've been doing it for a while, it seems so meaning-less and shallow you feel ultimately lonely and purposeless and it gets quite depressing.

Then again, I had been in relationships, and they were fun to begin with, but once you've been doing it for a while, you get bored and contemptuous of each other and they drag on too long and you feel lonely and trapped and it gets quite depressing.

So I figured that if I was going to be depressed *anyway*, I might as well be up to my plums in a 23-year-old. I mean, there's worse places to be depressed.

I had got into a repetitive cycle where I'd be single for a year, get miserable and unsatisfied, realise I needed to be with some-one, then be in a relationship for a year, get miserable and unsat-isfied, realise I needed to be alone, then be single for a year. Was that how it was going to be for the rest of my life? I had a chilling vision of myself as a lonely, old 80-year-old man, still hopefully sharking around the old folks' home.

Looking around the room I realised just how many girlfriends I had had. Ten years before I would have been impressed by the number of notches on the bedpost, but at this moment I realised that it was relatively easy to have sex with people (though not tonight apparently), even to date them for a while. What was difficult and genuinely impressive was to find one who would stick with you for ever.

Standing here in a daze, I felt like I had inadvertently bought a ticket to Richard Herring Ex-Girlfriend World, where tourists would travel around a mechanised track around a diorama consisting of convincing papier-mâché, animatronic models of the women I had loved and lost or shagged and then stopped shagging or snogged and then sobered up.

It was making my head swirl. And my head was already swirling from the cocktails. It was now swirling twice, and in opposite directions.

Worse still, in sharp juxtaposition to my internal torment, each of them seemed completely sorted and happy now they were no longer with me. Diane, who I'd spent a happy-go-lucky year with a couple of years ago, was happily single and flirting with all the handsome men. Next to her was Julie, who I'd had a thing with before I met Diane, and who I had really liked, but who'd decided to go back to her boyfriend. She was now single, or at least that's what I had thought when I invited her. I'd been hopeful we could pick up where we'd left off. But she turned up with a new partner, Tony. In a bizarre coincidence, five years earlier Tony and I had been in competition for indecisive Maria, who had also ultimately chosen him. He was my clearly my nemesis. Maria wasn't with him any more, of course. No, she was married to a successful and sensible lawyer, Gareth, and they were laughing together on the dance floor. What did he have that I didn't have? Apart from a proper career, a steady income, a slim, muscular body, a sense of rhythm... And Maria.

Nibbling awkwardly on a stupidly miniature burger near the unbalanced table of gifts was Catherine, who I had dated in my mid-twenties and who was probably the sweetest woman I would ever meet in my life. But she'd been away at university when we were together and I'd been persistently unfaithful to her, realising only when it was too late what I had had. It took me years to get over her, yet somehow she still liked me in spite of myself. Her long-term boyfriend returned from the bar and handed her champagne. He looked like he knew what he'd got and wasn't about to risk losing it and I was glad she had got someone who deserved her.

Sitting behind Catherine was another Catherine (I've been out with more girls called Catherine than anyone in the world, including Henry VIII), who was not only married but now heavily pregnant and looking radiant. We'd known each other for years before we became romantically involved. She seemed to understand me better than anyone I'd ever been with. But we'd never quite properly committed, finding it hard to make the transition from friends to lovers. Six years ago, as I had headed off to another Edinburgh Fringe, it felt like things might get serious on my return, but she met her husband that month and I met someone else too and by the time I was back the moment had more than passed. Why hadn't I snapped her up when I had the chance? Then that could be my baby in there and my life would have some meaning.

Was that what I really wanted? Because it didn't seem to be what I was aiming for in the short term.

There was a tug of war going on inside me where one side was pulling for me to carry on with my spinster (I mean bachelor) lifestyle and the other for me to settle down and have a family. Not that that made me particularly extraordinary. I guess it's the eternal internal battle for many men (and women). On a basic instinctive level I suppose both sides were urging me to reproduce, one side wanting me to scatter my seed as far and wide as humanly possible, the other wanting me to plant the lot in one furrow and hang around to cultivate it.

Didn't that side of me remember what had happened to my rubber plant?

As with so many areas at the moment (though I suppose ultimately it all led back to sex), my hormones were in hyperdrive. Recently my sex drive, always high, had spiralled out of control, like a British-made space rocket being piloted by one of those wobbly men you get at the end of the marathon.

I thought I'd get to my forties and find my libido with some relief tailing off at long last, but I was more libidinous now than I had ever been before.

It was as if I had this burning furnace of lust within me and it wasn't a pleasant sensation. At all times of the day, wherever I was I seemed to be fantasising about having sex with every woman I saw... who was under the age of 30 (I'm not sick!).

It felt like a disease, a virus in my brain, making me faint and fuggy and nauseous and unable to concentrate on anything other than the pursuit of sex. I wondered if all 40-year-old men were going through this. Because I was actually just grateful that I wasn't already married and going through this hormonal blitzkrieg. Men are mocked for the way they behave when they're going through this midlife crisis, but if others were feeling the way I was and staying faithful to their wives then they should be applauded, not lampooned.

Luckily for me I was single and I could act upon my desires if I wished. And had done so, hoping that if I gave in to it and had sex with a younger woman that that would quell the fire in my loins. In fact, all it did was make me more libidinous than ever. Don't be tempted to try it, married men, it's like throwing petrol on the fire. And you know what happened to Steven West. You'll prob-ably get your teeth smashed in when your wife finds out too.

Yet increasingly some force, whether it be God or fate, seemed to be intervening in my life, to let me know how shallow I was being.

Everywhere around me in recent weeks I had seen signs, odd occurrences and pointers: someone seemed to be trying to tell me something. A few weeks before I had been in a coffee shop where I happened to be sitting opposite some pretty young women. It was a lovely hot day and they were wearing floral summer dresses, which fittingly for the season were rather short and flimsy. I couldn't help noticing that they had rather attractive bare, tanned, slim legs. In fact, given their proximity with my eye line, I found I couldn't stop myself just staring at their legs. I wasn't even making an attempt to look away if I thought they were looking, I was openly gawping at them like a pervert. A normal man tries to mask his lechery; only the pervert is open about it. Yet the honest pervert is the one who receives society's disapprobation.

In any case, I was merely appreciating the legs in an aesthetic and sexual way.

It wasn't my proudest moment. These young women were probably about eighteen years old. I was over twenty years their senior. Even I had to admit it was a little seedy.

To be honest they might even have been seventeen years old. And I'm just sitting there, staring, at their legs. Awful.

I just want to make it very clear, they were definitely over sixteen. So you don't have to get all weird about it.

All right, they might have been fifteen, but I was only looking. That's not a crime. We can look. As long as we don't touch. They can't stop us looking! That is our democratic right. If a 39-year-old man can't stare lasciviously at the bare legs of a fifteen-year-old girl then Al-Qaeda has won.

Anyway, they were definitely over sixteen because they were in the sixth form: I heard them talking about it. So there's nothing wrong with this at all. It is almost a charming tale.

But that unseen force, God or fate or the Easter bunny or maybe Timothy Claypole from *Rentaghost* (I can't be sure), wanted me to know what I was doing was wrong, as if I didn't know that myself already. Because at that exact moment a man arrived, pushing a baby in a buggy, and unknowingly happened to place it directly between me and the girls I was leching over, with the baby facing me.

So now instead of looking at the girls' legs, I was looking into the face of a baby, who, and I am sure I am not imagining this, was regarding me with disdain and disapproval. It knew what I had been doing and it didn't like it one bit. It was judging me and finding me wanting. There is nothing worse than a judgemental baby.

The baby's expression seemed to say, 'Why? Why? Why are you looking at those legs? It's wrong. You shouldn't be looking at young girls' legs, you're nearly 40. You should be thinking about babies now, you should be looking at babies and wishing you had one of them. You're getting old. It's time for babies.'

I gave the baby a look which said, 'Well, I have to look at the legs first. That's how babies come about. That's the first step in the beautiful process of creating a child.'

But the baby looked more furious. 'Not young girls' legs like these! You should be looking at the slightly stockier legs, in sensible slacks, of older women, in their thirties. Women who have lived their lives and are just ready to squeeze out a couple of babies before they die...'

'Women over 30! Who'd want to have sex with them? Come on!'

'You're nearly 40!'

'That's different. Luckily most women aren't as shallow as me.'

'Grow up – you're disgusting!'

There's nothing worse than being told to grow up by a baby. A judgemental, telepathic baby.

But this was not the only unsubtle signpost that the higher powers that I didn't believe in had presented to me. The weekend before this miserable birthday party, fate or a leprechaun or Bruce Willis in *The Sixth Sense* had conspired to allow me to meet Siân, my childhood sweetheart, for the first time in nearly twenty years.

I'd been at the wedding of Chris, a school friend (this was his second – he'd managed to marry two women to my none before he hit 40) and I had known that Siân would be there. Of course that wasn't a problem, after all this time, but then again I had been surprisingly apprehensive about our reunion.

I had started going out with her when I was sixteen and as it turned out it was, as yet, the longest relationship of my life. We stayed together, on and off, pretty much until I went to university three years later, when predictably it finally fell apart. She was a couple of years younger than me and so it had always been a very innocent relationship, which we certainly never got anywhere near consummating.

And as with many first loves, it was a daily war of attrition where I, frustrated by her purity, was trying to persuade her to go a little further than she was prepared to go, and she was pushing me away, telling me I was obsessed with sex. Which weirdly I both was and wasn't. I was fascinated by it in theory but terrified in practice. I just wanted to kiss her and maybe get my hand up her top, but she was not yet ready for such things.

'So you'll have fingered her by now,' the crude and laddish Mark Harris had leered just two months into the relationship. I didn't even really know what he meant and didn't want to tell him that I hadn't even snogged her yet, so just gave what I imagined was a noncommittal smile.

'You're a lucky man!' he commented, sniffing his fingers and guffawing. It seemed like everyone else was on the train to Sexville, while I was locked in the toilets in the station. And it was a station where the Sexville train didn't even stop. On a line that had been decommissioned.

But I stayed with Siân because I loved her, or believed I did, and was more or less prepared to wait for her (and myself) to be ready. Neither of us would be until much too late for us. Still, I believed she was 'the one' and that I'd spend my whole life with her. I was more ethical and romantic (and frightened of everything) back then and my heart's desire was to make love with only one woman in my life and to stay with her for ever. Oh, how whatever puckish deity had written my life story must be loving that dramatic irony right now.

But there were some good times together and as we got older there was at least some physical closeness. I remember Siân used to sing to me, 'You are my first love and first loves never die.' That's a lovely memory to have. At least it was until it struck me that that means that she, at the time, must have realised there would be other loves after me, or it doesn't make sense.

I was pretty heartbroken when it didn't work out and it hung over me for a long time that I had never made love with the first girl I had fallen in love with. Her memory had haunted my life, which perhaps explained my queasiness at the prospect of being in the same room as her again.

The wedding was in Wales and I had driven two more of my unmarried and single school friends, Phil and James, up from London. The rural church was hidden away in the middle of nowhere and we'd spent the last half an hour driving down windy country roads, flanked by high verdant verges and flowering hedgerows that made it difficult to find our bearings. My sat nav was useless out here – we were so remote that I'd be surprised if they had any postal service, so there was no chance of a postcode.

Houses and people were few and far between, but the two pedestrians we encountered gave us wildly conflicting instructions of how to get to the church, almost as if they were enjoying sending these out-of-towner Englishmen on a wild goose chase.

Finally we arrived at the idyllic thirteenth-century church, although we'd somehow come to the wrong side and were nowhere near the field where everyone else was parked up. With only seconds until the ceremony, there was no option but to leave my car on one of the verges. Surely there couldn't be any traffic wardens out here. Or would that be where rural Wales suddenly become supremely sophisticated?

We got to the church a bit late and the rest of the congregation were already seated, but we found a spare pew in some transept or apse in the periphery with very poor sight lines for the main event. I couldn't stop myself from looking around for my first girlfriend, oddly unsettled, hoping I might not spot her yet desperate to see her again.

I wasn't sure I'd even recognise her after all this time. In my mind she was a teenager, but in reality she'd be 38 now. Again I mourned the rapid transit of time as I struggled to comprehend that so many years had passed by so quickly and quietly without me noticing.

I looked round the church, my eye resting on various women as I wondered, is that her? Or could that be her? That woman's about 60, that can't be her... can it? I felt confused and disorientated.

Then I spotted Siân, sitting way over on the other side of the church, looking almost exactly the same as she'd looked the last time I'd seen her. It made me laugh to myself about the ridiculous candidates I had been considering for the position.

She was sitting with her husband and three children. Even though I knew she was married and a parent, it seemed impossible to comprehend. Last time I'd seen her she'd been young, free and single and now in the blink of an eye she had three kids. Not babies either, actual grown kids. Her eldest son, a boy of about twelve, was sitting beside her and looked so exactly like her that it took my breath from me. He looked so like her and so unlike anyone else that it was impossible not to imagine that that would have been the child we would have had if we'd stayed together.

I knew I was being ridiculous. There was no way our puppy love would have lasted; there was no way I was going to be the kind of person to stick with one woman my entire life; plus we'd never had sex, which as I understood it was quite an important part of the baby-making process.

But in that moment there was no option but to fantasise about that alternate universe where I'd settled down with my first girl-friend and had a family, as I had hoped would happen, rather than sitting here on the other side of the church: single, childless, with all my other fuck-up 40-year-old friends who had nothing in their life. It was monumentally depressing. The floor fell away. I felt bereft and adrift. Like my whole life was meaningless.

I knew I was being self-indulgent. But she represented a time when I was full of hope and less jaded and where the idea of being with one person for my whole life was still a possibility. And I'd loved her. As much as any teenager can love another. It was a dress rehearsal for love, but that didn't make it any less mean-ingful. It clearly still meant something even now. A love of a time, rather than of a person, of what she represented, rather than who she actually was, because of course I didn't know her at all any more and all we had in common is that we'd shared those feelings for the first time as we played at being in love.

I met her outside the church and it was strange because for a few moments we just stood looking at each other and I wondered if she was imagining the alternate universe she might have been in if things had worked out differently.

Then she looked at me, slightly askance with a look of confu-sion on her face. 'That can't be Richard Herring?!' Mocking me, but with affection. And we laughed and we joked and I didn't feel bereft or adrift any more; it was lovely to see her. She intro-duced me to her son, who no longer seemed like the ghost of something lost, just a sweet boy with his mother's eyes.

How strange that she could still have this effect on me after all this time. How strange that despite the insignificance of those youthful days compared with the significance of present reality that it still felt like such a big deal to see her again. There was still an ember glowing. It was never going to burst into flame, thank God, but she'd been right all those years ago. She *was* my first love and it *would* never die…

And charming and sweet as it was to have that innocent connection through time with another human being, it was still yet another signal that my life, like my car, had taken the wrong turn somewhere down the line.

Clearly fate, or whatever it was that was sending me these heavy-handed hints, was telling me to get on with it. But I didn't seem to be taking the bait. It was going to have to take a man dressed as a giant baby confronting me with a big sign reading, 'It's time to have a family, you twat!'

And I would still be saying, 'So what exactly is your point here?'

At the party the band were playing 'Baby Love' as I continued to scan the room. There was one significant ex-girlfriend missing from the diorama, my latest failed love, Sarah-Jane. She'd been invited, and said she'd come, but we were halfway through the evening and she was nowhere to be seen. It was only about two months since we'd split up and the wounds were still fresh and tender. We had remained close and I'd still meet up with her and Buster and they both clearly liked having me around. Maybe tonight was the night when we'd get back together. I was certainly pissed enough to think it might be a good idea.

Emma, drunk, but in a way that only made her merrier and Frodofied, saw my plaintive stare and understood its meaning.

'Maybe it's best she's not here,' she suggested.

'Yeah, it is. I don't want her cramping my style,' I said with an attempt to look devil-may-care, but which betrayed my actual sorrow.

'No, you seem to be doing a good enough job of that on your own.'

'I really thought she might be the one, but she took everything so seriously… or maybe I never took anything seriously. It was so frustrating. I miss her. And I miss Buster.'

'Aaah, that's so sweet. You get on so well with kids, you should definitely have some.'

'You sound like my mum. Did she put you up to this?'

'No, it's just obviously true. You'd be a brilliant dad.'

'Would I? I think kids like me cos I'm a brilliant playmate.'

I had increasingly been suspecting this was the case. One weekend, a couple of months earlier, Sarah-Jane, Buster and I had gone to a play centre in Richmond in west London. Their website promised 'Endless play in our multi-level soft structure – featuring ball pits, slides, tunnels mazes, obstacles courses and much more,' though I had to question their use of the word 'endless', especially as the website also mentions the opening hours. I think even were the place never closed that most kids would be bored with it within two hours maximum. Not that it wasn't good. It just wasn't endlessly good.

My failure to procreate meant I had largely missed out on experiences this. It was like entering another world. Because although the place is designed for fun, there was a strange whiff of tragedy hanging over us all. As the kids jumped up and down on the equipment, the parents sat on plastic chairs, drinking coffee, reading the paper, looking tired, seeming relieved to have a few moments of respite as their kids went and kicked the crap out of the tunnels and ball pits. The play equipment was colourful and the kids looked like they were having the time of their lives, but juxtaposed with the greyness of the adult world and the sheer hard work of bringing up children it became an oddly depressing place.

Or did this observation actually say more about me? I wasn't comfortable being on the grown-up side of this equation. I felt out of place on the sensible grey side of the room, still feeling in my heart that I should be romping on the play stuff. And this was possibly confirmed when I went in to help Buster up on a shelf that was too high for him. I got to have a little go climbing around and suddenly the eggy feeling of gloom lifted. It wasn't endless fun, but it was better than reading the newspaper. Maybe I was aiming too high trying to be 21 until I was 40; maybe two and a half was more my level.

The significant thing is that I felt I fitted in on the kids' side. I was one of the children, not a father.

On one side I was clearly terrified of commitment and losing my independence and on the other I was aware of my mortality and the risk of departing this world without leaving my mark, or any progeny to continue my line.

I wasn't alone. Half my married male friends were telling me I should become a dad, that it had made them feel their lives were worthwhile, but half of them were telling me to stay single and childless for as long as humanly possible.

Recently I had overheard a conversation on the night bus that summed up all the forces at play.

I was returning from a triumphant performance of *ménage à un* at London's Arts Theatre and wondering to myself how many other West End stars would be travelling home on a late-night bus. Is that how Elaine Paige got home? Was Kevin Spacey on the lower deck?

Probably not, but bad luck to them. It's a cheap and efficient way to get around and the N207 stops practically outside my front door. And as long as you don't mind the terrifying mentally ill people, the gangs of thugs looking for a fight and the pools of vomit then you're laughing. Sometimes my anonymity is a bonus – and I enjoy listening into conversations and writing them down in case they prove useful for me in the future.

There was a couple sitting behind me engaged in quite an earnest discussion and I found myself tuning into it. I couldn't see them and I wasn't going to look round and risk being stabbed in the face, so it was like listening to a radio play. I was saving money *and* being entertained. Surely worth the small risk of death!

They were clearly inebriated, but surprisingly eloquent, discussing the state of their relationship and an obvious and eternal sticking point. The woman clearly wanted to have children, but the man was not quite so keen.

'Maybe in four or five years,' he told her. 'But you have to understand, men and women are different. I don't have the biological imperative that you do.'

'You could have a child any time in the next 40 years,' she

agreed, 'but I'm 30... Thirty's not that old though, is it?' she half asked and half stated.

'No,' said the man. There was no other sensible answer to give. 'And Jenny at work is 37 and she's having her first baby, so you have time.'

The woman was clearly disappointed in her boyfriend's attitude. She wanted babies and she wanted them soon and in her heart she knew that if she waited for him to be ready and he was never ready then she might miss the window of opportunity. The window was slowly shutting and if it got any more shut it would be a foolhardy man who put his penis through it.

She obviously liked this guy and wanted it to work out, but it felt equally clear to me that he was never going to go along with it. I mean, I could be wrong. I was a 39-year-old man on a night bus, alone, listening into someone else's conversation and trying to scrawl little bits of it down in the back of the book I was reading, so I could write about it later. I may not be the best person to ask for relationship advice.

But even I was amazed by the excuse he came up with next. 'I don't mind children,' he said, 'and I might want to have some one day, but just not yet. It's too soon for me. I think of the polar bears...' This was an impressive turn. 'There are so many human beings in the world, far too many, and we're sucking up all the earth's resources and because of us the polar bears are dying out and their environment is being destroyed. I just don't know if I want to add to the problem.'

This was brilliant. He was making it look like his wish to remain childless was down to a concern for the future of the planet, rather than him being a self-obsessed prick who didn't want to get tied down.

She was sweet and understanding, but clearly in the tone of her voice worried that her dream of motherhood was in danger of being crushed. The couple wanted different things, but it was clear they were going to postpone this realisation to a later date in the hope that something would magically change. In your early thirties, this is the way things are. By the end of your thirties, you are much more realistic and pragmatic. I thought about turning around and saying, 'I think you should end it. Nothing will change. You want different things. You can compromise on the little things but not stuff like this. Nice polar bear argument, by the way, mate.'

But I didn't.

'Thirty isn't that old,' the woman repeated. She was trying to convince herself that she was right. And she was right – she has plenty of time, but that still doesn't mean it's a good idea to waste some. The bloke wasn't all that, to be honest. If you're reading this, young lady, then I would advise you to move on, if you haven't already. He doesn't care about polar bears. He just wants to remain fancy-free and uncommitted. Believe me, I know.

Still, polar bears, though. Genius.

Emma was grabbed by one of her friends and dragged on to the dance floor. I looked around for a potential dance partner, just as the door swung open and Sarah-Jane, looking elfin and gorgeous in her best party dress, walked through the door. Perhaps my night wasn't over. In my heart I knew the relationship was dead, but we were still friends and maybe we could temporarily cure our blues with some graveyard sex (by which I mean making love once a relationship is finished – I'm not that kinky).

But my plans were thwarted as I saw that S-J was leading someone else into the room by the hand. My mouth fell agape as possibly the most beautiful man I had ever seen followed her in. He was tall and toned and bronzed, with flowing blond locks and dressed like a model from an advert for the most expensive and ponciest aftershave in the world.

As if I hadn't had my face rubbed in it enough by my exes already, here was my most recent girlfriend, less than two months after we'd split, hand in hand with a demi-god.

It was fair enough that she had moved on, but in my fragile state this was too much to cope with. I drank more, sulked more and tumbled further into the soul-shaped hole that I had found within myself. I felt Lilliputian in comparison. In fact like a Lilliputian that Gulliver had accidentally stepped on and was in the process of scraping off his shoe into a bin designed for dog muck.

Perhaps Sarah-Jane was trying to make me jealous; perhaps it was an attempt to send me running back into her arms. But it just sent me running off, hot-faced, into the cool of the night.

Then I came back up, because I realised I'd left all my crappy presents behind. I started aggressively and carelessly stuffing them into a plastic bag. A talking Homer Simpson doll said, 'Mmmmm, doughnuts,' and I punched it hard in the face, as it repeatedly said, 'D'oh!'

Who knows what trouble I might have got myself into if it was not for the kindness of my friend Nancy? She saw that I was enraged and insensible and shouldn't be left to my own devices and along with her female friend Alfie, she guided me outside and hailed me a cab (I might have gone for the night bus otherwise and who knows what adventures might have occurred then). Sensing I was a man on the edge, my guardian angels didn't leave me to it, but actually jumped into the taxi with me, to escort me safely back to my house. They did their best to cheer me up and patiently listened to my lamentations about the emptiness of my life.

'I've got nothing, Nancy. My life is a disaster.'

'No, it's not. Do you have any idea how lucky you are?'

'I've got nothing. Nothing!'

I kicked my bag and Homer Simpson said, 'You tried your best and you failed miserably. The lesson is, never try.'

There was an awkward moment as the girls tried to stifle their laughter.

'If I was in *The Simpsons*,' I conjectured, 'I wouldn't even be Homer Simpson – at least he's managed to have kids. I'd be the Comic Store Guy.'

'The big fat nerdy guy? You're nothing like him,' said Alfie unconvincingly.

'Have you seen that episode where he's walking down the road alone, reading what he would like to call a graphic novel, but is actually a comic? He's sneering to himself, having no friends to hear his pontifications, "But Aquaman, you cannot marry a woman without gills. You're from two different worlds!"' My impression was weak, but the girls kindly laughed along. 'Then he looks up and sees a neutron bomb about to hit him and in a rare moment of self-awareness exclaims, "Oh, I've wasted my life." That's me. Forty years down the toilet. This priceless, pointless opportunity – wasted. And the fact that I use a cartoon as my major cultural reference probably sums that up better than anything.'

'You'll feel better after a cup of coffee,' said Nancy.

Thirty minutes later I was sitting in my lounge with a hot drink and these two kind ladies talking me down and making me feel like there was some point in continuing.

At least I hadn't ended up coming home alone and a little voice in my head thought that maybe there was more on the girls' minds than being good Samaritans. I thought I'd chance my arm. After all, it was my birthday.

'So, any chance of a threesome?' I slurred.

The girls, God bless them, just laughed this off. It was, I suppose, so wildly wide of the mark that it could be nothing but amusing. Feeling sorry for me, they both came over and gave me a little hug, which was at least two women holding me simultaneously and probably as close as I was ever going to get to my dream.

'You're a really great bloke, Rich,' Nancy told me, despite all the recent evidence to the contrary. 'You'll feel better in the morning. Well, maybe the morning after. And you know I've got a fiancé, you big idiot.'

'What about you, Alfie? I don't mind if it's just the two of us.'

'Hmmm, tempting offer, but I think I'll pass this time.'

'Suit yourself.'

Now we were all laughing. Even in my drunkenness I could finally see I was being a self-pitying idiot. By now convinced that I wasn't about to top myself, Nancy and Alfie made their excuses and left and I went to bed. Alone, as was only fitting, but perhaps slightly aware that, in spite of their gifts, I had some good friends who saw something good in me, even if I was finding it hard to spot it myself.

The Road of Excess leads to the Palace of Wisdom.

But the Road of Excess is a two-way street and in the opposite direction lies the Hut of Stupidity. It's amazing how many of the confused travellers on that damned highway end up there.

CHAPTER 5
SPERM MARATHON

23 June 2007 – 19 days to 40

The next day I was woken by my mobile phone ringing on the bedside table.

'Hello,' I groaned as I fumbled it towards my mouth.

'Hello, it's only me,' came a much too bright and chirpy voice, cutting into my brain like a laser.

'Mum! What time do you call this to be ringing someone up?'

'It's two o'clock in the afternoon.'

'Is it? Oh, right. Well… Even so.'

'Sounds like you had a good party. Did you have fun?'

As usual she didn't need to know the truth.

'Yes,' I lied. 'It was brilliant.'

'You didn't drink *too* much, I hope.'

'You know I don't partake of alcohol, Mum. I don't like the taste.'

My mother chuckled sardonically. In the background I could hear my dad, talking loudly, but not this time for my benefit.

'Where are you?' I asked.

'We're up in Middlesbrough this week, remember. To pick up your grandma and Ken so we can bring them down to Cheddar for the party.'

'The party?' I asked, my mind still confused by the after effects of two hundred pounds' worth of cocktails. 'The party was last night.'

'Not your party, our party. You're not the only one in the world with a birthday, you know!'

Of course – we were just a week away from another shindig, this time celebrating both my 40th and my mum's 70th. 'Who's Barbara talking to, Keith?' I could hear my 95-year-old grandma asking. She is the most amazing woman, who stayed fit and active right through her eighties, but who was now finding it hard to remember very much at all.

'It's Richard, your grandson,' my dad was enunciating loudly.

'I can't believe I'm going to be 70,' Mum commented wistfully. 'Or that my baby boy is 40.'

'Not for another 19 days... Not that I'm keeping count.'

'He's a comedian,' my dad was explaining. 'Not a famous one. Not yet.'

'Is he good-looking?' asked my grandma.

'Well, he's a bit short and fat,' replied my father, unfortunately for him in a bit of a lull of my chat with Mum.

'Quiet, Keith,' said Mum. 'He might have heard that.'

The best way to play this from my dad's point of view would be of course to pretend that he had known I had heard all along and that it had been a kind of a joke. But instead he tried to talk his way out of it, somewhat ineptly I have to say. 'Nothing wrong with being short and fat, though,' he said. 'And he is very good-looking despite that.'

'He's not fat,' countered my mum, tellingly making no such rebuttals about my alleged shortness. These are my parents.

'You know I love you anyway,' was my dad's final attempt to make up for his rudeness – the 'anyway' not really representing any kind of apology.

Then my grandma said, 'Well, I wouldn't know him if I saw him,' which was the only thing in the conversation that made me sad.

'Any ideas for what you'd like for a present yet?' fished Mum, trying to change the subject.

'I don't want anything.'

'Come on, we've got to get you something.'

'But there isn't anything I need.'

'You can have anything you want.'

'A Rolex watch?'

'Up to a value of a hundred pounds.'

'I'm a grown-up now. If I want something I can just buy it myself.'

'There must be something.'

'I wish you'd been this keen to get me what I wanted when I was a child. Every year I told you I wanted a Scalextric, but would you get me one? No, you wouldn't. It broke my little heart.'

'I can't believe you still go on about that bloody Scale-electrics…'

'It's Scalextric, Mum. And it's all I ever wanted. Why didn't you get it for me?'

'It cost a lot of money. And we didn't want to turn you into a spoiled brat. What about all the other things we got you: the snooker table, the Subbuteo, the acoustic guitar that you only played about once?'

'Those things weren't important to me,' I lied. 'I only ever wanted one thing and you never got it for me. I hate you. I never asked to be born.'

'Should we get you a Scale-electrics this year then, to make up for it?'

'No, it's too late. I'm too old now,' I indignantly responded. Though I immediately regretted my haste because I realised I would really, really love one. But I couldn't backtrack now.

'So no ideas for what you want then?'

'I want to not be 40.'

'Really? Cos I'd love to be.'

'Bye, Mum,' I groaned and I turned over and tried to go back to sleep.

I was rather too used to hangovers at the moment. Even though I'd been getting into fights and funks and inappropriate fucks,

I had carried on with the drinking and carousing that caused all these things. I had to. Because in just a matter of days I would be 40 and my life would be changing for ever and I'd only be sipping the occasional sherry or medicinal port.

But because I was nearly but crucially not quite 40, those hangovers were hurting in a way that they never had before. Sometimes one could last two whole days now and they left me languid and lethargic. I would find it hard to get anything done except fester in my home with the curtains drawn, watching *Diagnosis Murder* and playing computer games, or just miserably lying on my sofa, nursing my sore head, before heading out to go through the whole sorry pantomime again.

The worst part of it was that after a night on the sauce I would invariably wake up at six o'clock in the morning with my mind in a state of confusion and panic, feeling nauseous and totally incapable of going back to sleep for at least two hours.

The only way to calm my fevered and usually still slightly drunk brain was to turn on the TV until the discomfort passed, but at that time I only had the choice of aggravatingly chirpy and inane breakfast television, or programmes for toddlers on CBeebies. I would usually plump for the latter. Which, as you've seen, would come in handy if I was having any conversations with two-year-olds, but was starting to drive me slowly but effectively mad.

I had recently visited Longleat safari park where the guide had told us that the gorillas had a TV in their enclosure and you could tell which programmes were their favourites because they actually applauded them. They liked stuff like *The Tweenies* because of the colours and music. In my booze-addled state I had clearly de-evolved to the mindset of an ape because I was becoming obsessed with programmes like *Balamory* and *Teletubbies*. I was joining in with the repetitive songs and shouting out answers to questions posed by actors who could not only not hear me, but would have had no interest in listening even if they could.

My current obsession was a show called *Big Cook Little Cook*. I loved the songs and the repetitive nature of the plot lines, which included about 40 per cent of the exact same footage in every show. I was mesmerised by this infantile entertainment.

For those of you without kids or alcohol problems, the basic premise of the show is that a normal-sized man and a tiny man (of about six inches in height) have for some reason decided to open a café together, even though the small man is no real practical help in the kitchen due to the disadvantage of his size. It is possible that it is actually a café run by a normal-sized man and a giant man – of around 1000 feet tall – but if this is the case then they live in a world where everything else is similarly gigantic and thus the normal-sized man is still of little to no use.

Each day someone (often a nursery rhyme character) comes into their cafe and then Little Cook tells a story about them which always, in fact, merely glorifies himself and shows how they owe all their success to this tiny red-haired man.

Then they decide to cook the character a meal, which is themed around what that character does for a living. Old Macdonald, for example, gets an animal smoothie decorated to resemble a chick. It made me cross as I lay there, dazed and confused, because if I was Old Macdonald and I got food themed on my job, I'd be tempted to say, 'Look, I spend all day at the farm looking after animals and when I come out for a bit of lunch I'd like to forget about my work for a bit and maybe just have some ordinary food, not based on what I do. It might be nice to be shown a menu rather than just be given whatever it is you think I'd like.'

The kitchen is always short of one ingredient, which smacks of inefficiency and bad planning, and so Little Cook is sent off on a flying spoon (which frankly stretches credulity too far for me) to track it down. He never carries the item back with him, but clearly possesses some unexplained magic which allows him to transport it to the café – probably negating the need for him to fly off on his spoon in the first place. Presumably these magic powers were what persuaded Big Cook to go into business with the otherwise useless and arrogant midget. Then they make the food for the customer, sing a song about cleaning up and get a present, in lieu of payment, from their delighted and satiated guest.

Some might argue that the show was not aimed at me, but it had begun to haunt my every waking thought. I was filled with questions about how these two people had met and how they managed to make a living when they never charged anyone actual money. And the songs were going round and round in my head on a loop.

Pots and pans will start to smell,
If we don't wash them really well!

I was 39 years old.

I felt like I was in danger of crossing the line between goofiness and madness. My preoccupation with children's television was just one of the reasons that increasingly I was hating the after effects of my bacchic overindulgence. I kept wondering if it might be better if I could give it up completely. It would certainly make my mother happy. Should I mourn the loss of my youth by totally forsaking booze?

But the prospect made my blood run cold. Not because I was an alcoholic, because I wasn't. At least I didn't think I was. I had friends who drank a lot more, which always makes one feel safe, despite the possibility that that just made them more chronic alcoholics than me. When I was 24 I had given up drinking for six months in order to prove I wasn't an alcoholic. Which was, a doctor friend later told me, exactly the kind of thing an alcoholic would do.

I feared sobriety because alcohol had been the lynchpin of my social life since I was fourteen years old when I'd dared to order a pint at the George disco in Wedmore, in the hope that it would impress Maria Barnes (it didn't, nor did anything else I was ever to do).

I recall the trepidation and fear as I approached the barman and had a conversation which went, to the best of my memory, like this:

'Do you have any beer?' I asked.

The barman looked me up and down and replied, 'Er... yes, sir, we do.'

'Oh good,' I said, pleased this was all going so smoothly. 'One cup of beer then, please.'

'Would that be lager or bitter sir would be wanting?' came the inevitable reply.

I turned to Maria and shook my head at the idiocy of this yeoman. 'No... beer!' I explained.

'Lager beer or bitter beer.'

'Oh er... The cheapest, I think.'

'Right...' He reached for the pump and then seemed to reconsider. 'Oh, you are eighteen, aren't you, sir?'

'Yes,' I said in my high, unbroken voice, before checking myself and lowering the register. 'Yes. Yes. I am eighteen. I was born in... that year that was eighteen years before this one. Yes.'

This was, of course, one of the forks in the road of my life. This barman held my destiny in his sweaty Somerset hand. He could have said, 'Look, Rich, you know you're only fourteen, I know you're only fourteen – do yourself a favour, mate, have an orange juice. The minute you taste a drop of this beer it will be too late. Immediately you will dislike the taste and be unable to understand what all the fuss was about. But you will force it down. Within two hours and one more glass you will be vomiting all over the toilet floor. And that is just the beginning. You'll get in fights, make girls cry, vandalise property, offend and upset with the foul thoughts it will dredge up from your subconscious. In December 1991 you will wake up in your own bed next to a naked old woman you do not recall meeting. And when you're a fat and lonely elderly man, you'll sit in bars on your own telling everyone about how life has treated you so badly and how your only real friend comes in a bottle. Eventually it will kill you.'

But as it happened, what he actually said was, 'One cup of lager beer coming right up, Grandad.' And my fate was sealed.

But at least if I could curb my enthusiasm for grog then I might get more done. Perhaps I should turn it into a comedic project that I could write about – maybe spending a year on the wagon and seeing what effect it had on my health, my weight, my social life and my productivity. Yet I kept coming back to the consequences for my social life. Alcohol is the glue that binds me to all my friends and is also an important icebreaker when making new friends or going out on dates. I probably wouldn't ever have sex again if I became teetotal.

Someone more sensible might ask why I couldn't just moderate, and maybe have a glass or two of wine a night, but I didn't have that kind of self-control. Well, not quite true. I have self-control, but can only have it in the on or off position, with no increments in between. I either eat chocolate or I don't. I diet or I don't. I exercise or I don't. I'm monogamous or I'm really not. And who would want to be a moderate drinker anyway? What's the point in that? I drink to get pissed.

I was conscious that precious days of the twilight of my youth were slipping away. Time I could have used in reading great literature, contemplating works of art or just spending outside in the fresh air and sunshine was slipping away. I had been alive for 14,591 days, but how many did I have left?

Shouldn't I be making the most of whatever time was left to me, rather than throwing it away in such childish pursuits?

I remembered on 9/12 (which for some reason no one ever talks about as much as its rather more showy predecessor) I was sure that civilisation as we knew it was about to end: planes were going to come crashing down on all our heads, and within months we'd be embroiled in an unwinnable world war and everyone would die. So I resolved to stop wasting time, to live for the moment, to seize the day, to make the most of every second. But within a week I was still sitting on my sofa in my pants at 3pm masturbating to the free previews on hardcore pornography sites. Which in case you're confused is NOT making the most of my time.

I considered just how many of my 14,591 days on this planet I had wasted. Because surely there can be no greater sin, no greater affront to God than to fritter away this precious gift of life. I would imagine that it must pain our creator to see people squandering what little time they have.

The chances of you being here now are astronomically small.

Think about it. In the ejaculation that created you there were 600 million sperm, yet yours made it to the egg first. Your numbers came up in the cock lottery. You won the Sperm Marathon (one of Mars's less successful chocolate bars). The odds are impossible: 600 million to one. Don't you owe it to those 600 million unborn babies who weren't as lucky as you to live the fullest life you can?

But it's even more unlikely still. What if your mum and dad hadn't had sex the day you were conceived? What if they'd had an argument or your dad had had a crafty wank that afternoon and spilt you on the ground. One of the back-up boys in the next ejaculation would have taken your place. You would have vanished into the ether. Slipped through the cracks of the universe.

But it's even more unlikely still. Both sets of grandparents also had to meet, get together, not break up and then have sex at the exact right moment; your mum and dad's sperm both had to beat 600 million competitors. Your great-grandparents had to do the same, all the way back through history, ancestors cheating death, meeting the right person, having sex at the right time, the right sperm getting through, the odds multiplying exponentially.

You are at the bottom of this massive inverted pyramid of shagging, the right gamete getting through every time to facilitate your existence. All the way back through history, an unbroken chain of sex, through all the humans, back through the monkeys, the fish, right back to the first amoeba, deciding he couldn't stand living with himself any more and was going to find a place of his own.

Doesn't that make wasting even a second of one of the 30,000 days you're likely to live seem like sacrilege?

I think if you're going to make up an afterlife – there obviously isn't one if you think about it for a second. When you're dead, you're dead. Grow up! – then why not invent something that would make people live their lives better, rather than the traditional notion that can only fill us with shame and fear?

Let's just say that, theoretically, when you die, you are shown into a gigantic room that is full of the 600 million babies who would have been born if their sperm had got to the egg first, in your ejaculation. They're sitting in little thrones and are sentient and can talk telepathically, like something out of *Star Trek*. And they're looking at you quite pissed off, because you beat them in the race. You got to live and they didn't and they resent that fact. Six hundred million judgemental babies!

And you have to go round each of them in turn explaining every single thing that happened in your life and only when they're satisfied that you lived the fullest life possible, a better life than they would have led, can you move on to the next baby to do the whole thing again.

If you knew that was coming up when you were dead, I think you'd pull your finger out and try and make the most of life. Just to avoid the shame of saying, 'Yes, I did spend every Sunday morning in the year 2007 watching the omnibus edition of *Hollyoaks*. Even though I was 40 at the time, and it wasn't really aimed directly at me. And I had seen every episode already in its original 6.30 evening showing. But I was enjoying the subtle variation of seeing the show signed for the deaf. It becomes like a new story. I imagine that bald, middle-aged man who's doing the signing is a new character who's just arrived in Chester and for some reason he's hanging around with a load of seventeen- and eighteen-year-old models. He can't quite cope with it. He's a bit bamboozled. He can only speak with his hands. He's the character I most identify with, if I'm honest.'

The baby would probably say, 'I would have cured cancer in 2007, if I'd lived!' Even though he'd probably have watched *Hollyoaks* really. But he can act all high and mighty, never actually having lived.

That's an afterlife!

It would take billions of years, endlessly re-examining your life.

Then when you'd finished, you'd assume that was it and you could go to proper heaven now. But then you get shown into a second room, which is full of all the babies who would have been born if every sperm you'd produced or encountered had created a child, rather than going into a condom. Or into a handkerchief.

Then you have to explain to each of those babies in turn why it is they never even got the chance to live...

That second room is essentially Catholicism.

Yet even with the realisation that I was frittering away precious moments, I still couldn't rouse my corpulent body. Or even get on with some work. I would be 40 in nineteen days and I couldn't deal with that.

I had six weeks between the end of my tour and the start of the Edinburgh Fringe to write a whole new hour of stand-up and I couldn't deal with that either. By any comedian's standards that is a tough ask.

I was considering leaving out some blank paper, some tiny clothes and an acorn cup of beer at night in the hope that some scatological elves would do it all for me.

Instead of facing up to the proximity and seriousness of these upcoming events, I just let myself slip further into the pit of depravity. Even without the boozing, my unhealthy lifestyle should have been a concern. One of my new year's resolutions had been to be thinner and healthier when I left my thirties than when I entered them. Even though I had been quite a porky 29-year-old, this was no longer going to be possible. I was getting fatter and fatter seemingly by the minute.

I have always been a bit of a yo-yo dieter, six months of healthy living, followed by six months of indulgence in a similar biorhythm to my dating life. But despite my good intentions, I had carried on drinking and gorging and if the evidence of my eyes as well as the carbonisation of my testicles was anything to go by, I was heavier than I had ever been.

When I finally peeled myself out of bed on that post-party afternoon, I dared to step on the scales to check. Sure enough, somehow my diet of beer and fried chicken and junk food had not resulted in miraculous weight loss. My eyes had not deceived me. Though I had been hoping against hope that I had always just had the misfortune to have been looking at myself in fair-ground mirrors that made me look bigger in the middle. And also that my eyes had become fairground eyes, so that when I just looked down at my belly, it became disproportionately big.

But while there are fairground mirrors and fairground eyes, there is no such thing as a fairground scale. I was depressingly and unhealthily fat. In fact, according to all weight charts, I was obese. It was so depressing that it could only send me back reaching for the Hula-Hoops and Mini Eggs.

Because even my eating patterns were immature. I gorged myself on chocolate and Blackjack chews and gingerbread men, I suppose deriving some comfort from the remembrance of things past. Which was as close as I would ever get to being Marcel Proust.

Chocolate was my ultimate downfall though. I have never had much interest in taking proper adult drugs, but chocolate is my heroin. I can't get enough of it. Some people say chocolate is a substitute for sex. For me, sex is just a way to take my mind off chocolate for a couple of minutes.

This obsession surely goes back to childhood, though my parents did things by the book and tried to limit consumption. But that just made me more single-minded and determined. I remember deciding that if a genie gave me three wishes I would ask for:

A Scalextric set.
To have the blonde one from Abba appear in my bedroom in just her pants (nice I let her keep her underwear on – I think I was a bit scared of whatever was in there).
To have a whole bar of chocolate to myself without having to share any with my brother and sister.

Funnily enough, now I'm grown up those wishes remain exactly the same. Though maybe without the pants.

Chocolate pervades my childhood memories. I'll never forget the smell that hung in the air when my mother baked a chocolate cake or the excitement of opening the one weekly packet of Minstrels that I voraciously consumed every Friday evening as I watched *Captain Caveman*.

Even today Easter eggs hold a special totemic importance. Then as now, whenever I had one I would gobble up the whole thing within five minutes. I used to hate those kids at school who were somehow capable of only eating a tiny little bit of their Easter egg every day and would still have loads left by September. There's no point in having chocolate if you're not going to make yourself feel sick.

But as with everything in life, sometimes the fantasy didn't live up to the reality. When I was about five I had become obsessed with the idea of having a knickerbocker glory ice cream. Who wouldn't be? It was, after all, gigantic and made out of ice cream, and on top of it all it had the word 'knicker' in its name. The idea of having such a treat all to myself seemed like an unbelievable and unachievable luxury. Maybe I was just a greedy little shit, or maybe being deprived of things (or feeling I was) has led me to focus too heavily on them and resulted in me being a greedy big shit in my adult life. Did such a puritanical attitude lead to me being unable to control my appetites in adulthood? I doubt it very much, but then again, when I see parents that never let their kids have chocolate or that carry carrots with them so that they can give them to kids at parties instead of cake, I wonder if they are setting off a time bomb which will leave these children sitting in a big pool of chocolatey sick the minute they have independent means of buying their own sweets. But then letting them have junk food when they want will have similarly bad consequences. Who'd be a parent? Only an idiot.

Still, it's fun to blame my mum and dad for things that are my own fault. Anyway, my parents can't have been as mean as I like to pretend, because I remember that after what seemed like an eternity of wishing (though was probably actually about a week or two) my dad finally bought me a knickerbocker glory when we were out in a café for dinner.

It arrived at my table, and looked huge (though not quite as huge as I'd imagined) and as delicious as I had hoped. But I recall that when it came to actually eating it, the thing was a disappointment. I don't know if there was too much of it, or whether

I didn't like the stuff that was in it or a bit of both. But my memory is one of overriding disillusion.

Of course this was to be a sensation that I would feel many times throughout my life, but with the possible exception of finding out that the mouse in *Tom and Jerry* was called Jerry and not Tom as I had always believed, this was the first time. So often the longing and the chase are the best thing and the actual experience is only going to be an anticlimax.

Most of the knickerbocker glory was returned to the kitchens and thrown down the sink. Or possibly it was just poured into another glass and then topped with some whipped cream for the next child to taste and then leave and so on.

Anyway, there's a lesson in there somewhere. Even if the lesson is that I am a selfish idiot and always have been.

I hadn't lost my Wonkaesque delight in sugary fripperies as an adult though. Just recently I had a new addiction: Flumps. Not the 1970s children's television programme, even though the strange furry puppets in that show looked like they might well be delicious (not Grandpa Flump – too stringy), but the ten pence marshmallow snack made by Barratt, consisting of a five-inch twist of yellow and pink fluffy mallow. I had discovered them in the confectionery section of my Sainsbury's Local and thought I'd give one a go, convincing myself that marshmallow was somehow a healthy alternative to chocolate. The minute I had tasted it and its unnatural head-spinning sweetness, I was hooked. One day I had bought six at a time, with the intention of keeping them in my cupboard for future use, but though four of them at least made it into storage, they were all gone before bedtime.

I was ashamed and embarrassed by this new mallow mania, yet still was unable to wait until I was safely home to eat them. And a Flumps (that is what the singular item is called: I presume the plural is Flumpses) might be the most embarrassing food for a 39-year-old man to be discovered eating in the street. What if someone I knew saw me? Or worse, what if someone who was only a vague acquaintance passed me, stopped to say hello and then noticed that I was halfway through a pink and yellow Flumps?

They probably wouldn't say anything, but they wouldn't need to. I would be a middle-aged man eating a candy treat designed for small girls – even an eight-year-old boy would be mortified to be caught in the act of consuming such a confection. Yet still I couldn't stop.

But my girth and unhealthiness were not only down to my sweet tooth. As in all times of depression and drunkenness, I was turning to fried chicken for comfort too.

A sign of the underlying tragedy in my life was that I'd taken to walking down my local high street of an evening, looking in the window of my local Chicken Cottage fried chicken restaurant at all the sad and lonely middle-aged men in there, sitting eating their dinner alone, talking to no one. It made me realise that there were people worse off in the world than me. Me, who ate my dinner sad and alone sitting in the window of KFC. It's a slightly better quality of chicken in there, in my opinion. It's about ten pence more for the two-piece meal. I had a bit more cash to flash than the Chicken Cottage idiots.

Occasionally I'd see someone staring in through the window at me, a look of pity and contempt on his face, and I'd think, hmmm, he's on his way to Nando's.

Fried chicken seemed to be symbolic of all that was wrong in my life. One night I was heading home after a few too many drinks. I was tired and anxious and depressed and my stomach cried out for fried chicken. I had already eaten, and so I tried to resist it, but I somehow persuaded myself that just one piece would cheer me up. Even though fried chicken had never done anything but make me unhappier. If chocolate was heroin then fried chicken was the crack cocaine of the 30-something overweight man who lives on his own, but is too scared to take actual drugs.

By the time I'd got to the counter I'd convinced myself I might as well have two pieces of chicken, and chips. I crumble so easily.

But in front of me in the queue I saw myself. Not literally myself – that would be weird – but another version of me. A more extreme version of me. He was about my age, a bit more over-weight, had more grey hair and was more of a nerd than me. He was such a regular of this Flavas fried chicken shop that he greeted the confused man behind the counter like an old friend. He actually insisted on reaching over the counter and shaking his hand. He was so addicted he didn't even appear to be ashamed to be here. Would I soon reach that stage?

He ordered the same thing I was about to order. Of course he did. He was a vision of me in the near future.

'Anything else?' enquired the man behind the counter.

'No!' chirped the outwardly happy man (though I was convinced inside he must be screaming in anguish at his loneliness… because he was me and I knew that was what I was doing). He then looked up at the board and ummed and aahed self-consciously as if the thought of having something else had just struck him. 'Oh, actually just four chicken wings as well.' He chuckled a little awkwardly. Thank God. He was embarrassed to be here, and ashamed of his greed. He just hid it better than me.

I ordered my food, quite pointedly not requesting anything extra. It was good to feel superior to the other sad fool whose fried chicken habit was out of control. We waited silently for our disgusting chicken. I wondered how many 30-something overweight men were spending this glorious summer night eating unpleasant, artery-clogging fried food, before returning to their flats alone.

I wondered about saying to him, 'Hey look, we are similar. I am a bit cooler than you, obviously, but we're both doing nothing – why don't we go and have a drink together in the pub and see if that eases the pain of solitude that fills our hearts?'

Then I looked into his eyes and realised he was thinking of saying exactly the same thing. Except he clearly thought he was the superior, cooler one. Perhaps he had seen me eating a Flumps that afternoon. I was *his* warning of what *his* life might become.

But then our chicken was ready, so we couldn't have gone to the pub even if we hadn't both been scared about having to talk to a more nerdy version of ourselves.

Instead we both went home to our separate houses. I was glad. The desperation of loneliness clung to him like a lingering fart.

*

Much as I wanted to stop time, the brakes on the juggernaut had failed and there was nothing I could do to postpone the inevitable. Three more days whizzed past in a blur and I found myself trying out material for the new show in a room above a pub.

Though it's nearly always a terrible idea to perform under the influence, it was so nerve-wracking having to stand up in front of strangers with untested jokes that I was now having a couple of pints before stepping on stage. This was a dangerous gamble. Ideally a comedian should have mental clarity on stage so he can deal with whatever is thrown at him, but sometimes beer could loosen my tongue and result in some brilliant improvised digression that would be good enough to keep in the next night. If I could remember it.

The audience had been a little quiet for the previous act and were for me too, but I'd had two pints of stout and was in an inventive and improvisational mood. Guinness, it seems, is good for you.

Two attractive women in the front row were enjoying the show and chipping in with supportive heckles and I flirted with them, directing my most sexually suggestive material to the pneumatic blonde on the right. She enjoyed the attention and gave as good as she got. She was so completely out of my league that I didn't take any of it seriously. She looked like too much of a grown-up to be interested in me.

Out of nowhere I decided to ditch my gags and melodramatically discuss the existential crisis I had found myself in. 'Jesus Christ, look at me!' I complained. 'So close to 40... yet still very much 39... and still making my living telling stupid fucking cock jokes. How tragic and desolate an existence! No wonder my life is in such a mess. I wouldn't mind, but here I am sweating my balls off, cutting open my heart and for what? A few weary chuckles, some half-hearted guffaws.'

'I think you're brilliant,' chipped in blondie.

'Thank you, a few of you appreciate what greatness you have in front of you,' I said, with fake arrogance and more than a tinge of bitter irony, 'but the rest of you wouldn't know comedic genius if it was slapping you in the face with its dick. Which to be honest, I'm about this far away from trying. I just want some response from you, any response.'

Most of the crowd were bemused and confused. Did I mean any of this? Was it a joke? Was it anywhere near being funny? It was a hot night and they stayed quiet and soporific, though I sensed they were slightly on the edge of their seats to see where this belligerent improvisation would go. 'I'm not sure I can go on,' I told them. 'Not just with the gig, with life itself. What's the point? If I killed myself on stage, would that at least get a reaction out of you? Would you applaud me as I died for my art?' They didn't seem to care. 'I wonder if I could kill myself by pushing this microphone into my eye. Let's give it a go. Just to see if it's possible. It'll be an interesting experiment.'

I took the microphone out of its stand and held the spherical end up to my eye socket and pushed. 'Nothing so far, but if I push hard enough perhaps it will pierce my brain and end this nightmare of being alive.' Everyone was rapt now and a few pockets of the crowd, including the two women at the front, were laughing hard and loving this dark and stupid interlude. 'If I can at least produce some blood then this will be a memorable night of theatre.'

The audience were unsure about how serious I was being, and to some extent so was I, but it was exciting to be at the centre of a happening. This is when stand-up is at its best, when something occurs in the moment that will never take place again and only live on in the memory of the few people there to witness it. At times telling gags can transform into art. Pointless and ephemeral art, but that's still something.

I pushed quite hard and quite long, but I didn't die, nor did I bleed, though I did get a slightly achy eye. But that wasn't much good to me as no one could tell how I had suffered.

As this was going on it occurred to me that the more my life fell apart, the funnier I seemed to become. While I worried about how I would write a show in such a short time, it seemed that essentially all I had to do was go in front of some people, discuss my problems and they would laugh. As long as I was unhappy I could make a living. But if I actually grew up then maybe my income would dry up too. This gave me a financial imperative to carry on being a juvenile dick. The exact opposite of most normal people. But at what cost to my long-term personal happiness?

I understood the paradox that it was my job to be a failure and the more I failed the more I succeeded and thus the less good I became. Which only made me better.

After the gig, the pneumatic blonde, who, now she stood up, I could see was a good four inches taller than me, asked me if I wanted a drink. I asked for another Guinness and it would have been rude not to sit with her while I drank it.

We fell quickly into a deep and flirtatious conversation, to such an extent that her friend was a little excluded and ended up having to fend off some of the strange old men who were drinking in the seedy pub.

My Amazonian friend told me that being 40 was nothing to worry about, telling me that she herself was 44. She certainly didn't look it and was in terrific shape. She looked like a mature Lara Croft and all eyes were on her. Surely I didn't really have a chance with her, did I?

But it seemed that I did. She said that she and her pal, Vicky, were heading out to a nightclub, asking me if I wanted to come along. Vicky was having a rare night out, away from her husband, but Lara, she told me, was divorced and tonight her mum was looking after her five-year-old son.

'What do you do for a living?' I asked.

'I'm a doctor,' she told me. I was suitably impressed. She had a proper job and was twice the age of the last woman I had slept with. I wondered if this was a good sign. Was I being mature for once? Shouldn't I be looking for someone nearer my own age? Someone I could have a proper grown-up relationship with? Someone who would help me put an end to my stupid, irresponsible, promiscuous life? For the moment I was, I have to be honest, just hoping I might get a chance to sleep with this statuesque beauty, but after that... who knew?

We were having a lot of fun. She was very funny and even suggested a couple of ideas that would improve my routines (something that pretty much never happens when strangers recommend a joke to a comedian). I told her I couldn't go clubbing as I had to get up and write in the morning (though when another pint of Guinness arrived this seemed increasingly unlikely), but wondered if she fancied coming back to mine for a nightcap. Lara fixed me with her deep brown eyes. I felt like everyone in the pub was holding their breath, waiting to see how she'd respond.

'I would *love* that,' she exhaled.

It was an amazing feeling to know that every other man in the place was looking at me with disbelieving envy.

'You jammy little git,' whispered one of the toothless old men.

Despite her desire to accompany me, Lara could not abandon her friend in this bar that had a stranger clientele than the Mos Eisley Cantina bar in *Star Wars*. And Vicky seemed very keen, if not insistent, that the pair of them should be heading anywhere but my home. Lara looked at me, pushing out her bottom lip to indicate her disappointment, but gave me her number and told me to get in touch.

Yet I knew from bitter experience that the chances were that in the cold light of day the impetus would be lost.

Somehow I managed to convince the disapproving chaperone that we could at least share a taxi. And as my house was first on the route they might as well come in for one last drink. As we walked the streets looking for a black cab with its light on, Vicky said, 'Why would you want to hang around with two old married women like us?'

But I knew she was speaking broadly. Lara had been married, but wasn't any more. Vicky was merely expressing her surprise that I wasn't chatting up young bimbos.

Soon we were home and for the second time in a week I had two women sitting with me in my lounge and the idea of a threesome was not a million miles from my thoughts, but the frostiness and clear impatience of Lara's companion told me that that was never going to happen. Lara though was keen to stay and was cuddling up to me as she sat beside me. It was unbelievably exciting.

Somehow we managed to persuade Vicky to go and have a little lie down in my spare room, giving us a few minutes to get to know each other better. Though we were on a strict time limit and were interrupted by impatient entreaties and taps on the door, we used those minutes wisely.

But then it was time for them to leave.

On a day like this it was a great thing to be a single 39-year-old man, even if, as was the norm, I still slept alone that night.

I was keen to see Lara again and in the next week or so had a perfect dating opportunity, as I'd been nominated for a comedy award by *Arena* magazine and there was going to be a big show-biz dinner and party to attend. I rather liked the idea of having this fantasy woman on my arm at such an event. It would certainly make me look a lot more successful than I was. Like a slightly less wrinkled Bernie Ecclestone.

A couple of days later, while on the fire escape outside another gig above a pub, I built up the courage to ring her number. The phone rang a couple of times, was answered and then with a bit of a fumble the line went dead. Perhaps it had been a mistake rather than a deliberate brush-off. Or maybe she was in the middle of a consultation with a patient. I rang again and was put straight through to the answer phone. I left a message, inviting Lara to the ceremony, saying how much I'd like to see her again.

Some minutes later she rang me back and in slightly hushed tones told me that she wasn't free on the night of the party and that in fact it was a bit too difficult for her to get away in the evening because of her son. My head dipped a little. The implication was obvious. She had been drunk the other night and behaved foolishly and that was that. 'But look, I'd really like to see you again. Can I come round to your house tomorrow lunchtime?'

It seemed a little unorthodox for a first official date and surely in daylight hours without alcohol to embolden us it would be a rather more civilised meeting than we had previously had. But I liked this woman and was intrigued by her and this wasn't just about sex, so I agreed.

She came round at midday the next day and once she was through the door grabbed me, kissed me passionately and said, 'Let's go to bed.'

It wasn't just about sex, but that didn't mean we couldn't have sex, did it?

Without her friend to interrupt us, we were able to carry on unimpeded. It was a very passionate encounter and a terrific way to spend the early afternoon, though I was somewhat astonished that things had progressed so quickly with someone I barely knew. But there was time for getting to know each other once the sex was over, though I was unclear whether she was also expecting some lunch. After twenty minutes of chatting, Lara seemed keen to have sex again. And despite being nearly 40 I was equal to her demands. But once we'd done that it was time for Lara to get back to work and she was gone, pausing only to arrange another lunchtime sojourn in three days' time.

I lay in bed once she'd left feeling exhilarated and amazed, not quite sure that any of that had really happened. Was it too good to be true? Was it some kind of trick? My mind was spinning, but I would be lying if I didn't say I was somewhat pleased with myself. I had just had mind-blowing sex, with someone who looked like a female superhero, without getting her drunk or even buying her dinner and by all indications she'd had just as good a time as me.

This kind of thing didn't happen to me. It didn't happen to anyone. Apart from Timmy Lea from *Confessions of a Window Cleaner*. And I had begun to suspect those films weren't the fly-on-the-wall documentaries I had initially believed them to be.

I may have been a little slow on the uptake here, but it wasn't until later that night, just on the cusp of falling asleep, when I bounced back to consciousness as my slowly cogitating mind finally put the clues into place and I realised, shit! She's married.

That explained the fumble to divert the phone calls, the sotto voce conversation when she had rung me and why she couldn't come out in the evening. It explained the desperate passion of her lovemaking. And it explained why her friend had asked me why I was out with 'two old, married women' like them. That was probably the most obvious clue, thinking about it.

I had just, unknowingly, committed adultery (although at least I was doing something adult for once). I was breaking one of the Ten Commandments. I was going to hell!

Overall, though, I was a bit gutted by this revelation. I had really liked Lara and had had hopes of it maybe developing into something serious and I felt uncomfortable about getting involved with someone who was married, even if just for fun. It made things complicated and dangerous and immoral. If I became emotionally attached to her it could only end in disaster for me. And even more so for her.

I decided that the next time she came over I would tell her I had realised what was going on and that this had to stop.

Once she was through my door and kissing me, it seemed rude not to carry on with things. I would tell her once we'd had sex. I had already committed adultery. I couldn't get sent to hell twice.

In any case she beat me to it, and as we lay beside each other, the post-coital calm was broken as she said, 'There's something I haven't been entirely honest about. I'm married.'

'Yeah, I'd worked that out, eventually.'

'Does it make a difference?'

I knew that I should say that it did, but then again I knew that just minutes previously it hadn't. There was an incredible sexual energy between us and it was hard to resist her. And at the end of the day it was her marriage and it was her call. I wasn't betraying anyone. If she wanted to do it, it was up to her, wasn't it?

She was as addictive as a Flumps and I would have had to have been crazy to turn her down. We had sex again and then she went back to work.

I lay in bed feeling a bit like I was just a sex object being used for my body.

I didn't really see too much of a problem with that.

I was a toyboy. I was the younger man. And I felt young. I was in my thirties, after all. For another thirteen days.

Peter Pan was the boy who never grew up.
So how does that distinguish him from the rest of the male sex?

CHAPTER 6
RELATIVITY

30 June 2007 – 12 days to 40

'Tell us about the time you kicked Grandad down the stairs,' said Andrew, my youngest nephew, who in my mind was four years old, but was actually somehow approaching twenty.

'Not this again,' groaned my dad. 'That never happened.'

'Yes it did,' I protested. And though I had recounted the tale at every family gathering in the last decade, I couldn't let my expectant audience down. 'I don't remember quite what precipitated it all, but I was about fourteen and me and your grandad were in the lounge...'

'No we weren't,' Dad interrupted. 'I don't think I'd forget something like this.'

'You've wiped it from your memory, because you were so humiliated,' I told him.

'Nonsense,' he sang back at me.

'Anyway, I think I must have sworn at him or been rude to him, because Grandad was furious. He was coming at me. He was going to hit me.'

'You were going to physically assault your own teenage son, Keith,' said Sarah, my seven-year-old though actually 21-year-old niece, calling her grandfather by his Christian name, as she was wont to do.

'It was a different time,' I told her. 'Parents could beat their children within an inch of their lives back then. In fact, it was pretty much compulsory.'

'I would never have punched any of them... They might have had the odd slap.'

'Well, that's all right then,' laughed oldest nephew Michael, who just couldn't possibly be 24 years old like he claimed.

'It was the only physical contact we ever had. We came to see the punchings as acts of affection,' said my sister Jill.

'Don't say such things,' my mum interjected. 'We were very loving parents who hardly ever hit our children.'

The whole family, my mother excepted, were laughing heartily at this rather qualified denial.

'Yes they were. We were very lucky!' I agreed. 'Anyway, I had scarpered out of the room to avoid another pummelling, but he was coming after me. He was furious. God knows what I'd said. I'd probably called him a wanker!'

My youngest niece Emily (who said she was seventeen but by my calculations was still a foetus) choked on her dinner and was aghast, but delighted by my profanity.

'Richard!' chastised my mother, playfully raising her hand as if to slap me.

'See... see,' I pleaded to the younger generation. 'They can't help themselves.'

'Just tell the story,' demanded Andrew impatiently.

'All right, all right. I ran upstairs... up those very stairs there.' I pointed through the open dining-room door. 'He was hot on my heels and my only hope to save my skin was to turn around and kick my father, T. K. Herring, MSc, down half a flight of stairs.'

'Balderdash!'

'His back smacked against the wall...' I clapped my hands loudly to indicate the strength of the impact.

'Don't be ridiculous,' shouted Dad over the laughter.

'I can still see your astonished, purple face.'

'If I'd fallen down half a flight of stairs you'd have killed me.'

'It felt like that. It might just have been four or five. Or a couple.'

'Or none,' suggested Dad.

'And maybe it wasn't so much a kick as a girly little slap,' added my brother David.

'Why would I make this up?'

'What happened then?' asked Andrew excitedly.

'I don't exactly remember…' I replied, secretly wondering whether this whole thing had been conjured up by an overactive imagination.

'Nothing happened because none of it is true,' Dad blustered.

'Can we just get on with our lunch in a civilised fashion?' requested my mother, with exaggerated dignity. 'This is meant to be a day of celebration.'

Indeed it was. I wondered how many more times I was going to be called upon to mark this unwanted birthday, which still hadn't actually happened. I was very much in my thirties. Why was everyone so keen to pre-empt it? There were twelve days of youth still ahead of me and in that period it seemed fairly likely that scientists might invent a device that could stop time, or reverse it. The chances were that I would remain young for ever and yet everyone else seemed to be ignoring this very real possibility.

But we were also celebrating another landmark. In two days' time my mum would be turning 70 and if she thought science was going to invent a time-reversing machine in just 48 hours she was living in a dream world.

Mum was 30 years and ten days older than me and I clearly remembered the day she turned 40.

'Happy birthday!' I had told her as I handed her the slightly wonky spice rack I had made in woodwork class. 'Thirty-nine again!'

'That's right,' Mum observed, 'I'll be 39 every year from now on.' She'd laughed along, but only now in hindsight could I see she'd been hiding a little pain behind her eyes. At ten years old I had just seen my parents as old people and would never have imagined they could suffer from existential angst, even if I had known what that was.

Yet to be celebrating her 70th birthday was more of a jolt for me (and presumably also for her), though it didn't make me consider that maybe I was being self-indulgent in being so affected by a relatively minor landmark.

In my mind, Mum and Dad are still 40. And I couldn't be the same age as them. My self-denial works to such an extent that when I mentally picture my dad he is brown-haired and youthful, broad-shouldered and in his prime. But if I actually stop to look at him properly then I see that he is in reality in his seventies, his hair is silver and his posture slightly stooped and if he tried to scoop me up and hoist me on to his shoulders now it would probably kill him. Though to be fair, even the fit 40-year-old version would have some difficulty shifting my present bulk.

But when it comes to visiting my old Cheddar Valley home, I find it astonishing and embarrassing how far I regress to childhood. It's something that I have long been trying to get recognised by the scientific community, with my new and immutable laws of relativity. To be honest, they crap all over Einstein.

My first theory of relativity states that time moves more slowly when you spend it with your relatives. No one can argue with that. But more pertinently my second theory of relativity states that time with your family and time in the real world move at different speeds. You could leave your family for decades, but when you finally come home again you find that even though you have aged, back here only a few seconds have elapsed. Nothing changes, the roles, the relationships. So even though my brother and I are both middle-aged, he is still expected to be the sensible and grown-up one, and allowances are made for my juvenile behaviour because I'm 'the youngest'. It's not just me still seeing my parents as 40-year-olds; they still treat me as if I was ten. Which gives me licence to be puerile and irresponsible.

It was time to give and receive presents. Mum had not taken the hint and another year passed without me receiving the Scalextric set that I had always coveted, but my sister had made me a birthday cake, decorated with the words 'Oh Fuck, I'm 40!', the childish title of my new stand-up show.

'I'd just like to remind everyone that I am actually still 39,' I said.

'Yes, just like I am,' replied Mum. 'Every single year.'

'No, no. I am really 39. I'm not 40 yet. And if my plans come to fruition I never will be.'

'It's not worth killing yourself over this, son,' observed my dad. 'You're worrying about nothing. Life begins at 40.'

'Or maybe it just seems like that because your brain is so raddled with dementia that you can't recall anything that has happened before.'

My mum shot me an angry look. My grandma had been so uncharacteristically quiet at the far end of the table that I had forgotten she was there, though of course she wasn't aware she had dementia. She was more worried about who all these strangers that she was eating alongside could possibly be.

My parents' gift to me was an album that they'd put together full of photos from my 40 years on the planet. It was genuinely touching, not that I would let them know that, but was also another reminder of the cruel and unforgiving swiftness of the passage of time.

I had struggled to think what I should buy for my mother – I don't know what 70-year-old women like – but had finally come up with the genius idea of arranging for her and Dad to spend a night at a posh hotel in Oxfordshire, with dinner at its Michelin-starred restaurant.

Which is a bit more impressive than a crappy album full of old photos, don't you think?

Mum and Dad were really delighted. It was nice to give them something back after all the deprivation and physical assaults.

A thought suddenly struck me. 'Have you still got that spice rack I made you when you were 40, Mum?'

My mother's smile froze.

'Oh… yes… of course I do. I loved that spice rack. I mean, I love it,' she blustered.

'It's just I haven't seen it around in the kitchen recently. Or at any point in the last 29 years.'

'No, no. That's because that spice rack is so beautiful and important to me that I only get it out on very special occasions.'

'Like a joint 70th and 40th birthday party.'

'Oh no, even more special than that.'

I flicked through my photo album for the third time in the five minutes that I had had it. It was such a lovely thing to have been given. There was my weary but smiling young mother, holding me in the hospital, just two hours old.

There I was, just nine or ten years later, high on the broad shoulders of my dad, the way that my imagination still pictured him. I realised that in that photo, Dad had been the same age as I am now. It inevitably made me consider the differences in our two lives.

When my dad turned 40 he had been married for seventeen years, had three children, two of them teenagers. He had worked hard as a teacher all his adult life and recently been promoted to headmaster, wore a suit and tie every day and had proper grown-up hobbies like gardening, golf and making elderflower wine. He had a tool shed and a garden and was capable of self-sufficiency if he and Mum ever wanted to emulate Tom and Barbara Good (who, thinking about it, they did somewhat resemble).

Now I was practically 40 (though still 39, in case you'd forgotten) yet I was single, had never been married, never even lived with anyone and had no kids. Like Dad I was sleeping with a married woman; unlike Dad I wasn't married to her. I was sloshing around in the insecure (in both senses) world of stand-up comedy. I spent most of my evenings out drinking with people in their twenties and if I so wished (and seemed to be doing with increasing regularity) could spend my whole daytime playing Scrabble on my Nintendo DS. I had the latest Arctic Monkeys CD (I hadn't listened to it, but I had it and that was what was important), wore Converse trainers and had lost thousands of pounds over the last two years playing online poker. I had no practical skills whatsoever, paying other people to mend broken stuff and even do my cleaning. If the Apocalypse came and I survived it, I would have nothing of use to contribute to the new society. People don't want to hear cock jokes after Armageddon.

My parents' generation pretty much had their life mapped out for them from the start: they had limited choices about what they could do professionally, needed to work to survive and got married early either because sex outside of wedlock was frowned upon, or because they had had sex out of wedlock and pregnancy had followed. A proper job and the responsibility of a family will soon make a twenty-year-old grow up, whether they want to or not. And the shame attached to divorce meant that couples mainly just made a go of it, no matter how unsuited to each other they were.

But my generation had more choice. While my dad almost automatically followed his father into the teaching profession, I had career options. Perhaps foolishly, but fittingly for someone who wanted to remain puerile, I chose writing and performing comedy. Even had that been a viable profession in the 1960s, my dad could never have followed it, a) because he had a wife and young children to support, which requires money and, b) because he is really not funny in spite of what he might think. I was in debt for the first decade of my career. If I'd had a family, I'd have had to get a job. Because I was single I could get by eating baked potatoes and wait for better times.

Effective contraception, along with the subsequent shifting social attitude to sex outside of marriage, meant that my generation has much more of a choice about when and if they have kids. It meant marriage and responsibility could be postponed indefinitely, allowing us to focus entirely on ourselves.

I looked at a photo of my five-year-old self, contentedly licking an ice-cream cone, between my 50-something, then lucid grandma, Doris, and my now sadly departed but much loved grandad, Don, from whom I had inherited my stature and fine mop of hair. He was the person who had first sparked my interest in comedy, always ready with a funny face or a silly pun or a magically appearing coin or a Chaplinesque piece of slapstick. Sometimes I didn't even understand the jokes, but I would still laugh, because I knew my grandad was funny. And I not only loved him for it, but wanted to emulate him.

I wondered what Don Hannan would make of my cushy life of irresponsibility, if he was still alive to witness it. He had worked his whole life in the building trade, proper hard labour, in order to earn a basic living to provide for his wife and child, yet to me, all the world's a playground and all the men and women merely hopscotch players. I made a better living than he could have ever dreamed of from pulling the funny faces and saying the silly things that he had given away for free.

I thought of the many ridiculous things I had done in my career: I had travelled to Inverness with a theatrical sword in an attempt to kill the Loch Ness monster. I had dated 50 different women in 50 consecutive nights, as part of my job. When Pope John Paul II had died I had written to the Vatican applying for the now vacant job, even though I had never been a Catholic and described myself as an atheist. I had dressed up as Pestilence, the horseman of the Apocalypse, and driven a milk float across Barnes Common. I had appeared bare-ass naked in front of a live audience and then simulated sex with a thousand-year-old skeleton. This was my ludicrous job. I got paid for doing this crap.

My grandad never travelled anywhere in a plane in his whole life. If he saw me, globe-trotting, drinking champagne high above the clouds, would he hate me or envy me? Or would he be proud and pleased that life was so much better for his grandchildren than it had been for him?

Then I wondered what my grandchildren, who I would probably never live to see if they existed at all, would make of my silly irresponsible life? What kind of world were the selfish antics of my generation going to create for them? And would they resent me just as much as I admired my grandfather his selflessness?

Sitting here having a birthday dinner with my parents and siblings, who had all lived a proper grown-up life, getting jobs and raising families, made me increasingly aware of how my lifestyle did not fit in with what was expected of a man of my age.

As a self-employed writer and comedian I rarely have to deal with businessmen or bank managers. I earn money, put it in the bank, take it out of the cash machine and spend it on booze and sweets.

But a few years ago, I'd had a bit of a purple patch, thanks to a sitcom I had written. I received a phone call from my bank asking me to come in for a meeting that would make an odd and lasting impression on me. I was to meet Alan Goodman, who was apparently my 'Premium Manager'.

I didn't know why he was called that. Was he better than all the other managers at the bank? Or was I somehow better than the other customers? And if it was the latter, was I better than other customers based on my financial position or because I had a nicer personality? I hoped that they had just judged me a good bloke and had asked me to come in for a pat on the back. It would be nice to think that the NatWest was not all about money, money, money.

I was still a bit nervous about being called in to my bank. It felt like I was going to be told off and reminded me of the time I'd had to go and see the headmaster at primary school. But this time I had not been smearing my bogeys on the underside of my desk. At least, there was no way that Alan Goodman could know that.

I turned up at the bank a little bit late, unshaven and lightly hungover. I had forgotten to set my alarm and hadn't had enough time to shower, though sprayed myself with aftershave to mask this oversight. Unfortunately, tardiness had forced me to jog down to the bank and I was conscious that I was sweating and fairly convinced that despite the Contradiction For Men (or possibly because of it), my perspiration was smelling of drunken debauchery. Anyone from my dad's generation would not contemplate meeting even a regular bank manager in anything but a suit, but I was in T-shirt and jeans, with turn-ups that had been dragging on the floor and become torn and frayed and hooked around my shoes like strange denim stirrups.

Alan Goodman could scarcely have been more different from me if he had tried. He wore an unpretentious suit and nylon shirt that I think he almost certainly bought from Marks and Spencer. He was balding, and though the crown of his head was entirely exposed, the hair that remained around his ears and above his neck was neatly trimmed. He smelt of neither booze nor sweat, but maybe faintly of Imperial Leather soap. I assumed that he was older than me, but then I still make that delusional assumption of anyone who has a proper job or a position of authority. He could have easily been my age or younger.

I liked him despite our apparent differences. He was polite and quietly charming and seemed bound to inherit the earth, thanks to an appealing meekness. He proudly informed me that he'd been working in banking for seventeen years and oversaw the accounts of 700 people. At the time I was writing an 80,000-word book entirely about the human penis.

I felt very quickly that I was not his typical customer.

He had filled in the details he already knew on his form. When he got to occupation he said, 'I've put this in pencil, "writer and comedian". Is that still what you do?'

From his perspective the idea of being in my thirties and making a living as a writer and comedian was a fantastical impossibility. Something that I had once claimed to be, while being an unemployed young man, but which time had shown to be a pipe dream. Surely the healthy state of my bank balance must mean that I had seen sense and was now working in the City.

Or maybe from the state of me he was assuming I was now a tramp.

In either case it gave me quite a kick to confound his expectations as I replied, 'Yeah, I'm still doing that,' before adding slightly archly, 'You can probably put that in pen.' He said he'd do it later. It would be neater. He was going to rub out the pencil and write it in again in ink. That was the kind of man Alan Goodman was. A good man. Like he'd been named by the uninventive mind of William Thackeray.

He inevitably asked me what I'd been working on recently. I told him about my sitcom which had aired on a satellite television channel. Like most of the population, he had never heard of it. And although he didn't ask, I couldn't resist telling him that I was also writing a book called *Talking Cock*.

His bald pate visibly reddened and he literally spluttered. He asked, 'Is that what it sounds like?' I told him it was. He was taking notes down as we chatted, but as he attempted to add this information, his shaking hand actually rebelled against him. The word 'cock' became a dyslexic mixture of those constituent letters. He laughed as he exclaimed, 'I can't even write it down!'

Two worlds colliding that were never meant to meet.

I was going to ask him at the end if I'd been called in because of having some money in the bank or because he'd heard I might be a good laugh to hang around with. But before I could, he tried to persuade me to sign up for NatWest Premier banking, where, it seemed to me, you paid £150 a year in order to look like a swanky tosser (though that isn't exactly how he sold it to me).

That pretty much answered my question.

So how had Alan Goodman and I taken such different paths in life and how frustrated must he be to know that this sweaty, sweary man in raggedy clothes in front of him was earning enough money to be considered for a Premium account? Would he have still chosen to spend seventeen years in the bank if he had known that he could make a living from writing cock jokes?

Perhaps Alan Goodman made such an impact on me because of a careers advice meeting I had had at school when I was a sixth-former, twenty years before. Mr Murray was seeing us all individually to discuss what we hoped we might do with our lives and to suggest avenues that we might wish to explore. I may be wrong, but I think he had employed some primitive computer programme to help him come to the correct vocation for each of us, but what is certain is that he had some method of determining from the information he had about each of us what we would be doing for the next 40 years. I remember it seemed less like advice than an absolute and impeachable vision of our future. Like he had a Harry Potter-style sorting hat that would tell us what we were doing and there was no point in arguing because the magic headwear was infallible.

Giving some pretence that there was to be some self-determination and free will in our lives, Mr Murray asked me what I hoped I might become when I grew up (nice that he made the assumption that that might happen).

'I want to be a writer or a comedian. Or maybe an actor,' I told him. I had enjoyed writing stories and making people laugh for as long as I remembered and while other kids loved music and idolised pop stars, I just listened to comedy records and my heroes were Michael Palin and Rik Mayall. I hoped beyond hope that I might somehow follow them into the exciting world of comedy.

'Well, obviously you can't do that,' said Mr Murray, rather casually and blankly, stamping on my fragile dream like it was a snail on a damp pavement. He could have let it live: it was doing no one any harm. But what the hell? Stamp on it anyway.

Maybe such a job wasn't on his forms and was thus void or maybe he was just being realistic and knew that this was not a viable career for a young man from Somerset in the early 1980s. I am sure he felt he was helping me.

According to the sorting hat or whatever magical process he had fed my skills and A level subjects and projected grades into, I, he proudly announced, was going to work in a bank.

'Really?' I said, unable to mask my surprise or disappointment.

While I knew that making a living as a comedian was fanciful at best, it was obvious to me that I was never going to work in a bank. If I was going to get a proper job, once I'd been to university, then surely I would go into the family business and become a teacher. That's what Mum and Dad did and that is ultimately what my brother and sister and even my eldest nephew would become. I had no interest in working in a bank and while I was good at maths, had very little interest in money or the economy. I could see immediately the whole thing was a crock of shit and my face betrayed this conclusion.

Mr Murray leaned in close to me, his nose against mine, and whispered in a sinister voice, 'You're going to work in a bank, Herring. There's no point in fighting it. Your future is etched in stone. So predictable that it can be calculated to 99.9 per cent accuracy even by the crappy computers we have here in the early eighties. Give up on your dream. You're going to work in a bank!' Then he threw back his head and laughed manically before adding, 'Do you think I wanted to be a careers adviser? Of course I didn't. But I did what I was told I would do. We must accept our role in society like the drones we most surely are.'

All right, maybe that last bit didn't happen exactly that way, but that's the gist of it.

Had he told me I'd be a teacher I might have accepted the unbending accuracy of his predictive powers and kowtowed, but

I was never going to work in a bank, so I rebelled against expectations and had a go at the comedy and writing thing instead.

And after twenty years, now I understand why Mr Murray was kindly trying to steer me in a different direction...

Looking at Alan Goodman was like looking into a Harry Potter-style mirror (like most adults nowadays, Harry Potter is my only literary frame of reference), which tells you how your life might have been had you taken the path that careers advice had dictated.

I wondered if Alan had gone into his careers advice meeting with dreams of being a beat poet or an astronaut and his Mr Murray had laughed in his face and told him he had to be a banker and he had just meekly accepted that, like the good man that he was.

Or was I being patronising? Maybe Alan Goodman's careers adviser had told him he was going to be a spy or a gigolo and Alan had turned to him and said, 'No way! I am going to be a Premium Manager to upwards of 700 people in the Balham area.'

'You can't be that, Goodman. The careers advice computer has spoken.'

'Well, fuck the careers advice computer and fuck you. I know who I am and what I shall be. I am not a number. I am a good man!'

I know that Mum and Dad had selected the cutest baby pictures for the album they'd given me, but it was still remarkable what a happy child I clearly was. In every one I was chuckling or merrily gurning or giving such a cheeky smirk that I could only guess what awful mischief I had been up to.

There I was, twelve months old, rolling in the grass with my big sister, smiling like the whole world was tickling me. And in the next shot, six months later, standing up now, a bulbous nappy round my rear end and an oversized police helmet covering my head, cheekily pouting for the camera. Then a couple of years have passed and I am coming in from the garden, as naked and innocent as Adam, covered head to foot in self-applied mud, my white teeth shining out from among the murk as I grin from muddy ear to muddy ear.

It appeared that I was always bound to be a comedian.

As soon as I learned to speak, I discovered that certain words gave me a rare moment of power and control: those that referred to bodily functions, to bodily waste and the usually hidden bodily parts responsible for most of this fantastic detritus. These words would amuse on the most basic level, but there was something subtler at play because they also had the potential to infuriate, and anger. In a world where adults wielded all the control, it was incredible to possess this slingshot which was capable of stopping this humourless, impatient, fractious Goliath in its tracks. To make them stutter and splutter and momentarily lose that air of unbreakable authority that they claimed to have.

It showed their hypocrisy too. They wanted to hide certain vital components of life from view, to pretend they didn't exist, to make believe that the world was clean and polite. They were ashamed of the bodily functions that as children we realised were natural and universal and should not be a source of embarrassment.

Pretty much the first thing I ever said was the phrase, 'Wee wee, poo poo, bottom,' which I thought was hilarious (and to be honest I still do). In fact, I found it so amusing that I repeated it on a loop for a good proportion of the next nine years. It was my first and in some ways purest catchphrase and interestingly is my adult stand-up act pretty much distilled down into its essential components. It was also a mantra against the unnatural world view that was being imposed from above.

I would sing out those words in staccato fashion, relishing the percussive finale of 'bot-tom' with unconcealed squealing delight. My parents would quickly tire of it, then become impatient, even cross, but nothing they could say or do would make me stop. I was insistent on proving them entirely wrong when they would casually remark to my siblings, 'Ignore him, he will soon get bored of it.' I never did. On and on it went. I knew it was getting to them, even when they feigned otherwise. And far from thinking it got more pathetic as I got older, I was (I still believe) right to realise it actually made it funnier. A three-year-old talking about wee is par for the course, but a ten-year-old doing the same? This was a work of art, a piece of theatre, as effective a satire of the world and humanity's pretensions to rise above the animalistic as anything by Beckett or Pinter.

The adult world tried to stamp this out right from the start. When I was just three years old, my parents would try and shame me into an unnatural maturity by telling me that I was acting like a baby, yet I paid no heed. I knew it was a trick and a lie. I looked around and saw I was actually behaving like all other three-year-olds. And if any three-year-old was being priggish and sneering about such puerile behaviour then it was them who was the oddball.

While with one breath adults would ruefully sigh, 'Why do they ever have to grow up?', with the next they were barking, 'Act your age, not your shoe size.' How oppressive that phrase is when you think about it. I was five, my shoe size was four. What kind of sane society chastises a five-year-old for acting like a four-year-old? If you can't be childish when you're a child, when can you be childish?

'Why can't you be like Jenny?' my parents would protest. 'She's your age, but she's so mature.' I hated people like Jenny and I didn't trust them. They were the same uptight prigs who saved up their Easter eggs for months on end. They were denying all their natural impulses, being sucked into the phoney world of adulthood, and in turn sucking up to the adults, claiming not to be amused by farts and bogeys and bottoms. I knew in my heart that they had to be pretending. These things were naturally just funny and, in fact, at that age, we only knew a tiny proportion of the functions of our bodies and the additional humorous possibilities. If we had only known the truth!

And if Jenny and her ilk genuinely were unamused by these things then it was actually because they, not I, were unsophisticated. They were unable to understand that this was much more than giggling at a smell or a word or a willy bouncing up and down as you danced (but come on, that is pretty funny on its own). It was about subversion. Adults had all the power and yet with the use of a well-timed belch or mention of one of those magical unmentionables, their pomposity could be pricked, their hypocrisy could be revealed, their world view of a genital-free, excrementless Utopia was debunked.

Even as a teenager, when so many people are yearning for the freedom of adulthood and trying to appear sophisticated and mature, I refused to leave my cherished childhood behind. The photos from my schooldays rarely showed a petulant, depressed adolescent: instead there are Cheshire cat grins, Hogarthian grimaces and a young man dressed up, not in the latest New Romantic trends, but in huge checked old man jackets and garishly coloured kipper ties (with no pun intended).

I had realised something many of my peers hadn't; that we were only truly free in this world when we were children. It was adults that were unliberated and confined. We were born free, yet everywhere we were in chains and so many of my school mates seemed to be forging their irons for themselves, then locking them tight around themselves and throwing away the key.

They believed Mr Murray, they craved the idea of getting a proper job and earning money and leaving playfulness and rebellion behind. My friends and I were suspicious of the girls in our year who were hanging around with older boys, pretending they were urbane and grown up, who pitied us for our continued juvenility. We were more sophisticated than them because we saw the truth and we knew what we really were and believed we had none of their pretensions, even though, in reality, we were mainly jealous that their sexual interest was directed elsewhere. We called them 'Premature Maturions', thinking them foolish for willingly opting out of these last few years of actual freedom.

But I managed to keep my youth on an artificial respirator long after everyone else had accepted that theirs was dead and told the doctors to pull the plug. First by going to university – which was less a chance to study and more a chance to postpone adulthood for three valuable years – and then by becoming a comedian. If you were going to try and create a comedian in a laboratory then you would surely take a student and a four-year-old and try and force them into the same telepod, knowing that if they fused during transportation that a wise-cracking cock-obsessed comic would emerge through the dry ice at the other end.

At the heart of it all I realised I wished that I was still at school. I wished I'd never had to leave.

I often daydreamed about a world where adults were allowed to stay on at school, not hanging around with schoolkids – I'm not strange – but you're still in class with people your own age, still learning, still having fun in that safe and familiar structure.

I didn't want to go to an evening class. I wanted to have to get up at 7.30am and then go to a school, where all my day is mapped out for me on a timetable and people teach me stuff and I get to have a break where I can play football with a tennis ball, against the other 39-year-old men, and then there would be after-school clubs where we could put on plays or have quiz teams and every now and again there would be a disco where I could snog some of the 39-year-old women who were in my class, after I had sneaked in some vodka to put in the punch. Why can't we have that? It would be great. Why do we have to work? Why can't we just learn stuff and have everything planned out for us? And then have a six-week summer holiday, where we hang out up Cheddar Gorge, playing on the video games and trying to get 39-year-old women to talk to us.

I pay taxes and a lot of those taxes go to education and yet I don't have any kids to benefit from the billions of pounds I donated. I think they should set up one school for childless adults and just see how it goes. I think enough people would attend to make it viable. It could work.

Especially if everyone had to wear uniforms.

Immaturity and childishness are seen as pejorative terms when applied to child and adult alike. Yet it seems to me it is the mature who retain the worst aspects of childishness – the belief that the world revolves around you, the impatience, the petulance, while the immature hold on to the many beautiful and superior aspects of puerility. There is an innocence and honesty to the child that makes them capable of seeing through much of the crap that adults have come to accept as normal and desirable. They are also able to express wonder at the world, rather than jadedly taking it for granted. To see the beauty and magic in everyday life, to be fascinated beyond boredom by a leaf or a cardboard box or a silly gag.

I have always admired babies for their ability to be constantly amused by exactly the same 'joke'. If human beings only carried this trait on into adulthood then my job would be very easy. All I would have to do is go on stage and move my hand over my face, alternating between a happy and a sad face as it passed, over and over again, and the crowd would be rolling in the aisles.

After lunch we went outside into the garden for some drinks. The sun was shining and everyone was in good spirits. Even my grandma was full of beans. She stood in the shade of a tree with her 85-year-old toyboy, Ken. When my grandad died, about twenty years before, Doris had still been voluptuous and lively and looked and behaved like a woman a quarter of a century younger than her actual 75 years. After a respectable period of mourning she discovered she, like an OAP Penelope, had suitors queuing round the block for her. She seemed keen to make the most of her life and I think that maybe I take after her in such aspects of my personality. Ken, a gentle and softly spoken old fella, had won the contest and despite their grey hair and wrinkles they were love's young dream and sweet and affectionate.

I hope I am still as frisky and disgraceful when I get to Doris's age. I love my grandma. She is the most amazing woman I have ever met. Pertinently, on her 85th birthday she had turned to me and lamented, 'I can't believe I'm 85. It doesn't make any sense. Inside I still feel like I'm 25.'

Even at her current 95 years of age, Grandma still had remarkable physical and mental agility, though her short-term memory was shot to pieces. Ironically she now seemed to genuinely believe she was at least 40 years younger than she actually was, her mind flitting around between different times and places, sometimes thinking she was in the house she had lived in 60 years before, sometimes thinking that my mother was Doris's older sister, Babs.

Grandma was still very crafty at concealing her mental disability. As I approached Doris and Ken in the garden she said, 'Ah yes, well, we know this young man, don't we?' Though I knew she had no idea who I was. 'Have you met him before, Ken?' she asked. Ken and I both said we knew each other, but she'd forget and ask again, perplexed about who I was and why I was here. 'How old are you?' she asked me.

'I'm 39.'

'Oh yes, and have we met before today?'

'A couple of times.'

'Do you know him, Ken?

'Yes, yes, I know him very well.'

'Of course we know you. Yes. How old are you?'

'I'm 39. Still in my thirties. Very much so.'

'That's a lovely age to be, isn't it?'

'How old are you, Doris?' I asked cheekily.

'I'm...' She went to answer but her brain could not keep up with her mouth. She looked confused and then laughed at this seemingly ridiculous situation. 'I don't know! How old am I, Babs?'

'You're 95, Mum.'

'Eeee, I'm not, am I?' She was bemused rather than upset, like life was playing some silly game with her.

'And who is this handsome young man?'

'Mum, this is Richard, my son,' my mother patiently reiterated.

Doris looked bamboozled. 'No, it can't be Richard. Richard's just a baby. How old are you?'

'I'm still 39.'

'Though keep on asking, because he'll be 40 any second now. It's nearly his birthday,' Mum explained. 'You'd better start saving up for a present for him.'

'Oh, Doris doesn't have to worry about that. She's given me enough,' I commented. 'My gran don't owe me nothing!'

Doris, sharp as a tack, came straight back with, 'Well, if I don't owe you nothing, then I owe you something. I was always a whizz at grammar.'

'I know that. You're my grammar grandma, that's for sure.'

We all laughed together and Doris smiled at me, before saying, 'And remind me where I've met you before, young man.'

It made me a little bit sad, but there was a lot to be positive about. Doris was still happy and feisty and she'd lived a long, full life and was showing no signs of giving up on it just yet. If I was going to stay alive as long and remain as vigorous and compos mentis and sexually active as she had, then I still had a good half a century ahead of me. Though at the back of my mind I was seized by the mortal dread that my brain and body would soon begin to atrophy. My hip was already starting to ache in the mornings and I sometimes suffered from a mild form of dizziness. Names and facts occasionally inexplicably slipped my mind.

And maybe Doris wouldn't have proved quite as hardy had she lived on a diet of Guinness and Flumpses.

I left Cheddar with another bagful of childish things given to me by my relatives: playing cards and shot glasses and some slippers that farted when you walked in them. My nephew Andrew had given me the slippers, subtly pointing out that I was not only an old fart, but one who deserved such a puerile gift.

As I drove home, I wondered if my continued immaturity was down to me trying to compensate for some perceived privation in my childhood. If my parents had just bought me that Scalextric set, would none of this have happened? Or if I hadn't had to share my sweets with my siblings might I have felt no need to stuff my face with them now? Was I making up for being so square during my teens and twenties? Or did I live this lifestyle simply because I could? Would my grandad have done the same if he had only had the chance? Was I the luckiest man in the world and if so why was I feeling like such a failure?

Virtue is its own reward,
But the unvirtuous need to be rewarded.
With awards.
Gaudy awards.

CHAPTER 7
I'D JUST LIKE TO THANK...

5 July 2007 – 7 days to 40

'You've been nominated for what?' choked Emma, so loudly that I had to hold the phone away from my ear.

'The *Arena* Magazine Awards Best Comedian of the Year.'

'Ha ha ha!' she screeched like a banshee. 'Surely there's been some kind of administrative error? What have you even done this year that's been funny? I mean deliberately funny.'

'I know, it does seem odd.'

'I can think of a hundred comedians who deserve that more than you. Proper comedians off the telly. Like Harry Hill, Russell Brand, Alan Carr, The Mighty Boosh...'

'Yeah, all right...'

'What about French and Saunders or Harry Enfield? Or Stewart Lee – he's miles better than you.'

'That's below the belt.'

'Best comedian? You? That's the funniest thing you've ever said. You deserve the award for that alone.'

'Yeah, I know. I obviously won't win. But, look, there's an awards ceremony and there's a dinner and loads of celebrities we can gawp at. And you never know, I might win.'

'You really won't. What about Paul Merton or Jack Dee or Al Murray...'

'Shut up. It'll be fun whatever. And I get a plus one, and I was thinking of asking you before you were so impertinent.'

'Oh, please let me come. Pleeease!'

'Well... All right then.'

'I can't wait to see your crushed expression when you don't win.' Suddenly Emma was suspicious. 'But why are you inviting me? Why aren't you taking one of your floozies?'

'Because, Emma, you are my best friend.'

'And?'

'And there will be loads of models from the magazine there and I am planning to get off with them all and you're the only person I can think of who won't mind if I ditch them to go off and shag a supermodel.'

'Yeah, good luck with that.'

'Plus the woman I wanted to take couldn't come, because she said her husband wouldn't like it...'

'Richard Keith!' barked Emma. 'You're not going out with a married woman.'

'Well, no, we stay in most of the time.'

'No, no, that's not right. You've got to stop that. Seriously. I'm not even joking. What would your mum say?'

'I know. I'm going to knock it on the head...'

'I'm very disappointed in you. I can put up with most of your antics. But that's beyond the pale.'

'I know, I know... You know who's going to be at the do? Only Harry Shearer!' I knew Emma would be apoplectic to be in the same room as the man who had appeared in our favourite film, *This is Spinal Tap*, as well as being the voice of (among many others) Mr Burns from *The Simpsons*.

'Excellent!' she replied, perfectly aping the boss of the Springfield Nuclear Plant, her *Simpsons* impressions being much better than mine. 'There'll be some crap celebrities there as well though, won't there?'

'There'll be tons of them. We're going to have the time of our young lives. Well, I'll have the time of my young life, I'm still in my thirties, remember. You can have the time of your dried-up old 40-something life.'

I was genuinely mystified about how I had come to be nominated for this award and that's not the false modesty you usually get at these events. This was a very unusual scenario for me.

I had been a stand-up and writer for almost twenty years and while I have worked constantly and had some limited successes, I think it's fair to say that I was not yet a household name. My dad could still justifiably question when I would be famous. I could walk down the street without being mobbed by fans. I might get recognised about once a month, but usually by someone who thought I was someone else, like Father Dougal from *Father Ted*, or Dom Joly.

Recently, for example, I had been sitting with my newspaper in a bar and a man had approached me with palpable reverence. 'I just want to congratulate you,' he said, holding out a quivering hand.

Instinctively I took it and said, 'Thank you,' though I wasn't sure what he was so impressed by. I was admittedly halfway through a medium *Guardian* sudoku and hadn't yet had to write in any little numbers in tiny writing in the corner of the squares to assist me. Maybe it was that.

He sensed my confusion. 'Well done on the *Long Way Round*,' he explained. 'An amazing achievement.'

I smiled and looked pleased with myself, but then I realised that that didn't mean anything to me at all. 'Sorry, I don't know what you're talking about.'

'You're Charley Boorman, right?' he told me, and when he saw my blank face he said, 'You motorcycled round the world with Ewan McGregor,' as if it was still possible I might be the man he thought I was and had merely forgotten this epic journey.

'You've got the wrong person,' I told him.

He looked at me with suspicion. 'Are you sure?'

'Yeah, I'm pretty certain,' I told him.

I certainly live in a strange hinterland outside the citadel of celebrity, but close enough for the light from that celestial location to occasionally fall upon me. I feel like some kind of chimera-like beast, living in a bush, eating grubs, who will look up to be blinded and confused by the bright lights in the near distance. Intermittently the gatekeepers of the diamond paradise will leave a dish of milk out in the back garden for me and sometimes even allow me into the servants' quarters of this ass menagerie to feast on the crumbs that Science from *Big Brother* could not manage to consume.

In a similar vein to Groucho Marx, generally I don't really want to attend a celebrity party that would want me as a guest. Because if I am invited then the barrel is really being scraped.

Earlier in the year I had got an email at 6.30pm inviting me to a media launch that was happening that evening at eight. Which I think shows how desperate they must have been at that stage to have anyone remotely recognisable, even, as in my case, if they were chiefly recognisable as someone else.

When you are invited to something with an hour and a half to spare, you can be certain that you were not very high on the priorities of the party-giver. You can only really conclude that they invited a hell of a lot of other people, giving them more than 90 minutes' notice, and that those people did not want to come. Concerned that they might not have enough people to fill the room (and obviously not wishing to throw the doors open to 'ordinary' people who haven't even been on a poor-quality reality TV show), they opened some long-forgotten filing cabinet and picked out an old list, blew the dust off and found my name.

Could anyone with a modicum of intelligence be anything but insulted by this? Did they expect me to be pleased?

The email went out of its way to make it perfectly clear that I was a last resort and even included a list of the 'other celebrities' that had agreed to come to the party and who thus must have been invited with rather more notice. Which would have been less insulting if it had been full of A-list movie stars, but I think if I give you just a few examples you will see my lowly position in the cavalcade of twats. Confirmed guests included:

Peaches Geldof – a woman who as far as I could tell was really only famous for having shot out of the cock of someone famous, though admittedly into the vaginal passage of someone else who was famous, so perhaps that's enough.

L'il Chris – a tiny boy who had appeared on a reality show and had put out a couple of records as a result, who sadly I was quite excited about having the chance to meet. I was glad to see his name written down for the first time, as I had always assumed when I had heard people talking about him that he was sponsored by Lidl.

Patrick Neate – no, I had never heard of him either, though have subsequently found out he's a novelist who apparently won the Whitbread Prize in 2001 and is thus apparently a bigger celebrity than me.

There was even a list of celebrities who *might* be attending the party, which included H from Steps. I decided that I did not want to go to a party that even H from Steps was uncertain he wanted to be at. I stayed at home and ate a tub of Phish Food ice cream on my own instead.

It was probably for the best. I am not very good at playing the game when it comes to these events. You're supposed to act all cool and relaxed, with an unbreakable sense of entitlement and not even be a little bit fazed by being surrounded by loads of people who you've seen on the telly.

I can't do that. Even after two decades in this business I still have the need to be both in awe of and to mock proper celebrities.

The first time I went to BBC TV Centre I was not only filled with wee-making glee to be in the building where *Swap Shop* was filmed and to see the fountain that Roy Castle had tap-danced around on *Record Breakers* and to be in the same vicinity as the *Blue Peter* garden which had been vandalised so callously and hilariously in the 80s,[1] but when I found myself standing next to

---

2. I had been genuinely disappointed to find out that all BBC programmes don't get their own garden. Why should *Blue Peter* be the only one?

Jeremy Paxman in the lift I almost expired from the excitement. I made a point of touching his briefcase when he wasn't looking. As if that would somehow confer some of his magical stardom on to me.

I was glad I hadn't lost that even as I was knocking on 40's door. But it did make it difficult for me to go to any events where lots of celebrities would be congregating.

I'd been invited to the ITV Summer Party because I'd written and acted in a drama for them that had just gone out that June. It was in the posh Orangery down a long drive in the middle of London's Hyde Park. I came on the tube and had to walk to the venue, but by the constant stream of taxis and posh cars going back and forth beside me as I trudged, I would say I was almost the only one to arrive on foot. Which gives another accurate representation of my status.

It was jam-packed with some of the country's favourite entertainers. If some insane fan or extremist terrorist had decided to stand on the Orangery roof with a machine gun they could have changed the face of British broadcasting. David Jason, Chris Tarrant, Ant and Dec, Amanda 'A-Hol' Holden and the bloke who does the voice of Nick Clegg on *Headcases* (but how would anyone know whether the impression is accurate?) were all there. These people can't be replaced. Apart from the man who does the Nick Clegg impression, as his role can be taken by anyone who is able to sound like he has the voice of a man.

I couldn't stop the child within me pushing to the surface and taking over completely.

I spoke to Duncan Bannatyne from *Dragons' Den* and was unable to resist starting the conversation by saying, 'I've got this really good idea for an invention...' This should be the one place in the world where Bannatyne is safe from such a verbal assault and all the other guests obeyed the code, but I couldn't and wouldn't. 'It's Shamgel!' I crowed. 'It's hair gel, but then when you get in the shower it's shampoo as well. Why take two bottles into the shower when you can take none?!'

Bannatyne smiled politely and then seemed to spot someone he knew on the other side of the terrace.

I really, really wanted to go up to David Jason and call him a plonker – in fact, one of my friends offered me money to do so. But I thought that I would probably be told to leave the party and never be allowed to be on television ever again if I did it. So I just said it quietly, just slightly too far away for David Jason to hear.

Everyone else was behaving as if this was the most normal situation in the world and I wanted to be as insightful as the child in *The Emperor's New Clothes* and shout at them, 'What are you doing, you phonies? Stop pretending you're all so unflappable and detached. You know that inside you're as excited as me to be here. You know you want to go up to David Jason and shout "Oooh Grrranville" in his face. And you know what? David Jason, in his heart, would secretly love it if you did it. Don't start believing that because you're on the TV that makes you any different or any better than anyone else. You're all just people. Very lucky people. Especially you, Vernon Kay.'

But I was too worshipful of the faces around me to do any such thing.

My friend Al Murray (who I have known since university, but who is now famous for his brilliant satirical character, The Pub Landlord) was laid-back and comfortable, talking to Gene Hunt off *Life on Mars*. I'd known Al since he was nineteen. I knew inside he was exploding with excitement, yet his lackadaisical face betrayed nothing. I couldn't join him because I knew I'd have just blurted out, 'You're brilliant. I love you. *Life on Mars* was amazing.'

And he'd say, 'I'm doing *Ashes to Ashes* now.'

And I'd say, 'Yes... *Life on Mars* was amazing.'

Underneath it all, even though I know celebrity is a transitory and ephemeral thing and doesn't mean anything, I still genuinely, childishly revere it.

I am not complaining about my lack of fame, incidentally. In many ways it is an advantage to manage to make a living in this job and yet go about unrecognised. Having spent time in the company of more celebrated comedians like Al Murray I can see how wearing and how disruptive it is to be recognised by everyone, everywhere you go, no matter what kind of mood you're in.

Also, as a writer it's nice to have anonymity and to be able to sit on a night bus, listening in to someone's conversation about polar bears, without becoming the focus of attention.

Yet inevitably, as with everything else in my life, I was beginning to question where all my obsession with my work was leading. I had to contend with comedians who were my contemporaries appearing in Hollywood movies, getting nominated for Oscars and filling up stadia on their tours, while I was still playing to 50 people in tiny arts centres in some of the United Kingdom's most obscure towns. And driving myself around because I couldn't afford to pay a tour manager.

I was writing scripts and every now and again one might get made (like the one that had got me invited to the summer party), but most of them were being stymied before they made it to the screen. I was lucky in that I would still get paid for writing them, but I wanted more than money by this stage of my career. I wanted acknowledgement. I wanted success.

As a self-employed man, I was also anxious that if I didn't soon have a hit that my career might go on the slide as well, that I might not be asked to write any more scripts, that the arts centres might not have a slot for me any more.

As with every aspect of my life, I was taking stock with the approaching milestone (though still with four whole days before it happened) and was asking myself if I had got to where I thought I'd be at 40, when I was starting out at twenty.

And I knew I really hadn't.

I thought I'd be married with kids by now and have a degree of professional stability, but I'd been so focused on my career that I hadn't had time to do the whole family thing. I felt like Jim Carrey in one of those awful films, where he neglects his family for his job, but then at the end of the movie, just in time, realises that actually family is more important. Except that I'd worked so hard, I didn't even have a family to neglect.

Which wouldn't be so bad if this self-centred devotion to my job had led to massive rewards of fame, wealth and orgies on my yacht. But I didn't have any of that either.

Despite my fixation upon comedy above my personal life, I wondered if part of the reason that my friends had enjoyed more success than me was down to a sharper focus, a more concentrated determination. I was wasting a lot of time getting drunk, being hungover, playing computer games. It was hard to commit myself to writing scripts when in my heart I knew that there was a good chance they would never be made. One has to invest so much of oneself in creating a project, both in terms of time and emotional commitment, that to try really hard and then to fail is almost too much to bear. Was I deliberately producing substandard work to try and avoid this heartbreak? In which case was this not a vicious circle, bound to end in failure?

Or was I simply not talented enough to have that kind of success?

If you were to look at the lists of winners and nominees of the various comedy awards down the years, then you might have to draw that conclusion, as my name was conspicuous by its absence.

My awards cabinet, which I constructed in 1989 in a fit of hubris, is filled with nothing but dust.

Admittedly, one of the first radio shows I worked on, *On the Hour*, won a whole raft of prizes, but I feel it might have done that without my involvement, giving the calibre of the team behind it (including Armando Iannucci, Chris Morris, Steve Coogan, Stewart Lee and Patrick Marber). In fact, given that all of those people had gone on to win many subsequent awards while I had won nothing should make you consider that maybe I was dragging them down to begin with. Indeed, Stewart Lee won awards before he worked with me, but only started winning them again once our association was over.

I have always claimed that I disliked the idea of awards, showing particular disdain for the Perrier Awards in Edinburgh, which had never even given me the smallest nod in the fifteen Fringes I had attended and the 22 shows I had done. I have always said I don't like the idea of having awards at an arts festival, which should be about celebration not competition, and that picking 'winners' is detrimental to everyone, but really I was mainly jealous and angry that no one has ever wanted to reward me.

The only things I had ever won were:

The Kings of Wessex Ex-Pupil of the Year 1996 – I received a £20 book token from the school in Somerset that I had left eleven years before, as an acknowledgement of my success. Not because I had been on TV, but because I had travelled beyond Bristol and not fallen off the edge of the world or been eaten by a dragon.

GamesMaster Golden Joystick 1996 – I won this for beating Stewart Lee at a video game during an uneasy and embarrassed appearance on this cult children's programme.

The Daily Telegraph Worst Comedy Experience 2005 Award. The critic Dominic Cavendish had picked out my stand-up show 'Someone Likes Yoghurt' as the worst thing to have happened in comedy in the previous twelve months. In a year that saw the debuts of both Tittybangbang and Balls of Steel, this had been quite an achievement. And if you're going to be the worst thing in someone's opinion, then who better than the Daily Telegraph?

None of these were likely to impress those grandchildren that I would never live to see. Not least because only GamesMaster actually presented me with a physical award, which I could have put in my fictional cabinet if I had not been stupid enough to bin the gilded plastic edifice when we moved offices a couple of years later. It would have made a fortune on eBay.

Now I could finally admit what had always been the case: I wanted to win a proper award. For being the best. Just one. Just something that would provide evidence that I had achieved something of note. Even though I have been on awards panels and know what a complete load of shit most of them are, how most of the decisions are political or fixed by the broadcasters to promote shows or performers that they want to do well. I just wanted some recognition!

So you can imagine my delight and slight consternation when this *Arena* magazine nomination appeared, seemingly out of nowhere. I didn't know what I had done to deserve this nod, or who had chosen me, and was aware that this wasn't exactly one of the most prestigious awards ceremonies in the world (in fact, *Arena* magazine was to go out of business just two years later). But in all honesty I didn't care about that. I felt delighted and validated to have had this unexpected nod.

I was realistic about it. I knew that I couldn't win. Like Emma, I knew that someone like Ricky Gervais or Russell Brand would get the trophy, but I was pleased to be invited along for the party and cancelled a couple of gigs so I could go. They were nice gigs – one of them was going to be a free one, in a museum – but I don't get nominated for awards every day of the year, and I knew there would be celebrities and supermodels at the event, so I binned the gigs, lured away by the empty glamour of showbusiness.

I didn't know who all the other nominees were, but had heard that Harry Hill was up for it, which was enough for me to know I could get drunk and enjoy myself, not troubling myself with preparing a victory speech.

The awards were taking place in a swanky bar-restaurant in Knightsbridge, with paparazzi outside hoping to catch sight of some of the many famous people who were expected. I walked through them, my eyes untroubled by their bright flashes, them not even giving me a first look, so palpable was my lack of celebrity. Emma was not turning any heads either, it had to be said, though the competition from identikit bleached blondes with grotesquely ballooning false breasts was somewhat intense.

Once inside, someone told me that the nominees also included The Mighty Boosh and Garth Marenghi. Again I was happy to accept that I had come in fourth. I spotted Paul Kaye as we entered the restaurant. He had enjoyed some success in the 1990s with his outrageous comedy character Dennis Pennis, who had dared to ask celebrities rude questions. I joked with Emma that if he was nominated in my category then at least I wouldn't come last. I mean, what had he done lately? Only acting. I assumed he was up for a drama award.

We had a posho meal and drank cocktails and Emma and I played celebrity spotting. Pop star Will Young was at the next table talking to the tiny but perfectly formed and beautiful Rachel Stevens from S Club 7. I was in love with her instantly. More impressively and less fake-ironically, I was gobsmacked when Harry Shearer walked past my table. Then alien-faced super-model Lily Cole seemed to float into the room and I thought, well, if I get knocked back by Rachel Stevens, there's my back-up. It was going to be a good night.

I noticed that none of the other comedy award nominees had turned up. Of course, all those guys were so used to winning awards that an *Arena* magazine bauble means nothing to them. But this was genuinely a big deal for me. This was my first-ever solo-performance award ceremony and though I knew I couldn't win, I started thinking, Well, you never know...

After dinner they started quickly handing out the awards for a variety of categories. It became apparent that every winner was there in the room. Emma noticed this too. 'I think you're going to win,' she said. 'You're the only one here.' With a tingle of excitement running up my spine, I had to agree that it was a possibility.

It came to the comedy award and the MC said, 'The comedy award winner first came to prominence in the 1990s, with his groundbreaking work on a cult TV show...'

'It's you!' said Emma. 'You're going to win!'

It certainly sounded like it. I prepared myself to stand up, wondering if my suddenly weak knees might support my weight.

'And he first captured our hearts with his outrageous celebrity interviews in the guise of Dennis Pennis...'

'Oh, it's not you,' corrected Emma. 'It's Dennis Pennis.'

My head dropped. I had allowed myself to believe and hope for a second and realised how much I actually wanted this appro-bation, and then my dreams were crushed. If I had been beaten by any of the other nominees then it would have been fine, but

Dennis Pennis? He was even more obscure and 1990s than I was. *Arena* magazine thought I was a worse comedian than Paul Kaye, who isn't even a comedian any more. It was more insulting than not having been nominated at all.

And I then started to feel a bit embarrassed. Every winner was in the room and hardly any other nominees had turned up. Obviously *Arena* had let the winners know that they had won in advance. Maybe if Harry Hill had won he would have been there, but he obviously had found out he hadn't won and so hadn't shown up. But me, so unused to being remembered or acknowledged, hadn't even thought about asking beforehand and had come on the promise of some steak and free booze and the chance to pretend that I might have the courage to chat up a beautiful woman.

If I hadn't been nominated I would never have heard of these awards and even if I had heard of them I would not have expected to be nominated and I would have been happy in myself. Now I felt embarrassed and sad, like *Arena* magazine had invited me along to an evening solely to wipe cat urine on my face. And it was doubly painful that this was an award that in the grand scheme of things meant nothing – it was just a way for a magazine to have a party and put a spread of pictures of famous people in their next issue. It would have meant nothing to anyone else, but would have made me feel like the king of the world. Even though winning nothing except an award from *Arena* magazine in your entire life would be more shameful than winning nothing.

'I don't care,' I lied to Emma, 'because I am going to have sex with Rachel Stevens tonight, so who is the real winner?'

Emma seemed to think that it was still Dennis Pennis and doubted my predictions of sexual conquest.

'Really,' I promised the woman who was already aware of the value of my promises, 'I'm only in my thirties for a matter of hours now and I am going to seize the fucking day. For once in my life I am going to give it a go. I am going to get more drunk and then go up to Rachel Stevens and say, "I would really, really like to have sex with you, just once. Let's just go outside now and make sweet love under the stars and then never see each other again. What do you think?"

'And if she looks at me strangely at that point I will then say, "I was nominated for the Best Comedian Award."

'And she might say, "Did you win?"

'And I'll say, "No."

'And she'll say, "And you still turned up?"

'And I'll look at the ground and say, "Yes."

'And then she'll say, "Who won?"

'And I'll say, "Dennis Pennis."

'And she'll say, "He isn't even a comedian. So you're a worse comedian than someone who isn't a comedian. How shit must you be?"

'And I'll say, "Look, are you going to have sex with me or not, because Lily Cole is over there and I'll give her a go if you're going to play all hard to get."

'And Rachel Stevens might say, "Isn't she nineteen? You must be at least 40. That's disgusting!"

'And I'll say, "I'm 39, Stevens, you pricktease. You make me sick. You've missed your chance, baby. Take a good look at what you could have won, because I wouldn't sleep with you now if you begged me." And then I'll say, "Unless you were going to say yes." And then if she looks at me like I am the lowest dreg at the bottom of the vat containing the lowest dregs of humanity, I'd be out of there.'

Having acted it all out, I decided it was probably best to just drink some more and then go home on the night bus. And let Lily Cole and Rachel Stevens forever wonder, who was that mysterious, brooding, silent stranger who kept staring at our breasts?

I felt genuinely and properly depressed, and cross with myself that I had given up the chance to do a lovely gig with people I liked because of the lure of unobtainable baubles (both awards and celebrity bosoms are covered by this).

As I stood at the bar a man came up to me and said he wanted to thank me because it was a love of *Fist of Fun*, the TV series I had co-written in the 1990s, that had brought him and his best friend together and they were still friends all this time on. I said to him, 'That means more to me than all the awards in the world.'

I was lying, though. I'd much rather have won the award.

On the last Saturday of my thirties, now just five days from the iceberg, this was my diary entry:

> I am coping badly with the run-in to my 40th birthday. I have been drunk or hungover all week, sitting on my sofa, mindlessly surfing the internet most of the day before just getting into a state of consciousness in time to go out for my gig. Really I should be working on the show, though it's been interesting how much it is coming together without any actual work. It is better to do all the graft in front of an audience, but even I am surprised at how quickly it is developing. Maybe this is a sign that I should just be drunk all the time.

That night's gig had gone pretty well considering. I got a bit drunk and inevitably perhaps I had fried chicken on the way home. So ended the last Saturday night of my youth. No cocaine, no hookers. Just some unnecessary and unpleasant fried food. How apt. It was how so many of them have ended in the past.

'Next Saturday,' I concluded, 'it will be bed at 9pm with a good book and a nice cup of Horlicks.'

Did I really believe that? If I kept the promise I had made to myself then from Thursday onwards I would be acting my age and not my shoe size, a new sober, sensible me. Was such a transmogrification possible? Or even desirable?

Looking through the photo album of those first 40 years, just before the start of a new decade, made me nostalgic for the other three times I hit a big something-zero.

10

I had been very excited about reaching ten. I can remember walking down to Cheddar town centre and proudly commenting to an adult I was with: 'I'm looking forward to my next birthday. I'll be in double figures.' That made me feel older, but in a good way. Like the additional number was a mark of maturity, rather than a result of the limitations of the decimal system. Back then each birthday was welcomed, coming round as slowly as they seemed to, as they pushed you closer to the seemingly unreachable time when I'd be able to do more grown-up stuff and find out about those adult secrets that I correctly suspected were being kept from me. The photo that summed up that time was of me in my Cub uniform, my chest puffed out in pride at my part in this junior paramilitary movement, my shoes polished. I was such a little creepy swot, a literal goody-two-shoes, working hard at school, trying to impress adults – not to say I didn't have my moments of cheekiness and naughtiness, but there I was. Ten, pleased not to be in single figures. A Cub.

20

Unsettlingly, I couldn't remember anything about my twentieth birthday at all. I don't know if I didn't find it significant at the time and thus not worth celebrating or maybe I just got too drunk. I am sure that I thought I was getting stupidly old. As a thirteen-year-old I had pronounced, 'I'm not going to get married until I am at least 22,' I suppose believing then that by such a wizened old age I'd be prepared for such responsibilities. At twenty I must have felt my lotus-eating days were almost over and I was on the threshold of having to grow up. Well, I got that wrong. That year I was up in Edinburgh for my first ever Fringe, with a student theatre group. Fifty of us slept on the floor of a Masonic lodge, where we stayed for nearly two months: rehearsing in July and performing in August. So I presume we went to one of the pubs we were frequenting (possibly the Deacon Brodie) and drank Scottish beer. I can't be sure, though.

I remember my nineteenth birthday, when I was in California working on a summer camp and got handcuffed to the flagpole and sprayed with water, and I remember my 21st, when my student comedy troupe were performing at a rival university. We drank Newcastle Brown Ale in one of the colleges after our dress rehearsal and then Emma and me prised some wooden signs off the wall and stole them as trophies. But the twentieth birthday is lost. My parents came up and saw the show a couple of weeks later and there is a photo of me doing a routine with an ancient ventriloquist puppet which had been made by my great-grandad. Already on the path to being a comedian.

30

I think I dreaded turning 30 more than I was now dreading turning 40. I had somehow got away with continuing my childish life for another decade, but now, most surely, things would have to change. My career was progressing steadily onwards, though that year the BBC had not recommissioned the TV show I was doing with Stewart Lee and there was some uncertainty about how things would progress (in fact, the Beeb gave us a new show, so there was a couple of years left in the partnership).

I had a party at Goblins, an eccentric wine bar that we used to frequent back in those glory days in Balham. It was good to have a local, where everyone knew your name and Dave and Sheila, who ran the place, laid on a buffet for me and I got all my friends together and had a good night. At least my friend Ewan found love there.

Balham's own poet laureate and self-styled mayor, the comedian and playwright and all-round genius Arthur Smith, turned up, writing me a poem for the occasion, which summed up my contradictory nature and entire personality in just six words:

Rage and Balloon
Sage and Buffoon.

I still have it pinned to my noticeboard. It might be the best gift I have ever received.

I had a big beard at the time, as I was heading off to the Fringe to perform in a play about archaeology that I had already written. A few days later I headed to the Montreal Festival for the first time, and there is a photo of me there, naked, but covered in bread (as part of a TV sketch – I'm not sick) with a piece of lettuce on my head. It seems that I had no worries about it being time to grow up once the big day had passed.

Indeed, I recall that all my concerns about being in my thirties evaporated the morning after that party. I enjoyed them a lot more than my twenties, which, thinking about, I actually pretty much hated. Once you're in your thirties you can be yourself and I'd had a lot of fun. All this made me feel a bit better. I hoped that the last-minute jitters would pass once the big day had come and gone.

July 11 was the last day of my thirties. Much as I wanted time to stop, my life had to go on. That night I was gigging in the slightly unlikely location of a room above the club house at West Ruislip Golf Course. The last night of my thirties in a place which is like a homing beacon for the middle-aged. The gig was disappointing – this time getting drunk beforehand probably hampered my performance – and the audience were quiet and seemingly uninterested. I was a bit bitter and angry and surprised when no one seemed to give a toss about how momentous this last evening was for me, probably, thinking about it now, because most of them had already passed it.

The last precious grains of sand were tumbling through the hourglass of my youth and I was in the middle of this mediocre performance in this isolated venue.

Some friends had come to see me, including Helen, a 23-year-old student that I'd been having a casual dalliance with over the last couple of years. She was going to accompany me home that night. I was at least going to spend the transition between my thirties and my forties up to my plums in a 23-year-old.

We got the tube back to Shepherd's Bush after the show. We were the only people in our carriage and at that point of the

Central Line there are long gaps between the stations – and so I drunkenly suggested that as a last-gasp finale for my thirties we should indulge in an activity that Bill Clinton did not count as sexual relations.

It was more of a dare than a genuine attempt to get up to anything, but Helen was game and gave it a go. Although such law-breaking recklessness made us laugh, especially when I noticed a man in the next carriage straining to see what on earth we were up to and hastily buttoned myself up, it was perhaps an ungracious and tawdry end to my youth. I am too self-conscious to be properly rock 'n' roll. Once again an incident that might make other men feel proud and virile made me feel a bit sleazy and sad.

And proud and virile as well. I am only human.

But I couldn't carry on like this. Could I?

As midnight struck we were walking along the fittingly anti-climactic Shepherd's Bush Green. I didn't feel any different, but then again I wasn't born until 8am. I had eight hours to go before everything changed. Would waking up tomorrow be like Bill Murray waking up when he finally got to the day after Ground-hog Day? Was my life about to change?

What do you think?

Give me chastity and continence, but not yet.
Saint Augustine

CHAPTER 8
OH FUCK... I'M 40

12 July 2007 – 0 days to 40

I expected to feel different when I woke up.

Like a butterfly emerging from a chrysalis and thinking, what's this? Where did these wings come from? I thought I was a caterpillar. Well, that's a bit of a mind fuck!

Or perhaps I would have attained some new level of consciousness, where my spiritual side would rise into the ascendant and suddenly I would understand the meaning of existence.

I thought, at least, as the dreaded moment arrived, my face would rapidly age and wrinkle and then I'd crumble into dust like the evil Nazi at the end of *Indiana Jones and the Last Crusade*.

But as the alarm rang out and I opened my eyes, I felt hungover and tired, exactly the same as every Groundhog Day before, and my face and body were holding together.

For a few confused moments I had forgotten what today was and was wondering why on earth I'd set my alarm to go off so early, but Helen leant over, kissed me on the forehead and said, 'Happy birthday, old man. Does this make me a gerontophile?'

I gave a sarcastic chortle.

'Wow, I'm in my twenties and you're in your forties. Suddenly today the age gap seems a little bit distasteful.'

'It is now completely inappropriate,' I agreed. 'But I have to tell you, from where I am, it's pretty bloody wonderful too. There's life in the old dog yet.'

I knew that many people my age would be looking down their noses at me if they could see me now, but I knew there were just as many who would be cheering me on, for showing that being 40 doesn't mean you're dead.

'So from today you're really going to be acting your age then, Rich? You're going to live the life of an abstinent teetotal monk?'

'Well, today's my birthday, so obviously I've got to celebrate that.'

'Of course.'

'And then next week I'm flying off to the Montreal Festival and it would be rude to my Canadian hosts if I did not enjoy their hospitality fully.'

'Otherwise there might be an international incident.'

'Then it's Edinburgh and I'm doing a show that's essentially a funeral for my youth, so nothing makes me want to live life to the full more than something dying.'

'After that, though, after your birthday and Montreal and Edinburgh...'

'Well, after that I'm going on holiday for a fortnight. Then there's a London run of the show. But after that. In October. I will definitely start to think about how it might be a good idea to change my ways.'

I didn't want to change my ways though. And I didn't feel any different. I felt exactly the same age as the woman I was now feeling. I remembered what my grandma had said about still feeling 25 when she was 85. Was that my destiny? While the shell of my body grew ever more fragile, whatever was at my core, the thing that made me me, was never going to age. Suddenly I kind of hoped so.

I wondered if everyone was the same as me and Doris Hannan. Whether truly as I'd thought at fourteen, that grown-ups were just pretending to be grown up because that was what was expected of them and everyone else was just better at keeping up the pretence than I was.

'I haven't changed a bit,' I told Helen. 'Forty *is* just a number. I am exactly the same man you went to bed with last night. Still young, still exciting, still exactly like a twenty-year-old.'

She gave me a naughty smile and pulled her naked body close to mine.

'Now stop touching me,' I told her. 'I've got to go to the British Museum.'

Good to my word, 45 minutes later I was walking through the gates of that august and architecturally stunning institution.

I had decided to have the whole day off, doing the things that made me happy. There was a strict itinerary, which I had sent out to all my friends, telling them they were welcome to join me for all or part of the day.

Because of my love for history and archaeology, the first stop was to be the Lindow Man exhibition at the British Museum. He is Britain's most impressive bog body. Back in the Iron Age, this unfortunate fellow was strangled, hit over the head, had his throat cut and then, if that wasn't bad enough, was thrown into a peaty bog in Cheshire. Unlucky for him, perhaps, but lucky for the world of archaeology as his body was preserved in the unusual conditions and they can study what he looked like, what he wore and even what he ate. Archaeologists have rewarded this man's gruesome death by nicknaming him Pete Marsh. I am sure he would have gone to his soily grave laughing if he had only known that.

I had partly come here because I thought it might make me feel more content if I came face to face with a man who was not only older than me, but whose skin was more leathery and wrinkled.

Perhaps not surprisingly, not many of my friends were keen to come on this 10am visit, but one did show up, my great mate Ben. This was appropriate as not only had we both studied history at university, we had both wasted our education by mainly doing comedy and acting instead of going to lectures. I couldn't even remember if the Saxons came before or after the Romans. But then it was early. And I was in my forties.

We also saw loads of other cool stuff, stolen from foreign countries by the all-powerful raping British Empire. The place is packed with treasure that never belonged to us and I thought that as it was my birthday it would be a nice gesture if they had allowed me to take one item home with me. But none of the guards seemed to agree. It was all right for them to nick stuff, but they had a very different attitude if anyone did the same to them. The fusty hypocrites!

More friends joined me for lunch at Pizza Express, which tells me that pizzas are more popular than corpses found in bogs. I wanted a Veneziana pizza, not because it's my absolute favourite, but because I enjoy creating havoc when I order it. On the Pizza Express menu it says 'a discretionary charge of 25 pence from the cost of this pizza will be donated to the Venice in Peril Fund'. Being the immature idiot that I clearly still was, despite being 40, I said to the waiter, 'I'd like the Veneziana pizza, please.' I then waited till he had written that down and added, 'But I don't want to give 25 pence to the Venice in Peril Fund, thank you.'

'I'm sorry?' he replied.

'I like the Veneziana pizza, but I don't like Venice. I think it was stupid of the Italians to build a city on the water and I don't see why I should have to cough up hard cash for their mistake, so I'd rather not give 25p to the charity. I am sure you must get this all the time.'

'Not really,' said the waiter. 'That's how much the pizza costs so...'

'No, that can't be right,' I said, enjoying my moment of pathetic pedantry, 'because the menu says the extra charge is "discretionary", which means that I don't have to pay it if I don't want. And I hate Venice. I don't want to pay it.'

Of course I don't really hate Venice. It's very nice from what I have seen (which is, I admit, almost exclusively from the perspective of the actual Lara Croft in the Tomb Raider game set in that city), but I like to spread mischief and the restaurant wasn't too busy, so I wasn't creating too much hassle for this innocent employee.

The waiter went to speak to his superior and then returned to say that he was very sorry, but on the till there was only a button for Veneziana and there was no button for a 25 pence discount. I looked disappointed, even though I knew this was the case, and said, 'But the menu says it's discretionary. Why does it say that if there is no way to deduct the 25p? I want to use my discretion.'

'I understand that, sir, and you are correct. The menu does claim it's discretionary, but as far as I know you're the only person who has complained.'

'Well, would it be possible for you to tell whoever writes the menu that maybe they should take the word "discretionary" off the menu, then possibly add after the words, "So, if you want Venice to sink into the sea, to find out if its inhabitants will drown or evolve into mermen, then please order a different pizza"?'

'Just say you'll do that,' said Nancy, having some sympathy for the poor man.

'Yes, I promise you I will do that,' said the waiter, beginning to understand that my complaint was light-hearted.

'Will you though? Because I've told other waiters and they've said they'd help change it, but it still says "discretionary".'

'Promise it,' whispered Nancy.

'I promise,' giggled the waiter.

'But for the moment if I have the Veneziana there is nothing you can do to stop the money going to the stupid Venetians.'

'There really isn't.'

'Hold on, I tell you what, can I order a Margherita pizza and then, as additional toppings, have all the ingredients that are on the Veneziana?'

'So you want a Margherita with onions, capers, olives, sultanas and pine kernels as additional toppings?'

'Yes.'

'I can do that, sir, but it will cost you more than just buying a Venziana.'

'Will any money go to the Venice in Peril Fund?'

'Well, no... but...'

'Then that is what I will have. I would rather that than have to contribute any money to people who built their city on water and are now complaining that it's getting a bit wet. I both hate Venice and am keen to find out if Italians can evolve into mermen, so it's for the best.'

'Please ignore him, he's being a cock,' said Nancy. 'Bring him a Veneziana and if you feel the need to get every member of staff to spit in it, then the rest of us will fully understand.'

The waiter left, thankfully laughing along. Hopefully at my little prank rather than because he planned to take Nancy's advice.

My friend Al turned up for dessert, before having to shoot off to appear on some TV show or other. He brought me a present – a Nintendo Wii console! Much as I'd complained about all the puerile gifts I'd received this year, I was pretty pleased about this one. It would make it difficult to give up playing video games in my forties. It would be rude to Al not to use his generous gift.

After lunch, other friends turned up to watch the ridiculous action film *Die Hard 4.0* at the cinema. Bruce Willis showed me that it was still possible for a man in his middle age to live a full life and be useful to society. He seemed to be able to jump out of exploding helicopters and walk away from car crashes with barely a scratch on him, so perhaps physical decline was some way away for me.

In the evening, with some of my friends leaving to be replaced by others, we went for a curry. I chose a restaurant called 'Gaylord', solely because I was childishly amused by the name, which had been one of the major insults of the 1970s playground. Perhaps the restaurant is only in business thanks to immature menchildren like me thinking they're being hilariously ironic by dining in such a place. 'Thanks for coming,' I said to everyone as we raised a toast for my birthday. 'You, my friends, are all a load of gaylords.'

'You're 40 now, Rich,' laughed Stefan. 'Do you still think that kind of thing is as funny now you're an old man?'

'No, I think it's funnier. I hope we never stop finding it funny to be curry-munching inside a Gaylord.'

That justifiably got groans and someone frisbeed a poppadom at my head.

'Well, that was a bit childish,' I complained.

Being 40 didn't mean I couldn't make rubbish jokes that didn't quite make sense. That was a relief.

And now here I was in the eye of the hurricane that I had been anticipating and fearing for so long and everything was almost supernaturally calm. I wasn't even knocked off kilter when Sarah-Jane popped in to the bar where we were having post-curry cocktails. We both knew now that we were never going to be anything more than friends and that that was best for both of us. I was pleased that the failure of the relationship hadn't destroyed this important friendship.

At the end of the evening there were around a dozen people, drinking and laughing in the bar. Interestingly they came from different parts of my life: James and Phil from school were there, Stefan and Emma from university, there were a couple of ex-girlfriends and some actors and comedians I had worked with. Many of them hadn't met each other before, but they were all getting on really well and commenting to me how great my other friends were.

I did have some amazing friends.

'I'm having a lot more fun here than I did at our stupid party,' I told Emma.

'I can't believe you didn't enjoy that. I had a blast.'

'I know. What can I say? I'm a prick.'

'You're not a prick, Richard Keith. Don't let anyone, ever, tell you you're a prick, because you're not.'

I waited for the undercutting punchline, but for once there wasn't one.

Emma could have, by right, pointed out that as I was now 40 and single I was duty-bound to marry her. But she remained silent. Perhaps she didn't want to spoil the fun or perhaps she was worried that I might actually call her bluff.

Here we both were at the apex of the hill, finally with a clear perspective forward and backwards, able to take stock of our lives. We sat beside each other, taking in the view, breathing in the imaginary, fresh mountain air.

'Can you blinking well believe we're 40?' said Emma. 'It's just proper crazy mental, isn't it?'

'It has whizzed by a little bit,' I concurred.

'A bit? It's whizzed by like Billy Whizz, up to the eyeballs on whizz, desperate for a whizz, whizzing around Whitstable... which famously has no public conveniences.'

I laughed. 'Are we ever going to grow up, Emma?'

'I hope not.'

'Because I can't work out if it's a triumph or a tragedy to be this old and to be the way we are.'

'Sometimes it's a triumph and sometimes it's a tragedy. But I think overall we're ahead on points.'

'Surely we've got to conform before we die.'

'Conform to what? Some archaic fifties notion of having 2.4 kids and a proper job? That's fine for some people, they need the security and the constancy, but not everyone fits into that template. Not everyone wants that and nowadays, thank God, hardly anyone bats an eyelid at anyone. You can be single or promiscuous or gay.'

'Do you think I might be gay?'

'And you express that homosexuality by having sex with dozens of women?'

'You never know.'

'I don't think you need to worry about it. I'm just not sure either of us are the kind of people who'll be ever happy to be with one person for ever. And you know what? Maybe that's just the way we are and if it is, that's OK.'

'It's OK now, but I fear getting to 60 and still having this life and having no one. I worry about being a sad and lonely old man.'

'Right,' said Emma, really hitting her stride, 'if that's what you're worried about then getting together with someone now won't guarantee anything, will it? In twenty years' time you could easily have split up, or she might die...'

'Yeah, let's be optimistic.'

'Seriously though. Or you might stay together, but just really, really hate each other and dedicate your lives to making the other one miserable. People who get married because they're scared of being alone in the future are idiots. If that's your concern then wait till you're old and then hook up with someone else – someone who is definitely still alive, someone you know you actually like.'

I had never thought of it like that. It was true. The chances of lifelong love were pretty small.

'Yeah and anyway I can't get married until I've had a three-some,' I said, accidentally out loud.

'I can't believe you've never had a threesome. All the mucky things you've done, all the mucky women you know.'

'I know… Well, maybe if you and me had another person in between us to stop us ever touching…'

'Do NOT go there, mister. It ain't happening.'

'It's not just the threesome thing though. I feel I wasted so much of my youth. That I haven't taken the opportunities that have come to me, that I could have done so much more.'

'Oh, stop moaning like a little girl who's dropped her lollipop. Do you know how many people would kill to have your life, Richard Keith? Do you know how lucky you are?'

'I guess I do, most of the time. Sometimes I think to have been born at this time, in this place, in my family, with all the oppor-tunities I've had, makes me among the luckiest human beings who will ever live. Past and future too, the way things are going. But even so, there's something missing…'

'So what if you've wasted some of your time? We all do that. You can't change it now. All you can do is to try to not waste more time in the future. You don't want to get to 60 and look back at all the time you wasted in your forties worrying about the time you wasted in your twenties…'

'I know. I'm just not sure I can change.'

'You are such a gigantic prick, Richard Herring,' she shouted, finally unexpectedly providing the expected punchline. 'But I love you. Now stop all this wanky soul-searching and get out there and try and go and chat up someone who might not be phys-ically repulsed by the idea of having sex with you.'

I went to talk with my other friends. But tonight I was happy to head home alone.

A couple of days later, my muscles surprisingly stiff from having played too much Wii tennis, I was in a plane heading for Canada and the Montreal Comedy Festival. With only another three weeks to write my Edinburgh show, this was in some ways an unwelcome distraction. But I had been flattered to be asked to take part in this invitation-only event and was aware that the place would be packed with industry bigwigs and if the right person saw my act and liked it, it might lead to all kinds of exciting new horizons for me. Comedians have come to Montreal and ended up starring in Hollywood movies or playing the kooky neighbour in long-running sitcoms or been given their own hour-long specials on HBO. Wouldn't it be something if I started my forties with a huge break which would send my career spiralling in a new direction?

The week started well and I was taking part in a show in a big theatre, where seven or eight British acts did ten minutes each. There was a nice sense of camaraderie between the comics and most of the gigs went down really well. But this show finished on the Wednesday night and none of the important industry people arrived until Friday. Fun as it had been to perform for the Canadian crowd, it seemed like a long way to come to do such relatively minor and abrupt performances. By the time the bigwigs started drifting into the Hyatt hotel bar, the hub of the festival, I was preparing to fly home and only had a couple of short spots to do, in tiny clubs on the periphery of the city. My dreams of playing a snooty English butler in the next series of *Joey* were starting to crumble.

I felt slightly sickened with myself for even caring about what US executives might think of me. Surely I didn't really even want the kinds of jobs they'd be offering. Did I?

By the end of the week I was dispirited and again contemplating whether this was any kind of profession for a man of my age. My last gig was a measly seven-minute spot in a tiny room above a bar. I was on a bill with around a dozen other comedians, all doing the same amount of time, one after the other, with no interval. At least I had a good spot in the middle of the bill, where there was a chance that the audience would still be fresh and up for laughing.

Down in the bar I met an American comic who came over to say hello, but he was quickly joined by an agent, who found out I was on the bill before one of his acts. 'Are you a Brit?' he asked and I told him I was. 'Oh fuck!' he shouted, spitting out the words with such venom that I assumed he was joking. But it became apparent that he wasn't, as he half-heartedly apologised, without giving me any inkling as to why it was so bad for one of his clients to follow me.

I was looking forward to getting my bit out of the way and getting back to the hotel to have a last drink with my friends, but then the coordinator of the gig came up to me and told me I was closing, because some of the other acts had other gigs to get to. My heart dropped. There would be little energy left in the room by the end of the show. The few crumbs of comfort that I had had were being swept up and thrown in the bin.

Still, you never know. A big producer might just walk into the room at the right time, see me and realise I was perfect for his toilet air freshener commercial and my career could be right back on track. The coordinator hadn't known who I was when I arrived, which I wouldn't have minded if ten minutes later he hadn't approached me again. 'What are you doing here?' he growled.

'I'm Richard Herring. I'm in the show.'

He checked his list with some scepticism.

'I'm on last. You just asked me to change spots.'

'Did I? You're a Brit, are you?'

'Yes, I am.'

'Oh fuck!'

He walked away. What was going on here?

At the start of the show, as expected, the audience were fired up and the comics were getting big laughs. But not from me. I found some of their stuff quite reactionary and offensive. One guy did a four-minute routine mocking someone at his school who was unable to read. The audience hooted as he put on a dumb voice and tried to go over a simple line from a book. I waited, thinking there must be more to it, there was going to be a sudden flash of brilliance that would subvert this and make the audience consider their own prejudice, but apparently not. This worked on only one level. Adults laughing at someone who was illiterate. While using the N word here can destroy your career, the word 'retard' causes no embarrassment or protest whatsoever.

As if to illustrate this disparity, a black comedian then came on and opened with, 'On my way here I saw an albino midget. I thought, hey, does this mean I get a wish?' It got a round of applause. Another female comedian overran terribly, while bringing the house down with reactionary material about how stupid men were and how they just wanted sex and sport and were incapable of discussing their feelings. But then she seemed to validate this negative stereotype by adding, 'But that's good. We don't want a man who cries, do we, girls? If any man I was with started crying and complaining I'd say, "Shut up, stop snivelling and be a man about it!"'

Again, no irony, no attempt to redress the balance for years of sexism in comedy by turning this on men; just a genuine declaration that all men were a certain way and everyone should accept it. As a man who expresses his feelings (a bit too much, you're probably realising) and occasionally thinks about more than sex and has little more than apathy for sport, I felt quite offended by the generalisation. And it's really hard to offend me.

It saddened me that all this stuff was going down brilliantly with the audience, with not one dissenting voice (and it would have been very bad form for me to start heckling another comic). I am all for pushing back boundaries and discussing any subject through comedy, and making people think about issues by deliberately confronting them with shocking and provocative material. But this was merely grown-up bullying.

By the time I finally trudged on, with the crowd flagging as I had expected, I was despondent about the whole concept of stand-up comedy, resenting being underused by the festival and wishing I could go home. I managed to contain most of it and do a solid enough, if underwhelming, gig to the tired crowd. But then I tried this throwaway one-liner:

To Be Or Not To Be... That is the first and only question on the University of Bee-keeping entrance exam.

The audience groaned at this, some seeming extremely disappointed with it, as if it was obvious and cornball. Some of the anger that had been building up all week bubbled over and I said, 'You know what, that joke was cleverer than you are giving it credit for. It's not just a pun about be and bee. What's funny is the ridiculous suggestion that there might be an educational establishment dedicated solely to bee-keepers, but that it would also have such a ridiculously easy question to try and select the best pupils.'

In some gigs that deconstruction might have got a laugh, but this crowd seemed a bit nonplussed by my post-modernism. So I added, jokily, but aggressively, 'Fuck you, Canada!'

The crowd were a little taken aback by this unexpected affront to them and their nation. They had no problem with disablism or sexism or a Korean woman doing a Benny Hill-style impression of her parents' inability to say the letter 'R', but when they became the butt of the assault it was suddenly less funny.

'Listen,' I continued, 'I've been doing stand-up comedy for eighteen years now. My sense of humour is better than yours... and all the other audiences who've heard that bee-keeping joke... and I'm telling you, it's funny.'

I was now getting a few laughs, as they realised I wasn't quite as pompous as they thought, but most people were just confused by me. I continued to the end of my short set, then walked off stage, past the few remaining comics and the coordinator, down the stairs, through the bar and out into the street. I didn't stop to talk to anyone, just carried on walking back to the hotel, some two miles away. I was feeling cross and unsettled, wondering if I would actually have been better off if I had just worked in a bank. Was Mr Murray up in heaven laughing at me? If he was, he was about the only one tonight.

By the time I was at the Hyatt, I had pretty much decided that comedy was a mug's game and I should give it up and try something else. To be fair I have thought this on a pretty regular basis, about once every six months, for the previous twenty years, but this time I was pretty sure I had had enough. I didn't know what else I could possibly do instead. Maybe I would go and work in a war zone for a charity and finally do something useful with my life. Not that I really had any skills that would be useful in a war zone. That was hardly the point.

In the downstairs lobby I got into the lift and as I reached to press the button, a familiar figure hopped in before the doors closed. It was one of my all-time favourite live comedians, Billy Connolly. I had met him once before but was sure he wouldn't remember, so shyness and respect for his privacy precluded me from saying hello. This lift, through a quirk of hotel design, took you only to the first floor and the reception and bar area, but not up to the actual rooms.

'What's the deal with this lift?' asked Connolly, with a cheeky glint in his eye. 'It only goes up one floor! What's the use in that? How do I get to my room?' Perhaps I was just so used to this man being funny that anything said in his instantly recognisable voice would have been amusing, but this was really making me laugh.

'Once you're out of this lift, there's another set of lifts across the foyer,' I explained.

'Oooh, I know that,' he said, bewildered by this unnecessary rigmarole, 'but why don't they just have one lift that goes all the way up the building? Would that have been so hard?'

I was laughing too much to respond.

'Or is this lift just a little security device? To keep the riff-raff from the streets out of this swanky-wank hotel?'

In this twenty-second trip, Billy Connolly was effortlessly more amusing and satirical and truthful than any of the comedians I had seen tonight and I laughed out loud, feeling privileged to have been in the audience for this free mini-gig.

In the right hands, comedy was an amazing tool and my faith in it was restored. It was as if Billy Connolly had been sent like a guardian angel of comedic arts to remind me that being funny could be life-affirming and not filled with hate or arrogance. It was worth carrying on. Especially with the Edinburgh Fringe around the corner and the chance to escape this madness and do a full hour show to people who appreciated me.

Back in London, Lara was sending me desperate emails asking for another lunchtime meeting before I headed off to Edinburgh for the whole of August. I was unable to resist her overtures, but I did so with a slight heaviness in my heart. I actually *was* finding it a bit dispiriting being used just for sex. I wanted to be able to go out into the real world with this woman, have a meal with her, maybe a conversation so I could find something out about her – I knew next to nothing. The secrecy and the breaking of sacred commandments were exhilarating, but I couldn't help thinking about her family and the repercussions all this might have on them. Her husband, I had discovered, was a professional sportsman, and perhaps some of this soul-searching was actually down to a fear of how many shades of shit he would be capable of beating out of me. I felt sure that an athlete would not be satisfied with seven and would continue to beat me, screaming, 'That last bit of shit was the same shade as the bit before. Produce an eighth shade or the pummelling will continue.'

I also wondered whether all people in relationships were up to the same tricks as my clandestine concubine. Is that how they manage to overcome the dread I was feeling about commitment, to simply secretly have sex with other people? Did I, in some ways the least romantic man, have overly romantic ideas about romance?

As much as I liked the mysterious woman who would come round, have sex with me twice and then leave, I was quite relieved that I was going to be out of town for the next six weeks (after the Fringe I had my much-needed holiday), hoping that the fireworks we were creating would just fizzle out while I was away. I didn't think I could cope with the long-term strain of being a mistress.

By the end of the month I had taken the train to the Athens of the north (so called because of the large number of kebab shops up South Bridge), Edinburgh, for my sixteenth year performing at the Fringe. I was 40 and it was twenty years since I had first been here. It was another milestone. Another indication of my age. Another nail in my coffin.

As I walked around this town with so many memories, I started feeling old. Not particularly in a bad way. Just in the sense that I have been in this town for sixteen summers of the last 21 and had thus spent a year and a half of my life here. Every corner held a memory of a drunken clinch or a lost love or a regurgitated deep fried pizza. The ghost of the dead young me haunted every street.

I wondered to myself whether maybe it was time to leave the Fringe behind. Maybe I had outgrown it or perhaps it had outgrown me. It feels like a young person's town at Fringe time and it was chilling to realise that many of the performers desperately handing me flyers in the street hadn't even been alive when I had first come here. Was my constant desire to return merely an attempt to recapture something that was lost for ever? Or did I just hope that through this sheer bloody-minded persistence someone important would eventually realise I actually exist and maybe give me one of those awards that I pretended I didn't want?

These were mainly idle thoughts. But putting on a new show is emotionally exhausting and paranoia and angst hold on to your back no matter how much you caper and jig to shake them off. There is a huge amount of competition, with literally thousands of shows for people to choose from, and it's massively expensive to put on even an hour of stand-up. Some years I have lost thousands of pounds up here and the fear of financial devastation if the reviews are bad and no one comes to see you only adds to the already unbearable pressure.

But still I love the Edinburgh Fringe. It's the best arts festival in the world. Even if I couldn't help wondering if never coming back would actually be a positive step. Maybe twenty years of anything is enough.

On the first night of the festival I had no show, but I did a 20-minute spot at a late-night gig. Everyone else went down brilliantly and I was closing so expecting great things. But it got a lacklustre and underwhelmed response. The audience were young and seemingly shocked and appalled by my rudeness and lechery. It wasn't a disaster, but wasn't very satisfying and may have stemmed from my pointing out that, for some of them at least, I was over twice their age. I imagined they were all thinking, who's this old fart? I might as well have worn my slippers.

I got through it, but it wasn't the start to the festival that I had hoped for and it didn't augur well for the new show that I was now pinning so many hopes on.

I walked home through the drizzly, grey streets of this imposingly beautiful but misty and Gothic city, the familiar smell of the hops from the brewery hanging on the air. As in Montreal, I felt unsatisfied with my career and was questioning again whether this was a job for a grown man.

Does Alan Goodman ever feel this low? I wondered.

I crossed North Bridge, which connects the Old Town on the hill to the New Town below. It vaunts high above the tracks of Waverley railway station and pretty much once every Edinburgh I consider throwing myself off it, with my bad reviews pinned to my clothes, hoping that that would ruin the lives of the stupid critics who hadn't understood my work. It would at best be a pyrrhic victory. Even I was impressed that I was already feeling like this on day one, before my Fringe had really even begun.

As I contemplated my mortality and that night's mild failure, feeling slightly disconsolate, chuckling at my own folly and predictability, I heard a shout of 'Richard!' Behind me at some distance was a shadowy, bearded figure in a cagoule. For a second I wondered if it was some random nutter, but it turned out to be a very special nutter, Daniel Kitson, a stand-up who produces work of filth and poetic beauty and is a serious contender for greatest living stand-up in the world. I watch his effortless improvisation when he's in front of the mic and am beguiled and bedazzled and usually wonder what's the point of even trying to be a comedian when there's someone that much better than me doing it.

He ran up to me and was so pleased to see me and cheery and funny that I immediately brightened up. Just as in Montreal when

I had started to have doubts about my profession, the comedy gods had sent me another comedy angel to guide the way.

'So, how are you?' asked Daniel.

'Fine, aside from the suicidal impulses,' I deadpanned.

Daniel laughed. Which was good, because it had been almost entirely a joke.

'I was just thinking,' I continued, 'that maybe I've been here at the Fringe enough times now. Maybe twenty years is enough.'

'Yeah,' he blustered, 'but 30 would be better!'

I chuckled, but thought about it.

'When you put it like that...' I replied. And genuinely the simplicity of the argument had won me over.

'You're certain to produce your best work when you're older,' he told me.

'Do you really think so?'

'I bloody well hope so. It couldn't get much worse.'

But there was a lot of truth in what he said. It was quite unusual to be my age and still trying to come up with new and interesting material. Most comedians are either propelled to greater things much earlier in their life, or alternatively realise the job is crazy and give up or possibly make a sideways move into production, promotion or writing. I was one of a handful of old trouts who successfully made it upriver to spawn every single year. I had the experience and the knowledge to produce something amazing, without the pressure of having some massive early career highlight to live up to.

'Where you on this year, Dan?' I asked.

'I'm at The Stand at 11.30pm... But not on Fridays and Saturdays!'

'You maverick,' I said. 'Those are the busiest days. How terribly contrary!'

'I'm not going to sell out and pander to what people might expect,' he joked in self-parody. 'I'm after quality, not quantity!' Though I knew that he would be getting both.

'If you really want to buck the system you should play the Edinburgh Fringe in September, when everyone else has gone home.'

'That would be keeping it real,' he agreed. 'Playing to two people in a venue with no lights or chairs.'

'Well, maybe next year.'

'Yeah, and I know you'll be back. You're addicted to this shit!'

We laughed and I felt better and banished my stupid doubts. Like Billy Connolly, Kitson reminded me of how great comedy can be and also how helpful it is to laugh at yourself when you're taking yourself too seriously. Acts of that quality give the rest of us something to aspire to and as my paternal grandfather used to tell me, 'If you aim your arrow at the stars, you might just hit the trees.'

It was time to banish ideas that this was no job for an old man. Billy Connolly shows that a comedian can mature with age and Morecambe and Wise demonstrated that there is little funnier than old men bickering like little boys. In fact, the older you become the funnier it is to be attempting to kill fictional monsters with theatrical swords or to run around with your arse hanging out your trousers.

I stopped trying to shake paranoia and angst off my back and instead just plucked them off with my fingers and threw them spiralling down on to the roof of Waverley station. In an instant I saw that being older in this environment was a positive thing. I had nothing to prove and could just concentrate on trying to do a show that I thought was funny and interesting on my own terms. If the reviewers didn't like it, then so what. Chances were they didn't know as much about comedy as I did and hadn't thought about it half as much. I have always been my own worst critic (though I have to say my self-criticism is mediocre at best) but I am one of the few that is actually worth listening to. I was just going to go out there the next day and enjoy myself.

And I did exactly that and had what was probably the happiest and most successful Fringe of all the many I had experienced. People came, I didn't lose money and the reviews were pretty good. More importantly I had lost the doubts that had been plaguing me. This was a brilliant job for a man in his forties.

It was a terrific Fringe.

Naturally I won no awards.

CONVERSATION 2

Scarlett, age seven

Midway through the Fringe I went for a coffee at the Pleasance Theatre, where I had once had water poured over my head by an aggrieved drunkard. I was meeting Al Murray and his young family. His daughter Scarlett had just turned seven and was play-ing with her younger sister Willow when I arrived. I have known Scarlett all her life and we have a fine history of childish badinage.

Three years earlier, when she was just four, I had recently moved into my new home and Scarlett had been round. Her mum had asked her what she thought of my house.

'Your house is wee!' she laughed. Scarlett is not Scottish and so was not casting aspersions on the size of my home. She was merely comparing it to urine.

I had feigned shock and anger. 'How dare you say that about my lovely home?'

'Your house is bum,' she added, clearly having grasped the concept that comparing things to naughty objects and substances made for an amusing insult, if not yet quite understanding how to use the arsenal of profanity that she had at her disposal.

I pretended that her comments had upset me. 'My house is very nice. It's not bum at all. It's not anything like a bum. Even though I understand that isn't what you said. You said it was "bum", rather than like "a bum".

She looked nonplussed.

Then after a pause she said, 'Your house is wee!'

And then for emphasis added, 'Your house is bum!'

The repetition seemed to make the whole thing even more amusing for her. Not that I can knock her for this. I had, as we know, a similar bent at her age.

I was with Scarlett on this one. I thought her childish dismissal of my house was highly amusing and also, in its simplicity, a much more effective satire of me and everything I stood for than her father or even her (genuine) great-great-great-great grandfather William Thackeray could have come up with.

Anyway, I'd enjoyed the humour of the impertinent youngster, so I'd joined in and said, 'No, YOUR house is bum. No, in fact, your house came out of a bum.'

The satirist's barbed words had been turned on herself. And rather than enjoying my puerile comments, Scarlett was stung. She stopped laughing and stopped comparing my house to excreta or bodily orifices and instead started to cry.

She cried very loudly. It was hard to hear what she was saying as she cried, but I think it was something like, 'Mummy, he said our house came out of a bum.'

Had Scarlett been an adult I would have taken the chance to inflict more wounds upon her and maybe said, 'Your house is fashioned from a mixture of sweat and bogeys.'

But Scarlett was only four and I had made her cry. So instead I tried to apologise. But she would have none of it.

'Oh, she can dish it out, but she can't take it,' commented her father.

'You started it, Scarlett. You said Richard's house was wee,' said her mother, attempting to mollify her. But Scarlett could not stand the fact that I thought her house had come out of a bum. I had insulted her and her family and all they stood for (or at least all that they lived in) and the cold logic that she had said my house was wee was not going to make any difference.

Though something within her was chastened. She howled, 'Sorry!' But that didn't make up for what I'd said. But added, 'I'm not your friend any more, Richard.'

'Oh, please be my friend. I'm sorry about the coming out a bum thing I said. It was the heat of the moment. I was riled by you saying my house was bum. Probably partly because you are right. It is a bit bum. There is something of wee about it. I just said that your house had come out of a bum because I was hurt and wanted to hurt you back. Your house didn't come out of a bum at all. I wish I'd never said that,' I pleaded.

That made no difference, so I tried a different tack. 'So if you're not my friend then you won't want the birthday present I've got you.'

Scarlett suddenly fell silent. She was deep in thought. Much as she wanted to cancel our friendship (to be honest she's not that much of a friend anyway: she's never even bought me a beer and she doesn't ever ring me), she also didn't want to lose the present (that incidentally didn't exist. It was a clever trick by me).

She said she didn't want the present. She felt that strongly about the whole 'your house came out of a bum' incident.

But a second later she had reconsidered. Her dad laughed about her getting upset and she laughed too.

'Give Rich a hug,' said her mum. And she did.

To a four-year-old friendships can be broken and remade this easily. I knew she wouldn't remember this incident. But I would always remember what she'd said about my house.

It still hurt now three years later, but I tried to rise above it.

Scarlett had matured a lot more than I had in the interim. She was charming to everyone she came in contact with. Everyone, except for me. She seemed to delight in being cheeky and calling me names. Somehow she instinctively knew that dismissal and disdain were the correct female response to me.

Even though she said I was stupid and stinky and so on (she is so childish), I think she still liked me a bit.

After a while I decided to do some leafleting and Al asked his daughters if they would like to help me. They both wanted to be a part of it and I gave them a wad of leaflets each and we went from table to table. Willow, who was about three, was rubbish at it. She kept dropping the leaflets and was too shy to give them to anyone. I should have shouted at her and sacked her on the spot, but bizarrely the public seemed to like her despite her total ineptitude. Luckily Scarlett was a bit better and would hand over a leaflet with a smile that charmed many of the punters in the courtyard.

'Have you seen the show?' one man asked her.

'Yes,' Scarlett lied. 'It's rubbish.'

'Don't say that,' I said, aghast. 'You have to pretend that it's good. That's your job.'

Scarlett just giggled and carried on slagging me off. We were quite an effective double act.

Willow's interest soon faded – luckily because I was about to give her her marching orders anyway – but Scarlett wanted to carry on.

'Are you helping your dad?' asked one woman.

'He's not my dad,' Scarlett protested with undisguised scorn, adding with justified pride, 'My dad is Al Murray!'

It was all causing quite a lot of amusement to the people we encountered. I had a bit of fun giving her a hard time for handing someone a leaflet the wrong way round, telling her that I would have to dock her wages. Suddenly, when she realised there might be money in it, her eyes lit up (like father, like daughter) and she briefly did a stint where she pretended that she thought the show was good. Which was just as funny. Every time I stopped to chat to someone she would bark, 'Come on, you need to get on with it. Those tickets aren't going to sell themselves. Not with your show.'

It was the most effective half an hour of leafleting I have ever done. My only worry was that people would turn up that night and then say, 'Where's the funny one? The little girl. She's what we came to see.'

When we'd finished I gave Scarlett a pound and she looked at me as if I had said her house had come out of a bum. She demanded more. I gave her another 37 pence and she seemed satisfied.

Travel broadens the waist.

CHAPTER 9
DECOMPRESSION CHAMBER

'Hello, Keith Herring speaking,' said my dad to the same singsong tune he had been using for as long as I could remember.

'Hello, Keith, it's Richard Herring here,' I replied, equally predictably.

'Ah, Richy! Rikki-Tikki-Tavi! Richmal Crompton! Are you famous yet?'

'No, Dad, not yet,' I wearily replied.

'Uncle Michael sent us the review from the *Guardian*. Very good.'

'Yeah, four stars. He hardly ever gives five.'

'Still, he did say it wasn't as good as last year's show though.'

'It was four stars, Dad. And a brilliant review.'

Dad made a sound that indicated that all that meant nothing, given the one criticism in the piece.

There was a bit of a silence, which there usually is at the 30-second point in any conversation between my father and me, which was followed as always by me saying, 'Is Mum there?'

'No, she's not. Opera society tonight.'

'Oh, right.'

There was another long pause.

'It's just I'm at the airport now, I'm about to get on the plane. I just wanted to say goodbye.'

'Ah well, I'll have to do it for you.'

'Right.'

'Where are you headed?'

'I'm going to Thailand, Dad. I told you.'

'Yes, I know that, but Thailand's a big place. Which part?'

'I don't know exactly. It's called Phi Phi Island.'

'Pee Pee Island!' spluttered my dad, childishly.

'Yes, that's how it's pronounced, don't be so immature.' Although that was a little hypocritical of me, because I was only really going there because I liked the funny name and I thought I'd enjoy telling people I was holidaying on Phi Phi.

'Where is it, though?'

'I don't know. I haven't had any time to research the trip. All I know is that the airport is in Phuket!'

'No need to swear,' said my dad, giggling like a schoolboy. 'You can use that one in your act if you like.'

'Yeah, thanks. I probably will.'

'And you're really going on your own?' he asked with some concern.

'Yes, I am, but that's what I want. I just need a rest. I want to lie on a beach, read some books and not talk to another human being.'

'Well, that's a bit weird if you ask me. Can't you take Sarah-Jane?'

'No, Dad, because we split up months ago and also I am just about to get on the plane this second.'

'What about Sally?'

'Sally and me broke up in 1996, Dad. She's married with a kid.'

'I know, but we liked Sally. Why didn't you stay with Sally? She's a lot more famous than you now, isn't she?'

'Oh, they've just called for boarding,' I lied. 'I'm going to have to go.'

'All right, have fun. Don't do anything I wouldn't do. I love you, son.'

'Yeah, good. Bye.'

It didn't strike me until I stepped off the plane into the clammy morning heat that I was a single European man in his forties, visiting Thailand alone. Was that a little flicker of disdainful judgement I saw in the eyes of the otherwise emotionless official at the passport desk as I stepped towards him with a conspicuous lack of partner by my side?

'No, it's not like that!' I wanted to shout. 'I'm just here to get some rest and relaxation... No, not the kind of rest and relaxation you're thinking about. I just need to recuperate. To take stock. All right?! And if I decide that it will help if I am wanked off by a ladyboy then that is no one's business but my own!'

But I genuinely wasn't coming here as a sex tourist. I had toured round this country about six years before and had been amazed to see how many middle-aged men seemed to be travelling with much younger Thai women, who were pretty, but dead behind the eyes. It was clear that most, if not all, of these men had come on holiday, hired a prostitute and were spending two weeks in their company. I have never purchased the time of a lady of the night, and I am not judging those who do, but I would imagine that if I were to ever do so, I'd pretty much want to be leaving the minute the dreadful, vulgar act was over. The idea of vacationing with someone I was paying to go to bed with me would seem just too tragic. And there seemed an extra level of unpleasant exploitation in these wealthy white old men taking advantage of the poverty of these young Asian women.

Then again, no one would ever find out if I did have sex with a prostitute or a ladyboy! Was my moral outrage in fact fuelled by jealousy or at least curiosity? Surely not. Even in my current debauched state of mind, I was sure I wouldn't stoop so low. Almost totally sure...

It was early morning in Phuket. I had barely slept on the plane and though it was 8am here, my body clock was set at 2am and I was starting to get weary. I was determined, though, to stay awake as long as possible to get into sync with the new time zone.

At the airport I was met by a man holding a piece of paper with 'Herring, Mr' written on it. Even this piece of paper trumpeted my single status. Just 'Herring' and the man could have been waiting for a couple or a family, but anyone seeing the sign would inevitably be thinking the worst. I tried to acknowledge that I was who he was waiting for, without drawing too much attention to myself.

He led me to his minivan. It was clear that he spoke little English and, basic O level French aside, I naturally speak nothing but. Despite his sign he was expecting a couple, but I made it clear I was the only Herring here. He gave a leery smile and wink and put his thumbs up. 'No, no, it's not like that!' I insisted. I don't know what the Thai for 'The lady doth protest too much' might be, but I am pretty sure that that was what he then said, with another bawdy chuckle.

He was going to take me to the port where I would catch a ferry to Phi Phi, though it turned out there was five hours until it disembarked. I could have done without that. After the long flight I just wanted to get to my hotel, get rid of the luggage that I was lumbered with and sit drinking cocktails in the sun. But none of this was going to happen, especially as just as the minivan of which I was the sole passenger pulled away it started to rain. The driver laughed as rain bounced off his windscreen. It was pouring. Had I arrived in rainy season? I really should have done some research.

About twenty minutes into the journey the driver pulled over and without attempting to explain disappeared into a nearby massage parlour. Was he going to have a massage? Or was he trying to fix something up for me? Five minutes passed and I contemplated how much trust I had put in the hands of a man just because he had my name on a piece of paper. He could be anyone.

What if there had been two 'Herring, Mr's on the plane and he'd actually been waiting for the other one? What if the other one was a perverted sex tourist? What if I ended up having to have his holiday and have sex with ladyboy after ladyboy? It didn't bear thinking about.

At last the driver returned and opened the passenger door, making a face which seemed to plead for forgiveness or understanding. He was followed by four young women in matching pink tops, who I presumed, given their uniform and the fact that they had emerged from a massage parlour, were masseuses. They seemed to be real ladies rather than ladyboys as far as I could tell, but you couldn't have everything. Their English was not much better than his, though they were keen to chat.

'Where you from?' asked one.

'London in England,' I told them.

They gasped and giggled and commented to each other rapidly in Thai.

'First time Thailand?' asked another.

'No, I've been before. I went to Koh Samui and er… Bangkok and Chiang…' I was too tired to recall the name. 'Chiang somewhere.'

They laughed at my stupidity, but I was weary and just wanted to get where I was going and not in the mood for chit-chat or getting massaged or something worse (or better, depending on your perspective).

We went on a twenty-minute drive and the women were dropped off at a complex of apartments and got out to go and do their work. 'Bye bye, Mr London,' one shouted.

'You want a massage tomorrow?' said another.

'Um, maybe,' I replied, as noncommittal as possible, and they disappeared in a cloud of giggles. In spite of my grouchiness I had enjoyed this little explosion of activity, this snippet of local life. I was aware that the driver was almost certainly illegally making a bit of extra cash on the side, but as I had so long to wait for the boat I was not that bothered.

As we drove on, the driver tried to talk to me but I couldn't understand what he was trying to convey. He had that same lechy look on his face and I didn't know how to make it clear through gestures and facial expressions that I really didn't want a massage with a happy ending or to be sucked off by a ladyboy. But maybe I was just being paranoid. After all, I had no idea what the man was actually saying and he might just have been commenting on the inclement weather. My presumptions probably said more about myself than I perhaps cared to admit.

Finally we arrived at the port. The driver bought me a bottle of water, which was kind of him, and I was unsure whether I had to pay him for it, but he didn't seem to be making overtures in that direction. Perhaps it was a bribe for me to keep quiet about the masseuses. He left me, with only three and a half hours to go before boarding. The place was devoid of both passengers and boats. It was going to be a long wait.

Though abandoned and fatigued, I felt weirdly calm and emotionally energised and happy. I was on holiday after an eleven-month stint of constant touring and writing and it felt like heaven just to have some time away from everything and be able to sit and read and observe an unfamiliar environment. There were minimal home comforts at the ferry port – a small kiosk selling drinks that was closed when I arrived and rows of plastic seats, under a high canopy. It had started to rain torrentially now and perhaps slightly hysterical from tiredness I was enjoying watching it hammering on to the car park and hearing it crashing into the thin metal roof above me. A cooling spray of splash-back rainwater ricocheted into my face. My senses felt heightened, I felt alive and super-aware, as if I had finally awoken after spending months in a half-asleep funk.

Gradually more tourists arrived, breaking my self-indulgent reverie, and after what seemed an age the ferry turned up, a small-ish but seaworthy-looking (what would I know?) boat with some steps down to a cabin with a bar selling drinks and snacks and maybe 50 seats in rows facing the front. I settled down for the jaunt to my island.

A boat trip is always a fun part of any tropical holiday but today mist hung around the ferry and the rain kept falling and there was very little to see. I tried to stay awake, but after an hour and no sign of land I felt my head dropping.

Though I snoozed for a few minutes at a time, the bobbling of my head would wake me up and I desperately wanted to stay conscious anyway, anticipating imminent arrival or at least hopeful of seeing some secret uncharted island with fields of marijuana plants blowing in the wind. Or possibly a hidden paradise, populated entirely with pliant ladyboys who would make me their king. But if such fantastical Gulliverian lands existed they remained hidden by the thick tropical fog.

Another hour passed and I wondered how far into the back of beyond we were heading, but kept myself conscious by observing the other passengers around me. This is one of the luxuries of travelling alone, especially as a writer. You can just sit back and see what everyone else is up to, not having to tend to the needs of a probably fractious travelling partner. I was thus able to allow my imagination to run wild and make wide sweeping generalisations about my fellow travellers, trying to guess who they might be and what their lives were like.

There were a group of three or more couples in their mid-twenties who looked Mediterranean and were speaking a language I didn't recognise. But I started obsessing over one of the women who I found very attractive. She was beautiful, but not in a totally obvious way, but that's always my favourite type of beauty. She had handsome features, very intelligent brown eyes that emanated warmth, wit and character. Even though I couldn't understand a word she said I knew there was something about her. If I had to marry someone based on first impressions then I think she would not be a bad choice. I was clearly in a slightly heady, unrealistically romantic frame of mind, but this was a happy and harmless mini-obsession. I was never going to act on my insane love. I was going to let it vaporise with the mist. There really was a great deal of mist.

Maybe I was envious, travelling alone and unloved as I was, but I couldn't help think that the man she was with was not worthy of her. While she radiated beauty and intelligence, he seemed ordinary, dull and insipid. Admittedly this came from the perspective of the casual, overtired, emotionally fragile and scarcely conscious observer, who had taken a fancy to his partner. I was well aware that I was equally if not more unworthy of this shimmering creature. But the man she had selected, the man whose sallow face and bald pate she was smothering in kisses from her angelic lips, whose unimpressive frame she was embracing with her willowy arms, who had somehow enchanted this creature enough that she could *love* him, just didn't seem to have what it took to deserve her.

He had none of her spark, no personality shining out from behind his eyes, he was like a black hole sucking all that was good and exciting from what was around him. If anything he was a damp tea-towel that had been placed over her smouldering form.

Within the group, however, was another man, who I felt was much more suitable for this Venus.

He was one half of a different couple in this happy group of holidaymakers. He was handsome and tanned and had a cheeky grin, an impish sense of humour and the deepest brown eyes. I didn't fancy him, but if I'd had to help the other side out when they were busy, then I'd be prepared to give it a go with him. It was just plain to me that he had the same luminescence as the woman who had captured my attention if not my heart. He wasn't (I guessed) my paragon of womanhood's intellectual equal, but there was something vital, special and rawly sexual about him. He was no tea-towel, but more of a panful of boiling cooking oil, and if he poured over this glowing ember of womanhood the whole thing would be explosive. In a good way.

When he stood next to my fantasy woman they looked like they should be a couple, they looked like together they would create something stronger and more amazing than they were apart. They were two plusses that added to one another, rather than a plus and minus that cancelled each other out, which was what was happening with their current partners.

Because the woman he was with just didn't seem right for him either. She was pretty enough, but just rather dull and ordinary and not worthy of this dark-skinned, chimp-faced Adonis.

It seemed obvious that my Romeo and Juliet should be together so they could make incendiary love and spawn beautiful, bright babies fizzing with spirit and vitality, but the saps were being held back and weakened by these saps. If the saps had any pride they would leave their perfect partners and hook up with each other and live out their insipid and pointless lives.

Of course I realised that this fantasy said more about me than them. Was I projecting my own failure to find the right person on to them? Was I actually just identifying with the doltish man, knowing that I too was not worthy of a woman that amazing? Was this why I was happily creating this fantastical alternate universe? Yet still I pined for their forbidden but beautiful love. If they acted on these supposed feelings then they would blow their social group apart. And yet... When something is so right would not the pleasure that the two of them would receive be worth the pain they would create? Ultimately weren't their partners the ones causing the pain by clinging to these people who were worth so much more than them and denying the very existence of their remarkable progeny? Most new loves break at least one or two hearts. Joy must always be balanced with sadness.

I knew I was being ridiculous and scurrilously overvaluing and devaluing people I didn't know. But a few moments later, in my sleep-deprived haze I thought I saw the amazing woman looking at the amazing man and catching his eye. And the look on her face made me wonder if I was the most perceptive man who had ever lived. They *knew* they should be together. Maybe this holiday would present some stolen seconds for them to declare their love and act upon it. Maybe the overt show of affection between the girl and her useless, balding boyfriend was actually all for the benefit of the man she truly wanted. Sometimes too much kissing in a relationship is worse than none at all. Who was she trying to convince?

As we approached Phi Phi Island (ha ha – pee pee) a few impressive cliff faces loomed through the mist, being all the more awesome after 150 minutes of shrouded nothingness. I was praying to the God I don't believe in (but still think deserves a capital letter just in case) that this group would end up at the same hotel as me, so I could watch the soap opera develop, like some kind of strange, loner Peeping Tom. My heart sank as they got off the ferry at the first port of call: I was staying on the other side of the island. I hoped that I might see them all again on the ferry on the way home, perhaps grouped into new partnerships, their exuberant happiness replaced with resentment and hatred, their social group blasted apart.

We would be cruising for another long, tired hour before we got to my hotel. This day was dragging on and on. It was going to take me almost as long to get from Phuket airport to my hotel room as it had taken to get from Heathrow to Phuket and I was regretting my failure to sleep on the plane.

The sea was getting rougher and the sky greyer and the rain even heavier, so I was excited and slightly scared when I was informed that there was nowhere to dock at my hotel, so we would have to climb off the ferry into a smaller boat which would carry us ashore.

We were well taken care of by the crew, who provided us with big yellow macs and practically carried us into the smaller boat. As the rain poured and the motor boat sped towards the hotel I huddled together with the bedraggled strangers who would be at least partially sharing my holiday. We must have looked like the soaked survivors of some maritime disaster rather than tourists about to start a holiday on a tropical island.

Finally, after what seemed like the longest day of my life, I was in the hotel restaurant, filling in my registration card, dripping rain and sea-water on to the floor. I had hoped that I might be given a towel, but instead icy flannels were handed out. This might have been nice on a hot day but were superfluous to requirements now. There was at least a cocktail waiting for me. 'Welcome to Paradise,' said the waitress, with no apparent trace of irony.

It rained for the rest of the day, but once I had changed out of my wet things and had a couple of beers and a delicious green curry, I was not too perturbed. It didn't matter about the weather. I was here to chill out on my own and do nothing else.

To begin with, at least, I made an excellent stab at keeping myself to myself. I woke up at 6am the day after arrival and was the first to get to the excellent and extensive buffet breakfast. I made the most of the fact that this was included in the room rate and ate bacon and eggs and pastries and fruit – all good waist-broadening stuff. I can't resist consuming as much as possible in a buffet situation or where food and drink is free.

Early on in my career, as a struggling writer, such occasions were often the only time I got to get properly fed. Of course that excuse was long gone and now I was not in such dire need of the calories, yet I couldn't break old habits.

I was glad to be the first here though, in an empty restaurant. I wasn't interested in speaking to anyone else or making friends. I had come on holiday for solitude. Partly because I didn't want to impose myself on romantically minded couples, but mainly because most people are idiots and I don't want to risk having to be friends with them for the next ten days. On holiday you are trapped in a tiny resort and allow anyone into your fortress of solitude and they might be bugging you every time you step out of your room.

The clouds cleared and the puddles quickly dried up and it became a much more agreeable day. I located a hammock within three metres of the front door of my luxurious beach hut, which directly faced the ocean, and started reading *The God Delusion* by Richard Dawkins. It seemed to be fitting to be in paradise and denying the existence of God.

The book discusses the gullibility of children and how religion (and indeed any philosophical system) can play upon this, quoting the Jesuit saying, 'Give me the child for his first seven years and I'll give you the man.' Of course a child's unquestioning belief in what they are told is one of the cute things about them, but also something that it is useful to grow out of. And yet it struck me that many of the people who use 'childish' as a pejorative term and who see themselves as sensible and grown up, also believe in life after death and a big man in the sky who is watching over them always and judging everything they do. These people, however, are rarely chastised for being puerile or silly or at least take great offence when they are. Yet one might argue that they are more childish and less knowingly so than I am.

As I thought about all this, I happened to look idly out to sea, just in time to see a shoal of flying fish, skipping and arcing across the water, like a swarm of tiny black insects. A small boy, neck-high in water next to his father, squealed with fear and then delight at this unfamiliar spectacle taking place just metres away from him. His dad reached out a protective hand, but smiled to see his son communing with nature and learning about the world. It was a beautiful moment.

But I was almost as impressed and in awe of this seemingly magical piscine, aquatic, acrobatic display as this small boy was. When you're away from home and see such unfamiliar sights, it is like looking at the world through a child's eyes.

It's not that the world we are more familiar with is any less amazing, but as adults we just get jaded and blasé about it. It's another way in which being a child is preferable to being an adult. Another positive about supposed immaturity. Childlike wonder is hard to beat. So much more positive than gullibility.

And affected as I was by the fish, perhaps I was maybe more beguiled by that moment between father and son. Conscious that not only was I 40 years old and on holiday alone, but also I had failed to reproduce, and thus wasn't able to share the wonders of the world by viewing it alongside someone who observed it with uncynical eyes.

That night I walked up some wooden steps carved into the hillside to get to the other side of the island to watch the sunset.

Sitting eating skewers of the meat of different animals, coated in peanutty sauce, while drinking Singha beer and watching the sun slowly descend over the green ocean was about as perfect as things can get. As I looked at it for the first time, it seemed that a path of gold light led directly from the sun to where I was sitting. I felt it was inviting me to try to walk across this shimmering carpet and hop aboard the burning ball of hydrogen, and hitch a lift to the other side of the world. It would mean me jumping off a sheer cliff, then rivalling Jesus' ability to perambulate on liquid and trumping Icarus's attempts to get close to the sun. For the moment I decided just to watch.

Behind me some Thai men were playing an impressive game crossing volleyball with football, kicking and heading a small hollow ball made from bamboo across a net. The smell of barbecued meat filled the air. As the sun went down, a strange chorus of insects clicking started up. I was drinking it all in; the holiday was having an almost narcotic effect on me. If I stayed here too long, even reading Dawkins, I might turn into a dropout hippy and start believing the earth was a living, breathing organism.

Every day I spent here I seemed to be more at ease as well as increasingly lyrical and poetic, albeit in an embarrassing sixth-form sense. A quiet voice in the back of my head wondered if I was going slightly crazy. Which worried me, as voices in your head is a sign of going crazy.

A structure had developed to my day: too much breakfast, hammock, lunch, hammock, satay, beer, dinner, bed. I was getting to bed at about 9pm and waking up with the sunrise. In fact, as the week progressed, this routine became almost a religious calling. At about 6pm I thought to myself, ah well, I'd better get up the hill and make sure the sun sets. It began to feel that my job was now to sit on a bench, drinking beer, eating satay and ensuring that the sun descended. I was like a slightly less visceral, crepuscular Mayan priest. If I wasn't there, who knew what the consequences might be on the smooth-running of the solar system. I couldn't believe I had never considered this as my vocation before and was thinking about trying to continue with it when I got back home, though I wasn't sure who'd pay me. Perhaps if I convinced people of my power they would contribute to ensure that the sun set each day. Though there's less imperative to see that life-giving orb of flame depart than there is to promise its return. Perpetual day is rather less frightening than perpetual night. Those Mayan priests knew what they were doing. But at least I wasn't pulling the still-beating heart out of a human sacrifice. But by the end of the fortnight, the way my mind was spiralling towards madness, who knew?

On the third evening the smiling waitress who brought me my beer said with disarming honesty, 'You very quiet!' If only she knew what I was like the rest of the year. 'You always on your own!' she added, without any apparent awareness of being impolite. I just smiled and told her I was OK. On the whole I was still enjoying being cut off from the world. I was like Robinson Crusoe, alone on a desert island, apart from the fact that there were dozens of other people there, some of whom served me food and alcohol and cleaned up my room for me. But apart from that, he and I were practically identical.

I liked the anonymity and the lack of interaction with other human beings. Sometimes you want to go where nobody knows your name.

At last I had found peace.

The next day there was a bit of a drama. I had been lying in my hammock reading, as my timetable dictated, when I became aware of a commotion coming from the next hut along.

A woman who seemed rather drunk for three o'clock in the afternoon, even on holiday, was shouting out seeming non sequiturs from the balcony of her hut.

'A Mars a day helps you work, rest and play!' she yelled and then laughed to herself a little bit too hard. Then she sang an isolated line of a song – 'You're too shy-shy, hush-hush, eye-to-eye' – in a raucous and unrestrained manner. It would have been funny, but there was a definite tension behind it all, something uncontrollable and potentially crazy. I knew that it would be a bad idea to look at her, fearing that eye contact would give her a chance to explode into hysterics or even violence. I couldn't afford to lose another fight to a woman.

'It's all right,' she leered at a nervous couple who had inadvertently walked along the path by her room. 'I've just got married.' I snuck a quick look at her from behind my book. She was swaying slightly and holding up her hand so that the passers-by could see her ring. They nodded and smiled with frozen smiles and ever so subtly quickened their pace.

But this was more than the giddy excitement of a blushing bride. There was something threatening in the air; her voice was just a little too hysterical, her manner too erratic.

'Giant steps are what you take, walking on the moon!' she sang-shouted and then came another chilling, leery laugh.

One of the members of staff, a Thai lady in an immaculate white dress, appeared within seconds, though looked impressively unruffled and unhurried. She went over to talk to the woman, whose slightly sheepish and seemingly sober husband had appeared out of the room. As I glanced over, the overexcited guest embraced the staff member and kissed her on the cheek. This again seemed an odd breach of staff/guest relations, especially as immediately afterwards she sang, 'Let's all do the conga!'

I wanted to laugh, but increasingly it became clear that something had cracked in this woman's mind.

'Come on, why don't we go inside?' hissed the exasperated man in one of those rasping whispers that carry further than one's regular voice.

'No, I want to stay out here and dance,' came the reply as the woman took off her shoe and hurled it towards the sea.

Then apropos of nothing the woman burst into tears.

I was curious to know what was going on, but also aware that I was almost intruding on this personal crisis. But I had nowhere to go but inside my room and it didn't seem right that I should be inconvenienced.

I was amazed how quickly and efficiently the hotel dealt with this mini-crisis. Within minutes porters were carrying the couple's luggage out of the room and the man led his wife over to the jetty where a speedboat had appeared to whisk them away from paradise to cope with whatever it was that had ripped through their lives to cause this hysterical scene. It was all dealt with very discreetly, but it was strange to have the real world encroach on this idle fantasy that I had been indulging in. We can hide from life, but we can't escape it entirely. And to witness someone being taken over by madness that at times I feared was bubbling under the surface and ready to engulf me, which like the singing woman I was pretending wasn't there, unsettled me for the rest of the day. That night at 3am I woke up with a start, confused as to where I was, feeling dreadfully, dreadfully alone.

For the rest of the holiday my observations from my balcony were rather less eventful, but strangely seemed illustrative of my concerns and worries. One afternoon I became engaged as a three-year-old boy (possibly the same one who'd been spooked by fish that flew) walked by, concentrating intently on the Cornetto ice cream that he was holding reverently in both hands. He pecked at it gently a couple of times, seeming as content as it is possible for a human to be.

And I realised that life doesn't ever get better than that – being three and having a Cornetto in the sunshine. There's no purer pleasure or indulgence in all that will follow in that journey from cradle to grave. But of course, you don't realise that at the time. Sadly you won't even remember. Still, I envied him that moment.

I knew I could still eat a Cornetto now at 40 – and in fact, I did that several times on the holiday, but no Cornetto I could eat now would ever be as awe-inspiring or perfect as the Cornetto you eat at three. It's like a Knickerbocker Glory that lives up to expectations and exceeds them. Which means that any Cornetto I ate now could only be a disappointment. Mainly, I realised, because at 40 I could eat a dozen Cornettos a day if I wanted – and I guess that's part of why it is special as a child. You have no actual control over what you eat and no power to choose beyond manipulating the adults around you. When a Cornetto comes along it is a wonderful and delicious surprise, an ice-cream oasis in the dessertless desert of life. Plus it's big and it's yours and you don't have to share it. You have no concept of it being bad for you and thus no guilt, no idea that there are better, more expensive, more delicious ice creams out there. You don't even really realise that soon the Cornetto will be gone. You just have a Cornetto in your hands and it's all for you and you are alive in the moment and nothing else matters. I could promise that child that there will never be such uncomplicated happiness in his life again. And the worst thing is that he had no inkling of the magnitude of this moment.

Could I grab him and shake him and shout at him, 'Remember this moment! Hang on to it! Because life gets no better than this!'? No. Partly because that would somewhat sour the indulgent pleasure but mainly because in this day and age a 40-year-old man furiously buffeting a young boy that he doesn't know while shouting feverishly into his face about pleasure is seen as some kind of crime. It's political correctness gone mad.

And of course if the three-year-old boy knew that the Cornetto was the best moment of his life then that would also spoil things a bit as well. He'd think, I'm three and I've experienced the zenith of my existence with maybe 80 more years to go! It's the fact you don't know that ultimately makes the moment perfect.

It was still impossible for me to tell if I wanted to have a child or if I just wished I was still a child.

At the end of a week of this isolated existence it struck me how little I had actually spoken on the holiday. I had spent the whole of August doing nothing but talking, on stage and in bars, but in seven days I estimated that I had uttered less than 50 words a day. I had not spoken more than two sentences to anyone at any one time. It'd been great.

I had also not stepped outside the grounds of the hotel. Sometimes on holiday I like to explore and the hotel certainly offered enough trips around the various islands that hung tantalisingly on the horizon. But I craved inertia.

On the eighth day I had had enough of hammocks and lounging and decided to get out of the hotel and see what was going on elsewhere on this crazy island, so I hopped on to the dragon boat (actually just a long, low wooden boat with a outboard motor – it didn't even breathe fire) down to Tonsai Bay with two other couples from the hotel. After such a slothful week it was incredibly exciting to be bouncing along over the waves, seaspray splashing in our faces. I had £200 worth of local currency, but had had no opportunity to spend any of it up until now, as the hotel did not deal in cash. I felt I should do something to help the local economy and spend as much as possible with local people, given that most of the money spent at the hotel was probably going into the pockets of American hotel-owning fat cats. The Thai people had been having a hard time of it of late, and it was clear even to the casual observer that Tonsai Beach had taken the brunt of the recent tsunami. Two and a half years had passed yet there was still a lot of rebuilding to do and a lot of damage still evident. The good humour with which these people had taken their recent tragedies was evident on a T-shirt I saw for sale on one of the many stalls:

Phi Phi island
2002 sars
2003 bird flu
2004 tsunami
2005 earthquake
What next?

The bay which I'd briefly stopped off at on the way to my hotel was stunningly beautiful, but the town itself less so. It was basically a maze of muddy alleys, lined with shops, cafés and market stalls, each selling what seemed to be exactly the same collection of cheap tourist-friendly trinkets. In certain spots it smelled of sewage and there was an awful lot of construction going on. I felt guilty about my privileged life and my self-indulgent worries about my charmed existence. I don't imagine that you'd find many kidults living in Tonsai Beach. In fact, the kids didn't get much chance to be kids at all: many of the stalls were manned (or childed) by sad-eyed youngsters.

I finally plumped for buying a couple of leather wrist-bands (ideal wear for the middle-aged man pretending to still be a gap-year student). The girl on the stall asked for 100 baht for each (a little under £2) but I haggled her down to 160 for the pair. It felt slightly sick to be arguing over a few pence, when the money meant nothing to me and so much more to her. The gulf between us was hammered home when I produced a 500 baht note, the smallest I had, and caused quite a stir as they went off to try and get me my change.

Can you imagine a market trader in the UK not having change for a tenner? I felt mean, and wanted to tell her to keep the change, but I think to have done that might have been insulting and patronising in a different way. The mark-up was clearly demonstrated in another shop where I was going to buy a notebook, mainly because there were lots of cute kids in the store and

I hoped that some of the money might filter down to them in the form of food. The woman asked 480 baht for it (I assumed it was one of those fancy handmade-paper notebooks – it had a wooden cover with tin figures on it) and I decided that was too much and put it down like it was on fire (because although I wanted to help, I wasn't prepared to part with £8 – charity must have its limits). She asked me how much I thought it was worth and I said maybe 200, so she asked for 250 and I decided that that was fair. Though none of this was fair. And I was a prick for not giving her the full amount, even if it turned out, when I opened it, that only the cover was handmade (and cheaply at that) and the inside was a lined notepad. They'd still ripped me off. And I deserved it.

It made me laugh because of my pretensions of magnanimity.

That night at the Satay Bar I started writing about my holiday and sorting out my many and contradictory thoughts in my cheap rip-off notebook. The friendly but bluff waitress who had remarked on my quietness the other day came up to talk to me again. 'Why you always read and write?' she enquired.

'I'm a writer. That's my job,' I explained.

'What you write about?'

'Just now I am writing about some people I saw on the ferry across who I felt were in the wrong couples and I was wondering whether they would realise this themselves one day.' I perhaps surprised myself with my sudden loquaciousness as well as my keenness to explain myself.

She seemed surprised, 'Why?' she scoffed, screwing up her face.

'I write about what I see,' I explained. 'Maybe I will write about you one day!' She actually jumped backwards in surprise and consternation. She clearly didn't want that or maybe she thought she wasn't interesting enough. 'We all have a story to tell,' I offered, but she was shaking a bit so I assured her, 'Don't worry. I will never write about you.'

I am nothing if not a liar.

That night I stayed up until after 9pm for the first time on the holiday and had a couple more beers in the bar. They were playing a U2 concert on the big screen. I think I hate U2 more than any other band. They are so phoney and portentous and ultimately vacuous. Apart from Larry Mullen, who seems OK, but the others are all dicks, especially Bono. And The Edge. And Adam Clayton, who isn't even clever enough to think up a new rock-star name. During 'In The Name Of Love', the big screens behind the band showed a bit of a speech by Martin Luther King and I shook my head in disgust at the arrogance of this trivial rock band daring to associate itself with someone truly important.

Later Bono was dressed as the devil and railing against capitalism (because U2 aren't part of capitalism) and I wondered if, in fact, Bono might actually be Satan. It made sense for a second and then I realised that the real Satan would be cleverer and less obvious than Bono. Or maybe Satan is so clever he's done a double bluff and is actually Bono.

The fact I was getting annoyed about this perhaps further demonstrated that being alone was starting to take its toll.

Luckily, the next day brought me some company, thanks to the second downpour of the week. The weather had been sunny and hot since my drenched arrival, but today a rainstorm of diluvian proportions had descended and there was no option but to take shelter in the restaurant and get drunk. After lunch I got talking to a couple of Australian women who had arrived the day before. They were both in their thirties and from Western Australia and had been friends since childhood, though seemed like polar opposites. Janet was plump and slightly dowdy and had left her husband and family behind to come on holiday with her friend. Kim was slim and attractive, and, I quickly ascertained, single. She was clearly a bit of a rebel, a chain-smoker with at least one tattoo and a slightly frosty demeanour. I liked her and was delighted to have found a single woman in this hotel full of couples.

Janet was the chatty one, though, bright and breezy. 'So where're you from?' she asked.

'London.'

'Oooh, nifty!' she said, smiling. 'Whereabouts?'

'Shepherd's Bush actually. You must have been there. It's a kind of Mecca for your countryfolk!'

They laughed.

My Garboesque claims to want to be alone, I thought to myself, seemed to be nothing more than self-protecting lies: it was rather wonderful to have met some people that I could have a conversation with and thus escape my solipsism.

They had an interesting story to tell. 'We set off two weeks ago,' explained Kim. 'We had two months to tour the world. We were going to the US, then on to the UK and Europe, making our way home via Bali.'

'It was going to be super-nifty,' Janet noted, rather dreamily.

'But when we got to immigration at LAX, the bastard at the desk says we can't go through. We had to go and wait in this little windowless room. We were there for fucking ages.'

'It was like being in Guantanamo Bay... you know... I imagine.'

'Then this bogan customs bell-end comes in and tells us that their computer records show that I had a drugs conviction back in Oz and I was like, "Yeah, the cops caught me with about an eighth of grass when I was fifteen!" and he was all, "A drugs conviction is a drugs conviction, ma'am." He called me "ma'am". He was so fucking sarcastic. So we weren't allowed in his stupid, stuck-up, shithouse country.'

'Well,' I observed, 'as I understand it they don't have drugs in America.'

'Yes, they fucking do,' Kim retorted, perhaps missing my joke. 'They have fucking loads of the stuff. If I'd had crack up me crack then I could understand their problem. But I didn't.'

'She really didn't,' agreed Janet, 'and they did check. Both of us,' she added with a degree of resentment.

'Fuck, it was awful. This wanker says I can't come into the country...'

'And obviously I didn't want to go in on my own.'

'And our flights to Europe were all out of New York, which of course we couldn't get to, so we just decided to make the best of a bad deal and get on the first plane out of there that was going somewhere hot. And so here we are. In the pissing rain!'

Kim's criminal status made her even more attractive. She definitely seemed to be a potential love interest and my resolutions to have a couple of weeks away from all that nonsense seemed to be falling by the wayside. Some casual holiday sex with a fugitive might snap me out of all my sunset gazing and navel gazing.

After a couple of hours of sharing a couple of jugs of cocktails, Kim went to the toilet (probably to shoot up) and Janet looked me in the eye. After having been light and slightly air-headed for all this time, she was suddenly serious. Solemn even. 'You've got the hots for Kimmy, haven't you?' she accused me.

'Well, I wouldn't say that exactly, but she's an attractive girl.'

'Oh, you're a smitten kitten, all right. It always happens. Keep away from her, mate, you'll get burned.' There was an apparent disgruntlement towards the person she'd chosen to travel the world with. Perhaps Janet was upset that due to Kim's misdemeanours, she had missed out on a holiday in the States, as well as getting a rubber-gloved hand up in places where she might have preferred it not to be. But her ominous warning only served to make this mysterious, shady figure seem more dangerous and thus even sexier.

Kim returned. 'Shall we get another jug of margarita?' she asked.

'Yeah, nifty,' chirped Janet, as jolly and untroubled as it was possible to be. I did an actual double take at this instantaneous change in attitude, but Janet just smiled at me. What was I getting into here?

We drank more and laughed more and Janet said 'nifty' a whole lot more as the rain dripped down from the bamboo roof.

'Hey,' said Kim, 'we're going out on a boat trip tomorrow. We're gonna to see some sea caves and the island where *The Beach* was filmed. You wanna come along for the ride?'

'Oh yeah, go on, it'll be nifty.'

'Yeah, yeah, that does sound nifty,' I readily agreed, again demonstrating that my protestations that I was happy on my own doing nothing were masking a real desire for adventure and company. I had had a bit too much time for introspection and now that I had agreed to go along I was really looking forward to escaping my desert island. A bit too much perhaps.

As I went to sleep that night, for a moment at least, I wondered whether master criminal Kim was going to spear me on a stalagmite when we were alone in the cave, rob me of my remaining bahts and leave my corpulent corpse to rot in the sea. Why did I find the prospect slightly arousing?

Though they knew which hut I was in, the girls did not come to get me in the morning, possibly forgetting an invitation that they had made when merry or, as my paranoid mind imagined, deciding they didn't want a whole day in my company now they were sober. With thwarted expectations, I had a bit of a miserable day, feeling abandoned and sorry for myself, before making my usual trip up the hill to ensure that the course of the sun continued unimpeded.

I sat and wrote in my notebook, perhaps a little ostentatiously, like a tragic poet, alone and unwanted. I tried to sum up my motives for coming away and to work out if I had achieved anything.

'*In my head*,' I wrote, '*I have slated this holiday as a kind of decompression chamber between the old me and the amazing new me who is going to emerge at the other end.*

'*I realise this is probably entirely unrealistic and that in all probability nothing will change. But maybe it is time. I hope I can at least try.*

'*I want to get fit and healthy again, get back into exercising regularly and lose some weight. This is probably achievable.*

'*But this is only a tiny part of what I sometimes feel I should alter. I feel maybe it's time to start growing up, to get my life in order, not waste so much time and probably most importantly, and this is the most difficult and unlikely thing to change (and I am only 40% sure that it is necessary), to make serious efforts in finding a serious girlfriend and in order to facilitate this to stop sleeping with women that I know for certain are inappropriate and where the relationship is going nowhere.*

'*This would mean finishing with the women who I am in casual relationships with. Can I do this? Will I do this? Do I really want this? Should I make hay while the sun shines, because surely the sun is setting soon enough (as I sit in the Satay Bar with the sun some thirty minutes from the horizon).*'

I then listed all the women that I was currently or potentially romantically involved with and shocked myself by the sheer number. My iPod was on shuffle and the song it randomly chose at this exact moment was by Ben Folds. 'There's never going to be a moment of truth for you,' he told me. 'Cos all you need is the thing you've forgotten,

'And that's to learn to live with what you are.

'You've got to learn to live with what you are.'

Was he right? I presume he hadn't written the song specifically about me, but maybe we can never change. But was this a moment of truth or, as seemed more likely, even at that very second, was I going to get home and return to my old ways?

I then wrote, '*I have a ludicrous life. I think that maybe the lesson is that I should enjoy it while the sun is still up...*'

The rest of the journal remains empty, because at that point my Australian friends turned up, cheerfully mocking me for being lost in the self-indulgent world of diary writing. I am not being racist, but there isn't an Australian on the planet capable of understanding anything emotional, so we just got down to doing all that Antipodeans can understand, drinking and eating barbecued food. Kim said, 'The boat trip was so awesome.'

'Yeah,' agreed Janet, 'it was nifty.'

'Just as you predicted,' I observed dryly. But no mention was made of the fact that I had not been with them. It didn't really matter. It didn't seem to have been anything personal.

After dinner we went for a walk up the beach. I had thought there was nothing beyond the hotel to the north, but discovered to my embarrassment that there was in fact a whole row of Thai cafés and a couple of little shops and bigger restaurants. Because of my assumption, I had spent nearly all of my time in my hotel and eaten all my meals there and now at the last minute I realised there were some other options. What a dick!

I thought Kim was being flirtatious, singing and dancing on the sand and encouraging me to join her, though self-consciously I just laughed and declined. But the fact we were getting on so well pissed off Janet, who definitely wasn't finding our interest in each other all that nifty. She sped up and disappeared along the beach. I don't know if she was jealous of her friend for being with me or me for being with her friend, but the atmosphere was turning sour just at a time when I thought it might be turning sweet. They were moving on the next day, so it was now or never.

I was left alone as my potential lover chased after her friend. The beach was dark and the waves were crashing against the shore. I breathed in the salty air and waited. I wondered what the argument was about. Maybe the plan had always been to lure me to this dark spot and dash my head on the rocks, but now Janet was having second thoughts, realising that I was a nice guy and the two of them were now debating whether they would go ahead with it. It was a sign of my continuing madness that I was hoping Kim would win the argument.

After some time, the stroppy gooseberry came back on her own and headed back to the hotel without a word. Kim followed her, no longer dancing on the sand or laughing. She was drunk and grumpy and as we chatted I discovered she had a less than liberal attitude to the Aborigine people of Australia, not in this case because she thought racism was funny. Everything had gone a bit wrong, even if it had really never been close to going right.

Kim and I got back to my hut and came to a stop. I couldn't work out whether we were about to part or if she wanted to come in. I was feeling powerfully tired after all that exercise and confusion and was actually slightly relieved when she just wished me good night and goodbye without too much ceremony. It was best that it had been a break from romance, though in my heart I know that if she'd been interested I would almost certainly have succumbed and immediately proved my pretensions of moving on with my life to be nonsense. We had exchanged email addresses, but of course we never heard from each other again.

*

Next day, as I lunched alone, my bad-weather friends having departed, the cheeky Thai waitress who I had promised never to write about asked me, 'Where your friends?'

'Oh, they've gone home!' I explained.

She then walked away, with a smile on her face, and almost sang at me like a playground chant, 'So you got no one to talk with now!'

This really made me laugh. Somehow in her childlike honesty there was a charm that might have been insulting in another circumstances.

When sunset came I was too engrossed in my book and weary to cross the island and was relieved when the sun did not stop in the sky. I had a great view of the effects on this side of the island, which were if anything more spectacular. The sky and thus the sea turned the most amazing shades of pink and purple. I had missed all this because of my routine.

With two days to go I was looking forward to going home now and thinking that these might be two days too many. But if at the end of the holiday you are looking forward to your own bed (which I'd only been in for one night in the previous six weeks) then that can only be a good thing. You can only have so much of paradise. You need some Shepherd's Bush to make paradise have any meaning.

On my last night I went up for a final beer at the Satay Bar at about 5.30pm and was rewarded with by far the best sunset of the holiday. Usually the sun has got lost in the clouds as it descends below the horizon, but tonight the ball of fire was clearly visible until it ducked behind the island where *The Beach* was filmed, that I had failed to visit. I love the sun – it will be a shame when it explodes or implodes or whatever it is that it's meant to do. Apparently that's not going to happen for at least 50 years though, so I should be dead by the time it occurs. It would make me sad to see it go, so I hope it outlives me. But even if it does, I will still be thinking as I die, that ultimately the sun will disappear, just like me.

When you're eighteen it seems like a good idea to have sex with loads of different people, but most of us, when we get a bit older, into our twenties, realise it's actually more satisfying to be in an exclusive relationship with someone that we cherish and respect.

Then we get a bit older into our forties and realise, 'No, no, I was right first of all.' But it's too late now, you're hitched. Best just sit it out, wait for the blessed release of death.

CHAPTER 10
THREE STRIKES AND YOU'RE OUT

'You see, when it's turned to hot water the boiler fires up...' The pilot light burst into life with a satisfying woomph. 'But when I turn it to central heating... nothing.' The light was out and darkness reigned behind the tiny window in front of the magical tiny furnace that heated my entire house. 'I mean, I'm no expert, but something has clearly gone wrong with it while it's been off over the summer.'

The central heating engineer was unimpressed by my inexpert synopsis. He gave me a look which either meant, 'We'll see' or 'This is going to cost you a lot of money.' Or maybe both.

'It might be the thermostat,' he opined.

'Yeah, of course,' I said, unconvincingly attempting to sound knowledgeable. I peered into the boiler cupboard. 'And where would that be exactly?'

'Probably downstairs somewhere.'

'Yes, right, that would be more normal.' Then with triumph I realised I might know what he was talking about. 'Yes! Come with me.'

Down in the lounge we located the thermostat and I was feeling quite the Handy Andy with my thermostat-locating skills.

'Well, there's your problem,' he told me. 'It's turned down to zero.'

I couldn't understand it. I hardly even knew this thing was here and had certainly never touched it. My central heating had worked earlier in the year, so at some point in the interim some visitor to my house had inexplicably fiddled with it. Presumably to ensure that my heating wouldn't work and that I would be forced to call out an engineer who would fix the problem immediately and make me look like the idiotic, infantile simpleton that I truly am.

If the engineer was gloating inside at my idiocy he didn't show it on the outside. He turned up the dial and then led me upstairs to demonstrate that my 'broken' central heating was now working.

He hadn't even got his hands dirty.

He got out a sheet of paper for me to sign. It didn't actually say, 'I am a hopeless excuse for a man with no idea of how to perform even the most basic DIY jobs,' but it may as well have done. I paid him for an hour, even though this had taken no more than three minutes from start to finish. He'd only had time to take two sips of the coffee I'd made him. He even made a comment about how he wasn't going to be able to finish his drink. Was he being sarcastic? Was he mocking me? Yes, probably. He'd been paid £80 to turn a dial. He must have laughed himself hoarse once he was back in his van.

After he'd gone, there was a part of me that felt I should keep him there for the full hour and make him do other things for me, with the time that I had paid for, like maybe he could have done my washing-up. But really I needed him to leave as soon as possible. I felt emasculated and inadequate.

I remembered being a teenager and showing no aptitude or interest in DIY, despite my dad's desire to teach me.

'What are you going to do when you've left home and I'm not around to do it for you?' he'd said.

'I'll just pay a man to come and do it for me,' I replied with startling foresight, not anticipating how mortifying it would be to do so.

*

I had been back home for two days. It was 12 September 2007, another significant date in my life. I was 40 years and 62 days old, by my calculations, the exact same age as John Lennon had been when he died. Had I achieved as much in my 40 years and two months as he had? Some might argue not.

I had had a similar feeling of lack of achievement when I'd got to 33 and realised I was now the same age as Jesus when he was crucified. Obviously he came back to life (and is presumably still alive), but he did all his most memorable stuff in those first 30-odd years and has been resting on his laurels since then.

Getting to the same age as Lennon seemed like more of a tipping point, not least because he definitely wasn't a fictional character. I also clearly remembered the day of his death. It was one of the first times that I was shocked and discombobulated by someone's demise. I was a thirteen-year-old boy, just having discovered Lennon's music for the first time and had been forcing Dave Tozer to listen to my one Beatles tape over and over again. Suddenly, unexpectedly, the news came that a Beatle was dead. The next day, Matt Wheeler, who I walked to school with, was wearing a black armband.

'At least he lived until he was 40,' I told Matt. 'I mean, it's not ancient, but it's still pretty old. He had a good knock.'

Of course, now I had reached the same age as Lennon, the tragedy of both the loss of his life and of all he might have subsequently created was much more palpable. As was the tragedy of how little I had managed to fit into the same span. And how much time I was still wasting doing nothing. I had to pull my finger out or alternatively find some old duffer who had done absolutely nothing with their long, long life and use them as my benchmark instead.

On the evening I got as old as Lennon had been I was in my bedroom and happened to look out of the window to see the sun setting behind the buildings opposite me. It wasn't as spectacular a sunset as the ones I'd enjoyed in Thailand, the sun somehow seemed much smaller and harsher in Shepherd's Bush, and the cloud cover was too uniform and concretey, so the sun's rays were unable to catch the cloud fringes and turn them psychedelic. But it is something that I would usually never have even spotted. Soon enough London sunsets would go unnoticed again, but for now some of the magical dust of holiday poetry was still lingering.

This was one more sunset than Lennon never got to see.

It was too early to see if my return home had coincided with the birth of a new and improved me. I was still as confused and conflicted as ever. I was making a few half-hearted attempts to make some changes for the better. I resolved to get some exercise and improve my diet, as I noticed with a heavy heart that all those Proustian Cornettos had tipped me over the 15-stone mark on the scales. I had also decided not to contact my lunchtime lover again, which was definitely a move in the right direction. But would I be as resolute when it came to looking for love, rather than loves? Could I find someone who would not only want me, but with whom I'd be happy to be exclusive?

There was perhaps a creeping desperation or infatuation to my behaviour and some internal tug of war going on between the part of me that still wanted to bask in my freedom and the part of me that hankered for something more meaningful. Perhaps as a result I was allowing myself to fall for unsuitable women, thus allowing the angel on my shoulder to pretend I was doing my best, while the devil on the other shoulder knew I'd be able to carry on living my grubby, wonderful, awful, wicked, genetically programmed life.

But the failures were starting to hurt. And were outnumbering the successes.

A week after my return and it seemed that I was going to continue drinking and partying like it was 1989. It was a Monday night approaching midnight and the pub that I'd been gigging at and then drinking in was closing, but I was not thinking about heading home and getting some sleep so I could get some work done in the morning. Of course not. I wanted the night to continue and when one of my fellow comics suggested heading up the road to a bar that stayed open until two, my only concern was that that would only give us two more hours of drinking.

A gaggle of us trekked the 250 metres up the road and I pushed open the door to reveal another hundred other blessed souls for whom a late Monday night on the piss was a wondrous reality rather than an impossible fantasy. I crossed the threshold, stepping from the monochrome and boring outside world, into a techni-colour, vibrant oasis of excitement. There was the sound of laugh-ter, of raised but friendly voices and gentle music from a live band in the corner. Why would I even consider leaving all this behind?

I made for the bar to order my companions in this adventure more drinks and found myself standing next to Eve, who had worked behind the scenes of one of my Edinburgh shows. It felt like an impossible and wonderful coincidence, even though we were in a pub that was also a theatre and is frequented mainly by people who work in the business.

'Hey, how are you doing?' I bellowed gleefully.

'I'm great. It's my birthday!' she told me.

'Hooray,' I replied. 'I'll get you a drink.'

'No, it's OK. This is our last one. We're going after this.'

She indicated towards the two pals she was celebrating with and I raised my hand in greeting. One had her back to me, but when she turned to say hello my mouth fell agape – she was breath-takingly, radiantly gorgeous. She looked at me, saw my unmasked disbelief and gave me the smallest but most encouraging of smiles. I was too astonished to speak to her, so just grinned back.

'I've got to take these drinks to my friends,' I reluctantly said to Eve, my eyes still fixed on the cheeky, pixie face of her compan-ion. 'Great to see you.'

I went back to the people I had arrived with, though now I didn't want to be with them at all. I was conscious it would be rude to abandon them so quickly, especially as I had had to persuade some of them to come along, but I wasn't paying any attention to anything they were saying. My eyes were as focused as they could be, given how much I'd drunk, on the voluptuous girl standing at the bar. She seemed to be bathed in an ethereal light that shone on only her and choirs of angels were singing in my ears. Was she floating ever so slightly above the ground? Or was I?

I was bedazzled.

I might have stood there for days, but suddenly I snapped out of my reverie, realising that the woman of my dreams was standing just metres away and was about to walk out of the pub and my life for ever.

'I've just got to go and say hello to some friends,' I told the comedian who had been babbling away unheard beside me and I stumbled blindly towards the object of my affections.

'I thought I should come and wish you happy birthday properly before you go,' I lied to Eve.

'We've decided to stay for another,' said Eve 'Emilia twisted my arm.'

'I did!' said the divine creature in front of me, with cheeky coquettishness. She had the exact same voice as Clare Grogan in *Gregory's Girl*. There is no sexier accent in the world.

'Emilia?' I repeated. 'What an absolutely beautiful name.'

She giggled at my clumsy flirtation and said, 'Oooh, smooooth!' But our eyes had locked and I realised I hadn't imagined whatever I had felt in that first moment and that there was some mutual interest. I made no further attempt to talk to the birthday girl and to be honest the rest of the bar and everyone in it might have spontaneously combusted at that moment and I wouldn't have noticed.

'What made you want to stay for another drink?' I asked.

'What do you think?' she replied, looking me squarely in the eye. I was almost so taken aback that I forgot to breathe and my heart stopped pumping, but I managed to gather my dazzled wits and come back with, 'Uncontrollable alcoholism?'

She gave a delightful, puckish laugh. It had been a risk to undercut her forwardness, but I had sensed that she'd find it funny. She gave as good as she got. She lightly brushed my chin with her hand. 'There was a bit of dirt there, from when your jaw hit the ground when you first saw me. I thought that kind of thing only happened in cartoons. I'd never seen it in real life!'

'That wasn't to do with you...'

'Oh, it wasn't?'

'No, no, of course not. I have a very rare condition – Loose Jaw… Syndrome.'

'I've never heard of that.'

'No, people are shamefully unaware of it. Even though Gordon Brown has a very mild case. Sufferers' jaws just spring open at the most inopportune times.'

'That must be a terrible disability.'

'Yes. Yes, it is. I sometimes lose control of my jaw muscles and the whole thing just flaps open like a trap door and…' I opened my mouth to its full extent and tried to speak. 'Oh look, it's happened again. It's a nightmare.'

Her own mouth dropped open too and she stared at me for a second with disbelief. 'Oh, I don't suffer from Loose Jaw Syndrome,' she said. 'I'm just genuinely astonished. Eve said you were a comedian. Is it your night off?'

I liked her sassiness and familiarity. Apparently most men (the idiots) don't like funny women, presumably they are challenged by them, but I really love anyone who can make me laugh and Emilia was hilarious. And also gorgeous. I was smitten.

After a few minutes of banter we were both suddenly lost for words, just gazing into each other's eyes as chemistry and biology did their unspoken, magical, yet ultimately base work.

'Wow! Well, that was a bit… weird,' I remarked.

'Let's move on and not mention it. We're both too cool to draw attention to it,' she advised.

It was hard to believe I had only known her for ten minutes. She was a singer-songwriter, although she was temping to make some money for the moment. I was looking forward to hearing her songs on her MySpace page.

'I wish I could go up and sing instead of the band over there,' she said, perhaps betraying the fact that she was a little inebriated. 'I am way better than them.' She seemed to be genuinely considering doing it.

At one point I stopped myself making a drunken, sick joke, but she insisted on hearing it and when I told her she not only laughed, but followed up with something even more off-colour. Had I found my perfect woman? I was besotted and all the signs said that Emilia was too.

Eve came over and whispered in her ear. 'We're going to be off soon,' Emilia told me, giving a little frown as she did so.

'Do you have to go with them? Stay and drink more with me.'

'I'd like to, but I've got work in the morning and I am already pissed off my face.'

'Well, could I see you again, maybe at the weekend?'

'For sure. I'd really like that.' There had been no question in my mind that she wouldn't. For some reason she didn't want her friends knowing that we'd been flirting, even though I thought it must have seemed obvious, so I slipped her my card and she said she'd email me.

In the cab home my head was spinning and I felt stupidly giddy. It's true that I was drunk and also true that part of me was already imagining undressing and caressing her, but another part of my brain was suddenly envisioning our whole future and it was unrolling like a cartoon carpet in my mind. The rest of our lives together was flashing before my eyes, like these things are supposed to do when you're dead. Though as far as I could tell I was still alive, hoping upon hope that this wasn't some cruel dream that I was about to wake from. I was envisaging us spending our days together, having kids, living to a ripe old age, before dying within days of each other. What kind of a romantic fantasy also envisages mutual death?

It was a bit freaky to me, even at the time, that this was the way my mind was working, and in hindsight I was clearly fantasising and reading too much into our brief encounter. Perhaps I should get to know her a bit first. Perhaps I was just showing my desperation to get into something serious. Perhaps I was actually merely overcome with lust for this beautiful young woman. She had the most spectacular body. How much was I projecting on to her after less than half an hour in her company? But she had seemed genuinely smitten too. I was sure she'd be in touch. It felt inevitable.

Convinced of our perfect future together, the very next morning I visited her web page. Her songs, I thought, were amazing and she also wrote a very funny blog. I wanted to let her know that I was thinking about her. Every sensible fibre of my being told me that this was a stupid thing to do, that I should be cool and wait for her to get in contact, as she had said she would. Unfortunately, most of the fibres of my being had gone all soppy and moony and they mutinied against the sensible fibres. I was drunk on love and possibly still on booze as well, and convinced she would love to know how she'd made me feel.

Hey Emilia

I've just been listening to your songs. You're right. It would have been way better if you'd taken over from the band last night. And your blog is hilarious. Not as funny as mine, of course, but that would scarcely be possible.

I just wanted you to know how incredible it was to meet you last night. You had a really profound effect on me and I've been thinking about you all night. I hope we can meet up soon. I'm free on Friday and Saturday, like I said.

Let me know how you're fixed.

Rich

She didn't reply that day as I had hoped and expected. Or the next. But her MySpace homepage informed me she hadn't visited the site for a few days. While I was checking it every few minutes, looking at her photo and listening to her songs. A bit like a stalker would. Maybe she didn't really use the page too much. She'd probably email me anyway, like she'd promised.

Friday passed and Saturday arrived and I could see that she had both visited her page and read my message, but unbelievably she had still not responded. I was heartbroken and confused, but there were plenty of reasons why she might have not wanted to follow things up in the cold light of day. She might have been drunk, she might have a boyfriend or be married (it wouldn't be the first time) or most likely I had just been ridiculously keen and uncool by getting in touch so quickly and had freaked her out.

I was feeling like a nutter and knew that if a woman had behaved like this with me I would probably have given her the cold shoulder too. But I had been convinced that this was the real deal and that there would be no need for game playing.

My heart was in the right place, it was just my brain that was drifting all over the shop, like an old woman driving the wrong way down a motorway.

I messaged her again.

Emilia,

How are things? I am surprised that I haven't heard from you yet and I hope everything is OK. Maybe you thought it was a bit uncool or weird for me to email you so quickly, but I had just been excited to meet you and it had seemed you'd felt the same.

If you don't want to meet up again, then obviously that's OK, if a little disappointing, but it'd be great if you just dropped me a note to let me know.

I mean, I'm still hoping you'd like to hang out, so drop me a note if that's the case as well, obviously.

I had a really good feeling about us. It'd be a shame if it all comes to nothing.

Rich

Still there was no response. I was just astonished that she would ignore me completely. I hadn't imagined the connection. She had admitted it was there. And I was aware that to continually message her when she was not replying was inadvisable at best and that sending a further missive could do nothing but harm me, but I wanted to see her again, or at the very least have some explanation as to why she was now blanking me.

Emilia,

Look it's clear that you don't want to see me and that's OK, obviously. I just don't understand why you're not even replying to me. Could you please just reply to tell me the reason you're not replying? Just so I know what I did wrong, if anything. Obviously if the thing I did wrong was to message you too early and too often, then this message won't help. I'm sorry if I seem crazy or paranoid, but I just can't believe that we went from such a promising beginning to such a horrible dead end.

I am not crazy, incidentally, although aware that stating such a thing in a message is indicative of the exact opposite.

Please just tell me what went wrong and I won't message again. And I won't message again in any case.

Richard

She didn't reply.

I remained good to my word.

Until about three months later when I sent another brief missive: 'Any news?'

She no longer found me funny. But I was genuinely hurt and astonished by the way she'd dropped me.

The unfurling carpet of our future life had been rolled up and thrown in a skip, where it was pissed upon by tramps. Our beautiful children remained trapped in that purgatory for those who will never be born.

'I met this girl in a bar the other day,' I told a room full of strangers in Cardiff about a month later. 'I liked her, she wasn't really interested in me. I was annoying her if anything...' A few laughs of recognition came from both women and men in the darkness, but the bright lights in my face meant I couldn't see most of them. 'I said, "Come on, I know it hasn't gone very well tonight, but give me another chance. Let me take you out for dinner." She said, "You? Take me out for dinner?! I wouldn't piss on you if you were on fire!"'

Some laughter intermingled with sympathetic 'Aaahs!' came out of the gloom.

'I said, "What if I wasn't on fire?"' I gave a leery wink. The audience erupted into a beautiful mixture of laughter and disgust.

It was the start of what was almost a perfect gig. The crowd were behind me, I was fizzling with ideas, improvising, in command and I tore the room apart. When I came down to the bar afterwards I stood chatting with Stephen, one of the other acts, when a ludicrously beautiful woman, with black hair and light brown skin, bounded up to us. She had been one of the few audience members I could see from the stage, sitting at a table at the front. I had directed a couple of my cheekier remarks to her and she'd seemed to enjoy them. Stephen was in mid-flow of an anecdote about snooker, but thankfully she interrupted him.

'How can you not be talking to me?' she said to me accusatively. 'How could you not have sought me out the minute you got off stage? I'm the most beautiful woman in the room – why would you not be talking to me?' Her boldness and confidence made me laugh, but as a comedian you meet a lot of crazy people at gigs and so I was cautious, in case she was barking mad or barking drunk or both. Indeed she was so self-assured that I wondered if she might have been indulging in some illegal stimulants. Despite my concerns, there was immediately something endearing and attractive about her exuberance.

'What do you do?' I asked her when I could get a word in edgeways.

'I break men's hearts,' she replied without missing a beat, before adding, 'And women's hearts too.'

'Yes,' I replied, 'I saw you nodding during the threesome section.'

'Oh yes,' she said, smiling, her dark eyes flashing at me. I was intrigued and excited but a little frightened too. It was all a bit full-on a bit too quickly, but it looked like being a sexual rather than romantic scenario, so my battered heart need not fear. The presumption that I would want to be with her was accurate, but to have it so blatantly expressed was slightly off-putting. I'm not a whore! I like to be courted – before having sex with someone I have only just met.

Then as quickly and effervescently as she had appeared, she vanished.

'I don't quite know how I blew that,' I said to Stephen.

Her tactic of feast and famine worked though, because I now couldn't concentrate on the conversation I was having. I was looking around the crowded pub for her, yearning for her to come back. Finally I spotted her at the bar, chatting and laughing with another man. She was in her thirties, voluptuous, wearing expensive clothes and, I now noticed, had the most perfect bottom. She had had a foreign accent, but I hadn't quite been able to place it and her skin tone could have originated from anywhere between Iraq and Mexico.

'She's fucking gorgeous,' I remarked, 'but I'm not sure about the shoes.' She was wearing these strange pink shoes that didn't really match the rest of her outfit. I have two judgemental warning signs about spotting potential unbalance in someone I don't know. Firstly I am always suspicious of pink being worn by a grown woman – I know it seems a fairly unfounded prejudice, but it just sets alarm bells ringing and had proven uncannily accurate in the past – and secondly I am also prone, rightly or wrongly, to assess someone by their shoes. I don't think it's such a ridiculous gauge of someone's personality. You have to make a lot of decisions when buying a shoe, about style, comfort, etc. It's a definite statement and surely a reflection on your personality.

A few months before, I had been sitting opposite a woman on the tube. She was reasonably attractive, her hair was quite trendy, her clothes were smart but stylish. You'd probably meet her and think, she looks nice, maybe we could be friends. Perhaps after a few weeks we may become lovers. Then when the time is right, I will ask her to be my bride and we will buy a place together, have a couple of kids. I might have an affair about six years in. She'd be hurt, but she'd forgive me and in a sense the whole episode would make our relationship stronger. We would become old together and watch our grandchildren grow up in a world that neither one of us really understood any longer. But we would be happy.

That's what you'd probably immediately think.

Unless you looked at her shoes.

Because her shoes told a whole different story. Firstly, they were an odd, unpleasant shade of blue. Darker than navy, but kind of dirty. Not that the shoes were dirty, you understand. Just the colour. What was more striking was that on the toe of each shoe was an incredibly unattractive representation of a flower. I suppose it was a rose, with that petal inside a petal effect. But it was more of a kind of blodge on top of another blodge and was too big for the shoe, and also in the same awful blue colour. The shoe itself was clunky and clumsy, seemingly painfully sensible from the front. But then I noticed that at the back it lifted up and was perched on a high and narrow heel. It was wrong. Like two shoes that had been involved in some kind of high-speed shoe accident and had been welded together by an unscrupulous cobbler.

One had to ask why anyone would choose to buy such a shoe, but anyone can make a mistake under the hot lights of a shoe shop, so more importantly what kind of person would actually *wear* a shoe like that? The kind of person who thought that this was the shoe for them must have something deeply wrong going on in their brain.

Far from forgiving you for that affair, a woman wearing that kind of shoe would take dreadful revenge upon you and the woman (or man) that you had dallied with. But she'd make you stay with her for the sake of the kids and make the rest of your life a living hell. However much you tried to explain it had been a midlife crisis, that both of you were to blame because you'd taken each other for granted, old blue-rose shoes would screw her face up at you and snarl and call you a bastard. You'd try to complain, but she'd hiss, 'Shut up, the kids will hear.'

You'd die at 50 having subconsciously deliberately drunk yourself to death. And she would dance on your grave in her blue-rose shoes (stumbling slightly due to the structure of the heel).

All because you had failed to look at her shoes.

The Cardiff girl's shoes were not quite as insane as that, but they made me stop and ponder. Their pinkness was concerning me.

Then again, she was spectacularly beautiful and funny and available and seemed to like me. And her bottom looked very good in the tight trousers she was wearing. Plus madness has always been a lure to me, rather than a repellent – the same poles of that magnet seem to attract (and I am more than aware of the irony that I was worried that someone else might be crazy, given the behaviour documented in this book). The dangers of being dragged on to the rocks by a wonderful siren were always too exciting to resist. I could kid myself that I was going to walk away from this, but she had me hooked.

I threw myself willingly to my fate and approached her and continued our conversation.

'Hey there, it's my turn to interrupt.'

'Ha ha, I knew you'd make your way here, but well done, you lasted almost three whole minutes without me!' She chuckled like a malevolent candle mocking the moth that it had just enticed towards its flame.

'You didn't tell me your name,' I remarked.

'I'm Julia,' she told me. 'Everyone calls me Joolz.'

'I'll call you Julia,' I replied, contrary as I always am in these situations. 'I couldn't work out your accent. There's some Welsh in there…'

'I'm American.'

Suddenly I thought I had worked out her ethnicity. 'Oh wow, are you a Native American?'

'Yes,' she proudly slurred.

How cool was that? And though it is wrong to be sexually excited by the prospect of an encounter with someone from such a rare ethnicity, I still was. I used to collect stamps and it was always great to find one from a country you hadn't had one from before.

'So are both your parents Native Americans?'

'No, my parents are from India…'

'I thought you were Native American.'

'I was, I was born in America.'

'Oh right, but I thought you were actually a Native American.'

She seemed confused, so I tried to clarify using the term I had studiously avoided up until now. 'You know, Red Indian.'

She was aghast. 'You can't use that term any more. That's terribly politically incorrect. How awful.'

'I wouldn't use it,' I defended, worried I might have inadvertently blown it. 'I was just trying to clarify what I meant because you didn't understand what I was saying when I used the right term.'

Stephen came over. He and I had agreed to go out for a drink before we headed back to our hotel, but this new distraction was tempting me away from my appointment. Stephen wanted to go to a bar in the docks. 'I live there!' she exclaimed and then fixed me with her brown eyes and said, 'Looks like you won't be staying in your hotel tonight!'

Surely only a fight with a trainee lecturer could stop the inevitable progress of biological imperative now. A voice in my head was telling me to walk away, but a voice in my trousers was shouting, 'Shut up, voice-in-his-head, what do you ever know about anything?'

Julia didn't want to leave the pub yet and asked me to stay and drink with her, so I advised Stephen (who was with his girlfriend in any case) to go ahead without me. I would take a chance on my unpredictable, brazen, olive-skinned, pink-shoed new friend.

But as soon as I had agreed to stay and Stephen and my safe escape route had gone, Julia and her two female friends disappeared and I was left conversing with a slightly strange man from her group who was significantly more drunk than me and a bit of a comedy nerd. He wanted to talk about my ancient television work. My heart sank. 'You look worried,' he slurred, accurately assessing the situation. 'Don't worry. We're not going to rape and kill you!'

That hadn't been something I had worried about until he had mentioned it. And just like you don't say, 'I'm not crazy' in an email unless you actually are, you don't tell someone you're not going to rape and kill them unless you were secretly thinking of doing so. The voice in my head was chiming, 'I told you so' while the voice in my trousers had suddenly gone a bit high and quavery.

Eventually Julia returned but she had lost a lot of her effervescence and her effusiveness and she revealed she had just flown in from Canada today and was starting to feel the effect of the jet lag. This probably explained her overexcitedness earlier. The drink had hit her befuddled brain quickly and effectively, but now she was coming down hard. The crazy, fun, sexually overt free spirit had vanished into the ether. She said she was going home and it seemed that the heavily implied offer that I would be accompanying her had been silently retracted. It looked like I would end up just talking to this man and his equally pissed and equally nerdy friends for the rest of the evening. Regretting my impetuosity, I was desperately looking through my phone for Stephen's number. But I didn't have it.

I had been led by my dick and for all my claims to be looking for someone special, my mission to sleep with as many women as possible was clearly continuing into my fifth decade. I was discovering that the bad taste it left in my mouth and the heaviness that it caused in my heart was getting less palatable as time went on. I felt foolish and frustrated. What was I doing wrong?

The comedy geeks had the address of a club that stayed open all night and the whole party left the pub to hail a cab, but Julia was in sensible mode.

'Don't be a party pooper, Joolz,' said the rapey guy. 'Come with us.'

'No, I wanna go home,' she told them. 'Get the cab to go via the docks.'

'You can't go home now,' growled Rapey. 'Don't listen to her, driver. Just take us straight to the club.'

'I don't want to go to the club. Take me home, please.'

'Ignore her, we're not doing any stop-offs. Just go to the address we told you…'

I was squashed between Julia and the dictatorial nerd and was not enjoying the confined conditions or the raised voices. I wasn't the only one.

'Can you just make up your fucking minds where you want to go and tell me, please,' said the sober cabbie, already at the end of his tether. I had only had a couple of drinks and was getting similarly pissed off, envisioning a very different evening from the one I had expected, culminating in my being found ravaged and beaten, dead in a ditch.

'You can't force someone to go where they don't want to go,' I said to Rapey McRape. 'Take us to the docks first, please, where Julia will be getting out, and then on to the pub.'

'Thank you,' said the driver and we set off.

'I'm getting out when you do,' I whispered to Julia. 'I only stayed so I could be with you. I don't want to end up with these drunk idiots.'

'We can hear what you're saying,' said Rapey.

'I don't really care... I'm going back to my hotel. I've had enough of this for one night.'

I hadn't been massively impressed with her change of heart, but I grudgingly respected her right to lead me on this merry dance.

Funnily enough, now she was less forthright I liked her a lot more. After the cab dropped us off and departed with its braying cargo of dorks, I walked through the swanky new development at the docklands to the place where she lived. I stopped at her door to bid her good night, but she gave me a sly smile and said, 'Do you want to come in for one drink? But that's all that's on offer.'

'Yes, that would be nice,' I agreed. In the quiet of the night, now she was more placid, I actually just wanted to spend some time with her and get to know her.

It turned out she was a high-powered and successful international businesswoman and was slightly embarrassed that the flat she was temporarily staying in was rather empty and impersonal. But we drank whisky and chatted more calmly and it became clear that she couldn't really remember much of the stuff she'd said in the pub. I was still a little guarded about the whole situation, but found myself unexpectedly opening up about my personal life, telling this stranger about the emotional quagmire I had found myself in. She wanted a photo of the two of us together and sat beside me so she could hold out her camera to capture the moment. It felt somehow familiar and pleasant to have her beside me. I tried not to imagine our future and how cute our children would be.

We arranged to meet for dinner the next day, as, unusually, I was staying in town for two consecutive performances. I kissed her full on the lips as I left.

'That was rather forward,' she said, smiling.

'That's rich coming from you. Do you remember the stuff you were saying in the pub?' I retorted.

But she genuinely didn't.

The next day this strange encounter was playing on my mind and I found myself keen to be back in the company of this flighty and changeable young woman. Perhaps in my heart I knew that it was a lost cause, that she was toying with me, probably not deliberately, that the shoes had actually told me all I needed to know. But I was hopeful, perhaps a little desperately so, that this might lead to something more meaningful.

Yet I was wary still, partly because of the many frustrations I had had in recent weeks, but also because I knew full well that I seemed to be falling for people with remarkable frequency. Since I'd got back from Thailand I'd been trying to latch on to anyone who seemed remotely interested.

The fact that she was so beautiful was also clouding my logic. Was this just lust dressed up as romance?

I rang Julia, but she didn't pick up so I left a message. And heard nothing back from her. I rang her again, aware that I was exhibiting the lack of cool that had almost certainly blown it with Emilia. This time she answered, but seemed a little awkward. Or was that me, reverting as I seemed to be, to the stuttering, embarrassing teenager who had so spectacularly failed to engage with girls at school discos? Something in her manner told me that she wasn't as keen in the cold light of day as she had been in the jet-lagged fug of night, but she agreed anyway to meet up for an early evening dinner before my gig.

'I am still pretty zonked out from the flight,' she told me as we sat down at the table of a tiny Indian café that she insisted served the best food in Cardiff. 'I think I might have to head straight back to bed after this.'

That's a pretty bad start to a date by any standards, and my recent romantic failures were already making me doubt my seductive abilities. I felt like my desperation was seeping out of my pores. There's nothing more off-putting than that and yet no deodorant in the world can mask it.

'That's a shame, I'd really like to meet up after the gig... you know, to talk again... It was fun chatting last night.' This was painful.

'I'd like that too, but I might just be too tired.'

Was I just being paranoid again? Or did I correctly sense that she wasn't being honest with me? Did she have a better offer for this evening?

Last night, filled with the confidence and adrenalin of a successful stand-up set I had been (mainly) funny and assured when we'd flirted, but now I felt insecure and nervy. Everything was a little bit stilted. The café was empty apart from us and lacked atmosphere, yet the waiters were hanging by the bar, and might be listening in, which added to the pressure.

She insisted on ordering food for both of us. 'But I'll warn you, because I'm Indian, I do like my curries very spicy.'

'Don't worry. I like it hot... You know, my food, I mean. I actually genuinely was talking about food there. I really like hot food.'

There was an awkward silence.

'Got any plans for next week?' I asked, like the dullest trainee hairdresser in the world. She looked at me for a second as if to ask if that was the best I could do.

'Not much,' she replied. 'I'm playing poker on Wednesday, but...'

'Seriously? You play poker? I love poker.'

'Yeah, I play quite a bit. I'm not too bad at it. Are you any good?'

Suddenly I was animated by our shared interest and turned on that this beautiful woman could play this wonderful and terrible game.

'Good? Yeah, I'm pretty good. Last year in a tournament I knocked out Joe Hachem.'

'The guy who won the World Series!' She was impressed, as was I that she knew who Joe Hachem was.

'Yes, he was the reigning world champion at the time. And I beat him. Which I believe makes me the poker champion of the world.'

'Well, until someone else beats you, I guess.'

'Which happened about half an hour later, but it was an amazing 30 minutes at the top!'

She laughed. 'I can't believe you're a poker player,' I told her. 'You are completely amazing.' She smiled uncomfortably. I was laying it on too thick, but I didn't seem able to stop myself. 'It'll be a shame if I can't see you later,' I said. 'We live in different towns. It's going to be hard for us to meet up again.'

'I am in London all the time. I'm coming down in a fortnight. Are you doing any more gigs? I'd love to bring my friends along to see you.'

'Yeah, I'm always gigging. And you could come and play poker at my house sometime.'

'I could,' and she seemed to mean it, looking at me as she had done last night. 'There's no need to rush this. I am absolutely certain we're going to be spending a lot of time together.'

'Are you? Good. I've been having some bad luck lately. I'm not usually this needy. Or awkward. And you are really gorgeous. You know, if I could just have you now, then that would really put me at my ease and we could just get on with our dinner.'

She laughed, but then said, 'Oh God, I did that once. I was in a restaurant with a guy. They had long tablecloths over all the tables and even though it was pretty packed in there, during dessert I got under the table and you know...'

'What?'

'Come on, you know. Under the table, I... Why am I telling you about this?'

I became a bit tongue-tied again.

I didn't know quite what to say, though knew the confident post-gig me would have come back with something suitably impressive. Instead I said, 'Oh right, well, the tablecloths here aren't really long enough.'

'I wasn't really offering that.'

'No, I... er, I know. But...'

It was a bit of a confusing mixed message. One minute she seemed into me and the next made me feel like I wasn't just barking up the wrong tree, I was in the wrong forest. And I was a cat.

She was a heady mixture of grown up and sensible and unpredictable and irresponsible. So she was just like me, only sometimes grown up.

I was aware that this might all be a bit of a fun game to her. As she had initially informed me, she was a heartbreaker. But the risk of disaster made everything even more tantalising. By the time I walked her back to her flat again, I felt pretty sure that things were progressing nicely. We came to a halt at her door. 'There's something going on here, isn't there?' I remarked. 'Between us, there's a bit of a spark.'

'Oh, don't spoil it by vocalising it,' she said with genuine disappointment. I think that might have been the moment where I definitively lost her. Or maybe I was never going to have her. She made a point of offering me her cheek as I went to kiss her.

I rang her after the gig, but the phone went through to voicemail. I never saw her again.

Having had two love affairs of such potential stymied before they really began, I was now more confused and cautious than ever. But also increasingly desperate for a success. I wrote in my diary, *'Must try to remember that being single – even when girls are interested – is not that brilliant.'* It's easy to forget that sometimes when you're in a relationship and daydreaming about having your freedom again.

I wasn't short of opportunities, thanks in part to the new phenomenon of social networking sites. Facebook and MySpace are a kind of heaven and hell for the minor celebrity. In the olden days people had to work hard to seduce you or stalk you, but now they can do it without even leaving their house.

On the nights I came home drunk and feeling lonely I would turn on my computer to find flirtatious messages from attractive young women I hadn't even met. In the past I generally wouldn't have taken the chance with any of them, given the danger that they might be twisted or crazy or in fact strange middle-aged men just pretending to be young women, but in the dead of night, when all else seems bleak, these tiny oases of friendship and potential shenanigans were proving very tempting. Most men in their forties don't have such temptations. With the greatest of respect to his sexual prowess, I bet Premium Manager Alan Goodman does not get 22-year-old women emailing him asking if he will have sex with them. Maybe he does.

In the past I have been very wary about getting involved with anyone who is overtly 'a fan'. There is an imbalance from the start and you never know how obsessed they might be or what the repercussions might be. But after my recent two knockbacks I found myself in a reckless and depressive state of mind and at least you could converse with people on these sites before you met them, thus weeding out the deranged and the disguised in advance.

For a few months now I had been conversing on MSN messenger with a young lady who had been to see one of my shows. She had a very striking photo on her MySpace profile, in which she resembled a young and pneumatic Nigella Lawson. It seemed harmless at first. She was funny and clever and also had a boyfriend, so it seemed to be safe enough to chat with her, yet occasional hints were dropped that she might be interested in me if things were different. Sometimes when she was drunk she might make inappropriate suggestions, which she would almost immediately recant. I knew she was a little bit flaky, but I wasn't in a position to criticise. I was as drunk and as flighty as she was. My exhausted sensible fibres were screaming for me to keep away, convinced it could only lead to trouble, but I was having fun or at least was filling the void of the long lonely nights with harmless flirtation.

I liked her and she made me laugh and like Oscar Wilde I can resist anything but temptation and unlike Oscar Wilde I am very tempted by tall, buxom 23-year-old women.

Just as I found myself at this new low, the girl emailed me to let me know that her latest relationship had broken up. She was distraught and emotional, but asked if we could meet up for a drink. It would just be as friends as she said she couldn't contemplate anything else at this difficult time. That suited me. I could meet up with her, see if she was just kooky or totally crazy and move on from there.

I was doing a charity gig for Children In Need in a pub in north London, so suggested she come along to that. I was working for free to help the poor children. Surely she could not help but be wowed by me being both funny and magnanimous.

As a comedian I had been all in favour of the new smoking ban that had recently been implemented in public places. I perform in a lot of little rooms above pubs and used to hate having to breathe in the polluting smog that invariably filled the space. I used to regularly get ill or lose my voice, but now those days were gone. I thought it was great.

The ban, however, has had some unexpected and less positive consequences, the most well documented being that now there is no cloud of tobacco smoke fugging up our bars we are suddenly able to smell all the unpleasant odours and emissions that were masked before.

Less noted, though, is the romantic advantage that smokers now have over non-smokers. In addition to the fact that smoking makes you cool and sexy, it also gives people an excuse to communicate with strangers under the pretence of looking for a light or a fag. Love is blossoming for the shunned as they huddle in doorways, meeting other smokers with whom they have at least one thing in common. It can get cold out there, so sharing body warmth is the natural next step.

What has been good for my lungs has not been so fortunate for another essential organ further south.

When I arrived at the venue, Nigella was already there. She had clearly been drinking for a little while as she was a bit tipsy and emotional. She needed cheering up and what better way to help her than provide her with more alcohol. I had met a lot of girls like her at university: posh and pretty and able to use those things to get almost anything they want. She was clearly from a privileged background and yet she had no money on her. I suspected that she never did and that she could nevertheless survive by relying on the kindness of strangers, most of them men, happy to be manipulated by such a beauty. So I happily bought her a drink and we got to know each other face to face, rather than via a computer modem.

We discovered some common ground and fell into easy conversation. I was conscious that she might turn into a bit of a handful if the drink kept flowing. But I think a handful was exactly what I wanted. I wanted to end the night with my bones sprawled over the rocks and seagulls eating my gizzard.

I bought her another drink and she commented that she really needed a cigarette, though she had none on her. She went round the room and cadged one from an old fella at the next table and went outside to smoke it.

On her return we decided to go upstairs to watch some of the gig, which was in full swing by now. We were having a fun time. She seemed to be cheering up and forgetting about her troubles and so was I.

Towards the end of the first half, Nigella needed another smoke and went downstairs to see if she could find a kind stranger. This, as you may have guessed, is where my evening took a turn.

She hadn't returned by the interval, so I went to look for her. She was in the beer garden, sitting with a couple of trendy-looking men, who were cooler and better-looking than me and who had cigarettes. But were they doing anything for charity? No. Surely that still gave me the upper hand. In any case the girl was out with me tonight, so obviously I had nothing to fear. Of course not.

The better-looking and cooler guy turned out to be a TV producer who currently (he claimed) was working with one of the biggest and trendiest names in comedy. 'I'm a big fan of yours,' he told me. 'In fact, I was wanting to talk to you about whether you'd be interested in working on a couple of projects with me...'

Just by knowing a smoker, I had ended up doing more networking than I managed at the entire Montreal Festival. Imagine if I was actually doing the smoking!

I've met enough smarmy bullshitters in this business to not take anything he said too seriously. If someone wants to work with you they don't wait until they bump into you in a pub to ask you. I think he was more interested in impressing my date than in actually giving me a job. Or possibly he was already cynically trying to put me at ease so he could cuckold me later. To be honest,

Nigella, now properly drunk, might have been a little more unpredictable and flaky than I had been counting on. A part of me momentarily wondered if it might be a good thing to engineer these two coming together. But that part as usual was shouted down by the other parts that liked the idea of spending more time with a drunk and emotionally vulnerable young woman.

I bought another round of drinks and then went upstairs for the second half of the show. Nigella stood behind me at the bar as we waited for my turn. In the packed room we were pressed together and she was squeezing my arm. My fears had been unfounded. She obviously liked me, even though I didn't smoke or look that cool or work with BAFTA- award-winning artists. And she seemed to be forgetting her earlier vow to keep things on just a friendly level.

I went up to do my bit and it went pretty well, but most importantly I helped the poor children and got nothing in return, except the kind of cachet that might hopefully lead to me getting a snog.

The gig over, I could now relax and was keen to see how the night might develop from here. As I went to get another drink for my now slightly tipsy friend, she went outside again for another cigarette.

I thought nothing of it and got chatting to some of the punters at the bar. Some time passed and I became conscious that Nigella didn't have her drink and so went to look for her.

The beer garden was closed, so I went to the front of the pub, opened the door and, inevitably (from your point of view; I had no idea that this was going to happen), discovered her in a passionate embrace with the producer who had so admired my work.

'Oh!' I exclaimed quietly to myself, before slipping back into the pub unnoticed by the new friends who were too busy trying to eat each other's faces.

I felt a bit betrayed, though I am not sure who I was more upset with. Clearly my romantic hopes (and to call them romantic raises them to a higher level than is perhaps entirely accurate) had been dashed, but also the duplicitous producer had ruined any chance of me ever working with him.

He had tried to ingratiate himself with me and used his superior coolness and attractiveness to steal Nigella off me. What a cad! But really it was the smoking ban that had made their stolen kisses possible. How many other connections have been made on pub doorsteps? How many other healthy non-smoker hearts broken by Cupid cosseting the cigarette-sucker, fate favouring the fag-fondler?

After a few moments' consideration, I decided the best course of action was to leave without making too much of a fuss, and I passed the treacherous twosome as they entered and I left the smoke-free establishment.

I am not the kind of man to get into a fight over a woman.

'Have a good night,' I hissed curtly, walking out into the cold night, not looking back, their exhaled smoke still hanging in the air.

Bristling with humiliation and disappointment, I couldn't believe I had been rejected again, this time so publicly and callously.

'Aren't you going to go after him?' I heard the producer ask. But she didn't and I headed hot-cheeked into the cold night.

Although this might classify as a lucky escape, I was at rock bottom. My life seemed to be tawdry and yet not even providing me with any sleazy pleasures to ease my pain. There was not to be a moment of truth, but over the next three weeks three things happened to me that were enough to put the brakes on, turn around and head in the other direction. I was about to leave my old life behind and step on to a path that would lead to enlightenment. In a matter of days I would take the first step on a journey of spiritual awakening.

It was, I'll admit, an unusual first step.

She said to me, 'You've got enough trouble satisfying one woman at a time, what makes you think you could cope with two?'

I said, 'That's the whole beauty of the system. When I'm done, you two can finish each other off for me... while I sleep. A woman knows what a woman wants... and has the patience to see it through to its tedious conclusion.'

CHAPTER 11

THREE'S A CROWD, BUT WHAT'S WRONG WITH A CROWD?

'I just can't believe it has never happened for me, that's all.'

'Not this again,' moaned Emma. 'Why don't you just hire a couple of prostitutes and have done with it?'

'No, no. It doesn't count if you've had to pay for it.'

'It's still a threesome.'

'It would be seedy to use prostitutes.'

'Right, and of course it wouldn't be seedy to sleep with two women at the same time as long as you weren't paying them.'

'Exactly. It's not fair. Everyone has done it apart from me.'

'That's not true. How many people here have had a threesome?'

Emma turned to the other comedians, musicians and technicians in the green room. We were five minutes away from recording a comedy radio show and could already hear the audience in the theatre next door, buzzing with anticipation.

'Come on,' chided Emma, 'hands up who has had a threesome.'

About half of the assembled group raised their hands.

'There, it's not even half of them.'

A couple more sheepishly admitted the truth.

'It's just over half. That is by no means everyone.'

'I am still in the minority.'

'These people are in show business, they don't count. If this was a random selection, then it wouldn't be anywhere near as many.'

'But I'm in showbiz, Emma,' I protested. 'That just makes my failure all the more tragic.'

'I'm sure it's not all that,' Emma said, trying to comfort me. 'Who regretted it afterwards? Show of hands.'

No hands were raised. Everyone looked smug.

'This is just so unfair,' I sulked.

'I don't regret it,' chipped in Steve, 'but it wasn't as much fun as I imagined it would be. It's quite a lot of work, you know, to keep two people... *involved*. Someone usually gets a bit left out or jealous.'

'Usually? How many times have you done it, Steve?'

'I don't keep count!'

'Too many times to count? Jesus!'

'I've heard that a lot,' said Emma. 'It's never as good as you imagine it'll be.'

'I don't care if it's not as good as I'm imagining. Even if it's only a tenth as good it'd still be the best sexual experience of my life... By miles.'

'Mine was with one girl and another guy,' said Dave. 'It was a bit embarrassing. Me and him were facing each other and I didn't know where to look. What do you say? "Nice day, isn't it?" "How's it going your end?"'

'No, it's got to be me and two girls,' I interjected. 'I can't be doing with all that.'

'I'm not sure you can afford to be that choosy, can you?' laughed Emma.

'Don't you do that routine where you beg women in the audience to make your dream come true?' remembered Elizabeth, the producer. 'Hasn't that ever worked?'

'No, it hasn't. I've probably done that bit 500 times. You would think that in all that time, just once, a couple of girls would have come up to me afterwards and said, "You've given us 90 minutes of entertainment –"'

'"Let us give you 90 seconds of entertainment in return,"' interrupted Emma.

'That's all it would take,' I concurred. 'But I can't settle down until I've done this. It would hang over me. I'd be wondering what it would have been like. And I can't have kids unless I'm married...'

'You're an old-fashioned kind of man, aren't you?' said Emma sarcastically.

'Yes I am. I say it in the show – any woman who doesn't have a threesome with me is effectively murdering my unborn children.'

'You wouldn't want that on your conscience,' admitted Elizabeth.

'Exactly. Or looking at it another way, if they do have a threesome with me, they'll be saving the lives of maybe two or three beautiful little babies. And as a reward, when my kids are about six or seven years old – old enough to understand what's happened – I'll introduce the women to them and say, "These are the ladies, kids, to whom you essentially owe your existence. Thank them. It's amazing what they did... I mean, they're not your mums. I wouldn't have kids with slags like these... but still..."'

'I can't understand why no one has ever taken you up on that, Rich,' deadpanned Emma. 'There must have been times when it's been on the cards, though, surely?'

'Yes, there have,' I confessed, 'but something always happened to screw it up. Or not, as the case may be.'

The closest I had got to fulfilling my ambition was when I was in my mid-thirties. I had been having a bit of a thing with a girl named Andrea and one night we'd been out with one of her friends, Kate, and got a little bit drunk and Kate had got talking about the idea and Kate had said, 'I might be up for that sometime.'

'Really?' I spluttered, not wanting to look too keen, but entirely failing in that desire. 'Well, we could go home and...'

'Not tonight,' she'd reconsidered. 'I'd need to think about it. But it might be fun.'

'We should definitely think about it,' agreed Andrea.

'Yes, yes. We definitely should.'

A week or so later we'd arranged a rendezvous at my flat. There were no guarantees and we were going to see how things went, but it seemed very, very likely that it'd be green lights all the way. Nothing could possibly go wrong...

We sat in my lounge drinking and chatting and then drinking some more and then having a chat, trying our best not to think about or discuss what must surely inevitably occur. I didn't want to appear too keen and ruin the atmosphere. I would just be cool and wait and maybe help oil the wheels a little with some more alcohol. None of us had ever done anything like this before. We weren't going to rush into it. But it was hard to work out how to get started.

But it would probably have been an idea to instigate things a bit sooner than I did, because before too long I was opening a fourth bottle of champagne. We'd been relaxed and giggly, but suddenly things got a bit too drunken and lairy.

Finally the subject was broached and despite their previous bravado the girls were being a little bit coy. They offered to make out with each other on the sofabed. I was a little concerned that my sofabed was a bit uncomfortable.

'Why don't we move into the bedroom,' I suggested tentatively. 'It'll be easier to relax.'

Andrea, filled with alcohol, took umbrage at this suggestion. 'I know your game – you want us on your bed so you can join in!' This was faintly ridiculous given that it was implicit that things would involve all three of us sooner rather than later.

But it was my turn to feel that my intentions had been slighted. 'No,' I slurred, 'I was just thinking it would be nicer there for you.'

'Don't lie!'

'Well, all right, but we all know where this is going, so we might as well take it there.'

'You're an idiot!' yelled Andrea, storming out of the room.

I followed to try and remonstrate with her and in our befuddled state we ended up resolving our disagreement with an explosively passionate, one-on-one sexual encounter, ironically enough in my bedroom, after which I immediately fell asleep. The girls spent the night on my sofabed and in the morning we were too sober, hungover and contrite to do anything but wish each other a good day.

I had blown it. And not in a good way. But I wondered if that had been deliberate. Subconsciously was I scared of the prospect of making fantasy reality? Why otherwise would I have allowed this silly spat to prevent something I had always claimed I wished to witness? Sofabed or bed? It's surely about as important as whether you use 'a' or 'the' in a sentence.

In truth I was rather more into Andrea than Kate. Perhaps I backed away from the certainty that was on the cards because actually I just wanted to be with her. Although I must admit even now I still replay the incident in my head, changing just a few tiny details and imagining the outcome, knowing that if this had been my Groundhog Day, 99 times out of 100 I would have been ticking 'threesome' off my sexual to-do list.

More recently I had been casually seeing Becky, a high-flying and seemingly respectable lawyer, but who rather delightfully seemed to enjoy letting her hair down when she was off work. She had seen an early version of the *ménage à un* show the previous summer and when I got back from Edinburgh that year delighted in telling me that inspired by my routine she had resolved that she should take the plunge and have a threesome with an old boyfriend and a woman she vaguely knew from her local pub. It was rather galling to discover that while I had prompted her to make this experimental leap, I had not been one of the participants.

She did tell me that the night, while having been a lot of fun, had descended into chaos, recriminations and petty jealousy, which had ended at 4am with the man having orgasmed and fallen asleep (do you see a theme developing?), and the other, as it turned out, slightly unhinged woman from the pub furiously angry, storming out into the man's front garden, shouting obscenities and waking up his neighbours.

Even so, claimed Becky, it had been an amazing experience. She seemed willing to give it another go, but perhaps petulant at being an inspirational but non-participating individual, I didn't pursue it and our friendship petered out.

It seemed that Pandora's box is best left unopened – especially if Pandora has a friend with her at the time.

But in November, while in the deepest, darkest recesses of rejection and confusion and at my most out of control, I was suddenly presented with a new opportunity. Not in the heat of the moment, but in a planned and premeditated fashion.

I had been communicating, via MSN Messenger, with Chloe, who I had met at a gig a few years before. Nothing had happened between us at the time because I had had a girlfriend, although Chloe had been very flirtatious. We'd struck up a friendship and occasionally emailed each other over the years, though not met up again. Just recently our online conversations had got a little bit more raunchy, but we'd just been having fun on late drunken nights. She had sent me a link to a website in which there were pictures of herself, modelling with not many clothes on. The other women who posted on this site were into tattoos and blood and bondage, though her photos were not quite as extreme. It was still a little bit scary.

Part of me felt I was sliding further into the slippery pit of depravity, from which I might never escape, even though it provided me with some temporary comfort. And Chloe had a softness and a sweetness to her and genuinely seemed to like me and care about me, without being desirous of any kind of serious relationship. But I also liked the fact she was clearly naughty and adventurous and sexy. I was nothing if not a man in the middle of a midlife crisis. And conversely, we were both adults and both single and so where was the harm?

Unless she turned out to be a psycho stalker, intent on selling her story of celebrity sleaze to a tabloid. If so she'd miscalculated wildly by choosing a celebrity who no one had ever heard of and who was more than likely to be the one brazenly writing about the experience himself. Though at the time I was slightly ashamed of what I was up to and keen to keep my shameful secrets to myself, lest I be judged as some kind of perverted, dirty old man. It is awful to be judged, especially so if the judgement is pretty much on the button.

During one of our chats she told me she was coming to a gig to see me in the flesh and mentioned that she was bringing a friend, Tara, along with her. A friend that, so she told me, she was interested in having a sexual relationship with. She thought there was more than a possibility of this turning into a threesome. I had written in my diary, '*It is almost certainly a terrible idea to go through with it,*' before adding with great self-awareness, '*but I obviously will do it if the opportunity presents itself. Maybe I can just get all this out of my system, but I worry it might destroy me in the meantime. I am a little bit out of control.*'

That was something of an understatement. Yet there was nothing I could do to stop the inevitable and for the rest of the week my body was jangling with hormones, my mind full of thoughts of what was to come, a heady mixture of excitement and fear. Yet I was certain that as usual something would happen to scupper the plans, as it always had before. Or that these women that I didn't really know would turn out to be lesbian vampires who would kill me and eat me. If they ate me before they killed me then I might still be up for it. But I knew my luck – they'd kill me first.

I met up with Chloe before the gig for a pizza. Last time I had met her she had been very drunk and rather forward, but now she was sober and timid and surprisingly reserved. My experiences with her on the internet had made me think of her as feisty and in control, but she was delicate and insecure and had huge inno- cent eyes like a cartoon bird. It felt like a mildly awkward blind date between two shy and slightly reticent strangers, rather than the prelude to debauchery, but the possibility of things to come hung unspoken in the air. Which felt strange in the cold light of day as although we had had a degree of intimacy online we had scarcely spoken before. Chloe was drinking, but I had driven to the gig and so would have to remain sober. Wouldn't I have to be drunk to go along with this? At least to give me the excuse for behaving so badly. Maybe the future was not already written in stone. Maybe man had been given free will. But surely not so much that he could resist such a temptation.

Even at this early stage the reality, as promised, was already seeming more complicated than the fantasy.

We met Tara in a pub next to the venue I'd be performing at. She seemed quite drunk already and was certainly much more outgoing and brash than her much more timid friend. She was talking loudly and seemed volatile and unpredictable, interacting rather readily with the slightly scary men who were sitting having a Sunday evening pint. I was reminded of the woman shouting crazily outside the house at the threesome I hadn't been invited to. Never having really been into taking drugs, I am useless at spotting when other people have indulged, but with hindsight I now realise that she might well have had a little bit of cocaine.

I knew next to nothing about her and all good sense said that I should back away. But both girls were attractive and I was a man and so it was going to have to take me spotting that they didn't have a reflection in the mirror to make me question the wisdom of all this. And even then I was still pretty much up for it.

By the time I came off stage at the end of the gig both girls were pretty blasted and I was conscious of my sobriety. They were still sitting in their seats, their arms around each other, already touching each other rather intimately and overtly. The people in the row behind were clearly amazed by and enjoying the spectacle. For someone who had just been on stage, talking openly about my filthy mind, I was rather self-conscious of the attention. I was also about seven or eight drinks behind them, embarrassed that what I had hoped to keep as a secret shameful night was already playing out in public. I felt like a bumbling square from one of those American fraternity films being seduced by some cheerleaders as part of some awful bet or humiliating prank.

Tara was very up front about it all. 'Look,' she told me, matter-of-factly, 'we're going home to have sex. You can come and watch if you like… and maybe join in.'

I felt the eyes of everyone in the row behind turning towards me, like this was some game of sexual tennis. I'd rather have been having this discussion in private, or rather less blatantly at least. But then again I didn't want to let the opportunity slip out of my hands again. 'Well, why don't you come to mine for a drink and we can discuss it?' I mumbled, blushing as I did so. I was keen to get out of there, but Tara needed the loo and Chloe wanted a cigarette. As she headed outside I became convinced that some goal-hanging smoker would step in and seduce her. Part of me again hoped that they would, to save me from myself.

The people behind had still not left their seats, enjoying this unexpected addition to the evening's entertainment, unaware, I think, that I knew the girls already. 'They were snogging each other during your set,' said one incredulous man.

'What are you going to do?' asked his girlfriend.

I tried to remain noncommittal. I didn't want my sad sleaziness to become a public issue. I just wanted to get out of there and get it over with. Where were they? They were taking ages. I could go and look for them, but was conscious of what had happened last time I'd done that. To lose out with one woman was bad enough, but if I got usurped with two at the same time then I'd know there was something wrong with me.

Despite my certainty that something would go wrong, fifteen minutes later I was driving them back to my house, them snogging on the back seat, me watching them in the rear-view mirror, feeling like a perverted but fortunate taxi driver, now convinced that I would crash the car and kill us all. Surely that's how fate would confound me this time. Laughing at me as I died in a heap of twisted metal and entwined limbs in a grotesque parody of what I had hoped to achieve.

It was quite a long drive and by the time we were home things seemed to have cooled down a bit. We politely sat in my lounge drinking champagne (had I learned nothing from the last time?) and chatting as if nothing unusual was happening at all. I was now glugging back the booze, as if I could somehow be excused retrospectively for a decision I had made while entirely compos mentis.

Suddenly everything was rather demure; perhaps we were all wondering about the logistics of getting this thing going, being worried about the one who made the first move in case the others recoiled and said, 'We were only joking! You didn't really think this was going to happen, did you?'

Maybe the moment had passed. Maybe I could turn back at the last minute and thus avoid the inevitable future where I became a tragic middle-aged swinger, only able to get my kicks at those strangely unerotic and antiseptic suburban orgies that they occasionally make documentaries about.

Chloe went to the loo and Tara came over to me and rather aggressively snogged me. I was a little bit scared of her and strangely, given our shared intent, felt like I was being unfaithful. Chloe was the person that I had met before and who I had set up the date with, and yet I had never kissed her. Was it bad form to kiss her friend first? Would she feel slighted or angry if she came back and saw us in an embrace? Coyly I told Tara she'd better leave me alone for the moment. It felt like things would never get started.

But when Chloe returned, the girls started to kiss each other and then I became involved and things progressed onwards from there. It was happening. The fantasy I had always dreamed about was finally happening. I had always assumed that I would find this situation impossibly erotic and that it would all be over for me with embarrassing haste, but if anything I was having the opposite problem. I was tense and nervous and finding it difficult to let go and lose myself in the moment. My fantasies were indeed, thus far, a lot better than what was taking place.

Perhaps I was worried about the repercussions, or what this meant about me as a person, but it was hard to focus on the task in hand. My central heating had broken down a few days earlier and this time it was going to take more than a man turning up my thermostat to fix it. I was waiting for a new boiler to be installed. It was a cold November night and prosaically I was more concerned about the temperature of the room, feeling a bit embarrassed that it might be a bit nippy now we'd got some of our clothes off. Also that week I had a friend staying in my spare room and couldn't help considering the fact that she might overhear us or come downstairs to see what was going on. It might turn into a foursome, but more likely it would just look strange and mortifying and lead to tension in the kitchen the next morning.

As you may have spotted by now, I do tend to overanalyse and I couldn't help wondering why these women were doing this. Chloe seemed so timid and shy and some things she'd said made me think she'd been badly treated by unpleasant and violent men in the past. Tara's aggression and detachment and determination to escape reality through drink (and probably drugs) was perhaps also the symptom of some deeper issue. I couldn't help thinking that there was something broken in both of them and I wasn't sure whether I was just adding to their problems.

But then I realised with a jolt that they weren't the only ones who were broken. My participation was just as much down to me feeling lost and hurt and seeking some salvation in physical, emotionless release.

Just as I was brooding over whether I was somehow taking advantage of these innocent girls, Tara attempted to insert a champagne bottle into my anus, which rather made me reconsider my position (in both senses). I made my discomfort with such an unexpected intrusion rather clear.

'Sorry, I thought you might like it,' she said.

'No, I don't really,' I replied, as politely as possible, as if I was making it clear I appreciated the thought. The realisation that we were all taking advantage of each other was enough to help me to relax a little, even if I was in fear of which object might be introduced to which orifice next.

Yet such banality would keep intruding on the attempts to transcend morality and bring us all bumping back down to earth. I suppose we were all acting a little bit, pretending we were in a porn film. But porn films always run to script and everyone is supersexy and committed. Real life isn't like that and sex is embarrassing enough between two people who know each other, let alone three who don't.

Everyone had been right; it just wasn't as fantastic as I had imagined it would be. Even so, it was still a pretty amazing thing to be a part of and once I'd got over my self-consciousness I managed to forget about the central heating and my other rather mundane concerns and make the most of it, trying not to consider the emotional hangover and shame that must surely follow.

Yet it still remained a struggle to keep everyone happy and all our insecurities were coming to the surface. Tara thought that Chloe's breasts were nicer than hers and so wouldn't take her top off. Chloe worried that she wasn't as experienced or as sexy and forthright as Tara. Tara was clearly bisexual, but Chloe, while saying she was happy to give it all a go, was overly self-conscious about being intimate with a woman and kept making jokes, which stopped Tara in her tracks.

At one point Chloe disappeared to the loo for half an hour and it transpired she'd been playing 'The Legend of Zelda: Phantom Hourglass' on my Nintendo DS. 'That's probably not something you want to mention when you're telling your mates!' she said later. 'Doesn't reflect too well on you.' Though it might be something Nintendo want to consider placing on their advertising for the game: 'More entertaining than a threesome!'

And then when Chloe emerged, Tara went into the bathroom, making this less of a threesome than a tag-team twosome. When Tara returned I was indulging in some dirty talk while having sex with Chloe, during which I called her a whore. Tara was genuinely affronted. 'How dare you?' she exclaimed. 'Chloe is NOT a whore!'

'We were just playing around,' I told her. 'Getting into a role play thing. She knows I didn't mean it.'

But the interruption had somewhat put me off my stride.

Then again, I wanted to say (but didn't), Chloe is taking part in a threesome with two people she barely knows. She is a bit of a whore.

Not that there was anything intrinsically wrong with that. We were all being whores. And that's an OK thing to be, in my opinion, if that's what you want.

It just seemed an inappropriate and vaguely amusing issue to get offended by. Especially given that Tara herself had recently tried to anally violate me with a Veuve Clicquot bottle.

Much as I enjoy pointing out the seedier and more ridiculous side of the affair, I certainly enjoyed the night. It was a rare and wonderful mixture of feeling pleased with myself and disgusted with myself in equal measure and I am not sure there is a better state for a human being to be in than that.

Thankfully I did not end up killed or cannibalised or with an aggrieved woman yelling outside my front door. In fact, a lot of it was surprisingly tender and sweet.

I walked them both to the tube station the next morning. It felt like what we'd been doing was written all over our faces and that anyone passing could tell what we'd been up to. Though a little tired and hungover, I felt more invigorated than if I'd hit a trainee university lecturer in the head.

I kissed them both goodbye and walked back home. I was not experiencing the pangs of regret that I had expected. In fact, I felt elated and self-satisfied, if not a little virile. Not only because of what I had done, but also because I had done it. Finally, after all the times fantasising about it and talking about it, I'd achieved what had once seemed impossible. And in that moment it felt like the fuggy mist that had been surrounding me for so long had evaporated in the morning sun. As I walked back to my house I realised I no longer had the excuse that I'd been holding on to. I realised that the threesome had not just been a milestone, but a millstone as well. Now I could leave it behind and get on with my life. I felt truly ready for something more serious. Having shared my bed with two women, I was now prepared, instantaneously, to share my life with one woman – though not one of those two obviously, for all the reasons I would later acknowledge when introducing them to my children. I had seen that I was broken and that I needed to take a step back and fix myself.

It was a road to Damascus moment, though I was actually on the road to Uxbridge. I had been spiritually awakened by a three-some, which has to be the best ever way that anyone has ever reached enlightenment. I can see a lot of hermits kicking themselves now.

Finally, I was sure, there was nothing to stop me finding someone special.

You know, once I'd had a foursome, obviously.

Within a week I had met a woman who I thought might be the one.

Predictably, though, there would be some complications.

All's fair in love and war.
Though in love, the use of machine guns is frowned upon...
As is kissing in war.

CHAPTER 12
YOU HAD ME AT 'BUM RAPE'...

Greetings,

I'm a lecturer in Creative Writing at Southampton University. I am keen to send my students out into the real world with a little more knowledge than they receive from their course. Would it be possible to entice you down from London to give a talk about your experiences? What would we have to pay you?

By the way, I think you know my partner. She's also a stand-up – Catherine. You gigged with her at the uni here in December.

Hope you can make it down. Let me know when would be good for you.

Many thanks
Simon

Hey Simon,

I'm very flattered to be asked, and think I am well placed to give your students a lengthy lecture about the grim realities of trying to make a living in this stupid way. Hopefully I can put most of them off completely and so nip any competition in the bud. I don't need anything in return: crushing the hopes and dreams of the young is payment enough for me.

I am gigging in Portsmouth on 23 November. Any chance we could do it that afternoon?

Yes I remember Catherine. Say Hi.
She's awesome. You're a lucky guy.
Rich

Rich
That's great news. You're a legend!
Simon

'Tell Dad that if I'm not famous, then how come I've been asked to give a lecture about myself to students at this country's four-teenth most prestigious university?'

'That is impressive. Though I don't know what you can tell them about anything. They're students. They know full well how to spend all afternoon watching TV and sleeping.'

'Not today's students, Mum. Because of student loans, young people today actually have to do some work at college. They need educating in the layabout, kidult ways of the comedy writer.'

'So you're on your way there now, are you?'

'Yes, just on the M3.'

'You're not driving, are you?'

'No, my chauffeur is at the wheel of the Rolls today. Of course I'm driving.'

'Well, you shouldn't be on the phone. You'll crash and die. Plus you could get more points on your licence.'

'Don't talk about points on your licence,' my dad growled in the background. He had recently been caught by a speed camera, rather impressively driving at 35 miles an hour in a 30 mile an hour zone while towing a caravan. For a man who had never broken the law in his life, this was an annoying blot on his record. 'It was at 4am, that's what annoys me,' he said for the hundredth time.

'It's OK, Mum, I've just got one of those Bluetooth things...'

'What on earth have you been eating?'

'No, it's those little hands-free receiver things that you put in your ear. You know that I like gadgets...'

'They're toys.'

'Whatever, but even I think this one is a bit pathetic. You see serious businessmen walking everywhere with these in their lugholes. They look infantile. I don't like it. I feel like one of the Borg.'

'You feel like Björn Borg?'

'No, you know, from *Star Trek*.'

'I know. I'm not a total ignoramus. It is possible for your mother to make a joke, you know. That's where you get it from.'

'So what's he been up to this week, anything exciting?' asked Dad.

'No, no, not really,' I lied. I really could never tell my parents about what I had done. I'm printing up a dummy version of this book with all the dirty bits taken out for them to read.

'You're sounding a lot brighter. Have you met a girl?'

'No… not exactly. I'm just happy to be talking to my wonderful mum.'

'Ah, you're a good boy. He says I'm a wonderful mum.'

'What about your wonderful dad?'

'Well, you can't have everything. I'd better go.'

I met Simon for lunch in a smart restaurant by the sea. 'It's the least I can do,' he told me. 'It's so kind of you to do this.'

'Not at all. Nice to be asked… Will Catherine be joining us?'

'No, she couldn't make it.' I felt an unexpected pang of disappointment. 'But she'll be at the lecture this afternoon.'

'Great!' I said. I surprised myself with how pleased that made me. I had been looking forward to seeing her again, but hadn't realised quite how much. Seeing her name had certainly made me more open to taking this job, but I think I'd have done it anyway. Wouldn't I?

After all, I scarcely knew her.

I had only met Catherine once before, at that gig at the university, though she had made an impression on me, almost without me even realising. Often newer comedians are a bit derivative or hackneyed, but she was properly funny. Her act was smart and sarcastic and occasionally joyously filthy, which was made all the funnier because she had a shy, slightly awkward manner on stage.

Because she was a demure, tall, slim and strikingly pretty woman, the audience didn't expect her to be so sly or dirty.

She had been incredibly timid offstage and had smiled coyly when I'd told her how much I'd liked her act, but not said too much in return. As I chatted with other people, she was standing close by and though I wasn't looking at her and she wasn't talking, when I think back on it I remember sensing her presence and liking having her close to me. I'd been rather intrigued by her and was keen to break away from the dullards who were preoccupying me so I could speak to her some more, but when I looked for her again she had disappeared into the night.

I was curious enough to look for her on MySpace and had been disappointed to see from her status that she was married. I had messaged her, expressing my surprise that she was tied down so young. She was only 26.

She messaged back and revealed that was just something she put up to deter unwelcome male attention. I wasn't sure if that included me.

A few months later she let me know that she was going to be up in Edinburgh for a couple of days during the Fringe and was planning to come and see my show. I recall being excited by that prospect. The night I thought she was coming I remember peeking out from the door behind the audience, watching them as they came in, hoping to see her. In fact, I was convinced I'd spotted her. For some reason her presence made me determined to do a better show than usual.

As it turned out that wasn't her at all; she had been unable to make it. I actually felt a little dismayed, though at least that explained why she hadn't hung around to say hi afterwards. Why did I even care? I didn't know her.

I think I would have done the lecture anyway, but it was an extra cherry on the cake that I'd get to see her again. In any case, I knew she had a boyfriend (though had heard from a mutual friend that they'd been through a few ups and downs) and he was making me very welcome, seemed excited to meet me and was, annoyingly, a lovely fellow. Though I had had my run-ins with one lecturer this year, I didn't have any kind of vendetta against the staff of our colleges and universities. This one was a good one, who was buying me food and not trying to punch me. Yet as things turned out he would soon have an incentive for giving me a beating.

We made our way down to the college and my thoughts turned to trying to work out what on earth I would say, if any students even bothered to show. Perhaps ten years ago I might have created a slight wave of excitement if I was speaking at a university, but most of these students would have been eight or nine the last time I was on TV. Would they even know who I was?

As it turned out, about twenty to thirty students drifted into the 200-seater lecture theatre. I don't know if that counts as a good house – I never went to lectures at university, preferring to sleep.

I hadn't prepared anything in advance and just hoped that I would think of the right things to say. I was just telling the story of my career. How hard could that be? But I am used to getting laughs when I am in front of an audience and though I tried to chip in the odd gag, all I could see were blank faces and glazed eyes staring back at me. I worried I was being a bit dry and boring. I droned on and on, cataloguing my triumphs and disasters, venting my frustrations at a TV commissioning system in which the people in front of me stood a much better chance of selling a script than me purely by dint of their age. When I finished I assumed I'd been talking for about 45 minutes, but actually managed more than 90.

It was perhaps more illuminating for me than any of them to dissect the twenty years of my career. I explained how tortuous and random the process can be, how much luck plays a part, how many classic TV series were nearly stymied at birth by un-imaginative executives, how I had started out wanting instantaneous fame and recognition, and to be acknowledged as the funniest man on the planet, but how now with two decades of experience I had the perspective to realise that those things were not important or really attainable. That, in fact, it is preferable to grind away for years as a writer or performer, learning your craft and building up the skills and mental attitude you'd need to cope with mass exposure, rather than burst on to the scene, flying high like a distress flare and falling and fading just as quickly.

But if a 40-year-old man in a leather jacket had come along to tell the student me that I should be patient and that a successful career was about longevity and integrity, then I would probably have looked as bored and dismissive as the lads in the back row. We think we know it all when we're twenty, and sometimes I wonder if we actually do and that in getting old we actually get more stupid and miss the point. But obviously most of the time I think that I know more now. And the more I know, the less I realise I actually know.

After an awkward question and answer section, where, as I remember from being young and in the audience, nobody was particularly keen to ask me anything and were suddenly much more interested in examining their shoes, I got a smattering of applause and it was all over.

I wasn't sure how it had gone, but Simon seemed ecstatically pleased and Catherine, who I had seen sitting at the back of the auditorium, came up to say hello and to tell me how great and informative she thought I'd been. I was touched by her genuine enthusiasm, but was also delighted to garner her approval. And I was just as happy simply to be in her company.

I wanted to stay and have a drink, but needed to do another interview and then head up the road to my gig. Catherine and Simon were making their own way to the gig, so I'd have a chance to catch up with her then. I left them sitting in the bar, again with this strange, almost imperceptible sensation that I didn't want to leave. I had heard of sexual magnetism, but only now as I struggled to pull away did I start to understand what people had meant.

The gig in Portsmouth went well and afterwards we made for the bar and had a few drinks. I was staying in a hotel in town so could have some wine and let my hair down. But as with the last time we'd met, I ended up talking with a different group, while Catherine and Simon sat at another table. It would, I suppose, have been difficult to chat to her too openly with him sitting right opposite her, and I wasn't consciously considering her as a romantic possibility. But I found myself gazing over at her on several occasions, noticing with a start what beautiful long legs she had.

Just as the bar was closing I managed to pull myself away

from the other people and joined Catherine and Simon. He was still effusive with gratitude for my visit to the college but I just wanted to talk to Catherine, and with just a few moments of proper conversation was reminded of all I had liked about her when I'd met her before. She was smart, but shy, a little bit self-conscious, strikingly attractive and, I correctly surmised, unaware of how incredible she was. I was wishing she was single, that the man who had kindly bought me lunch and without whom I wouldn't be even talking to this woman would just disintegrate into dust. Not that at any point I had any pretensions that Catherine might feel the same about me. Like the girl on the ferry on the way to Phi Phi, she was just a fantasy figure for me to project my dreams upon. And like the girl on the ferry, her boyfriend did seem a bit of a poor match for her. He was nice enough, but she was so amazing, so bright, luminous and scintillating.

I didn't for a second think I was any more worthy of this goddess.

The theatre bar closed and it was time for me to head back to my chain hotel and time for Catherine and the others to drive back to the college. The car park was on my way so I walked them all out of the theatre and found myself at the back of the group, having fallen into step with Catherine (or had she fallen into step with me?), while Simon foolishly and trustingly went ahead with the others.

We talked about comedy and Catherine's regrets that she had not been able to gig so much since she had moved down south to live with her boyfriend. She was, it turned out, planning to move to London in January, while he remained at the university, so she could concentrate on her career.

That didn't sound good.

For him, I mean. It sounded quite promising for me.

She clearly coveted my life as a touring comic, even though I was trying to tell her how lonely and relentless and depressing it could get.

We fell silent for a while and again I sensed an electricity hanging somehow magically in the air between us. Something extra-ordinary was happening between us on some pheromonal level. Or so it seemed to me. It was as if my heart had flown out of my body and was flying around us, invisibly, entwined with hers. It was such an extraordinary feeling, quite different than anything I had ever felt, and such a surprise to experience this unexpected tension between the two of us that I involuntarily gasped and uttered a surprised 'Oh'. I caught her eye and she looked away.

Was I imagining something where there was nothing?

As the rest of the group turned right to go to the car, I looked further ahead on the road I had to continue along, where a group of threatening-looking men were loitering on the corner.

'See,' I told her. 'Touring is pretty dire. This job isn't as amazing as you think. You're off home with your friends and I'm probably going to be bum-raped by some men.'

Expressing her desire to be as lucky as me, she protested, '*I* want to be bum-raped by some men.'

This was so unexpected and hilarious that I laughed all the way back to the hotel. That was the moment I think that I knew I had fallen in love with her. I looked forward to telling our grandchildren when I absolutely knew I'd met the one and what their grandma had said to capture my heart.

Back in my lonely hotel room I couldn't sleep for thinking of this filthy-mouthed angel, annoyed that she was spoken for, wishing that something would go wrong, feeling guilty for wishing to cuckold a man who had been nothing but decent towards me.

Was I more deserving of her than him?

It didn't seem likely. I felt like I was nothing but a liability.

The next day I was travelling along the coast to a gig in Brighton. I had the day to kill and not too far to drive. But I was astonished how preoccupied my mind was with this woman I knew so little about and who had given me no indication beyond a possibly imagined connection that my interest was in any way reciprocated.

Plus less than a week before I'd had two naked women on my bed at the same time, you know, when one of them wasn't playing video games. How could I have turned so readily from debauchery to romance? Was I kidding myself? I was reminded of my adolescent diaries where one week I profess undying love for one girl, then the next, with no apparent self-consciousness, I am championing an entirely different one altogether, dismissing the old love as just a 'childish phase'.

Was I starting to behave like a mature adult here or just regressing further into my irresponsible and teenage 40-year-old lifestyle?

I wanted to get in touch with Catherine straight away and find out what she was thinking and whether I had just gone crazy, but I had learned the folly of desperation when I had been in love with someone I barely knew just four weeks before. But that had just been a childish phase. I would play it cool, play the waiting game, make her sweat it out.

Plus I could only contact her via social networking sites and I had no internet access. Ah, the cold dark days of 2007, when we had no iPhones or mobile broadband. How did we live back then?

I was fully aware that I had to keep things in perspective and conscious that I might be losing the plot, but Catherine was occupying my every thought and affecting my every breath and in a way that had not been the case in the previous failed entanglement. Because this time I had no actual indication that she felt anything at all for me, yet my feelings for her were overwhelming almost to the point of incapacitation. There was something divinely pleasurable about the state I was in, but it was also a devilish torture. Love, it seems, is the point where heaven and hell touch.

But this was the kind of mood I was suddenly in. My brain flooded with hormones, telling me that this girl was the one. Everything looked bright, even though my chances were so bleak and my mental state so questionable. What had I picked up on a subconscious level that made me so sure that she would be mine? Because on a conscious level there was only bum rape.

I had been driving languorously along the coast, looking for something to occupy my day, without any idea of what delights lay along this road. So I was pleased to find myself driving into the town of Fishbourne, home to Fishbourne Palace. It's the ruins of a massive Roman villa with some of the finest mosaic floors in the country. Which isn't saying all that much, admittedly, but I had read about it, always wanted to see it, but had never bothered to go. Fate had brought me here. Fate and the A259.

But why?

I love Roman ruins – Pompeii is probably my favourite place in the world – and love to potter around the remnants of this once proud, now vanquished Empire. It reminds me of the impermanence and transience of our culture, which seems just as solid as the Roman Empire must have felt to the Romans. I also just think those Latin-speaking, laurel-wearing Italians were just really cool with their togas and aqueducts and their imaginative recycling of Christians (as lion food).

Though nothing in Fishbourne would rival the palaces of Italy, I was still thrilled to be here and my senses were at their height thanks to the excitement that Catherine had brought to my world.

The north wing of the palace is housed in a long building which protects it from the elements and there really are some wonderful mosaics there. One shows Cupid riding a dolphin (why not?) and is almost entirely complete and extremely beautiful. But even as I stared at the little god of love, my mind was preoccupied with Catherine and my chest fluttering with the emotions she had produced in me. Had Cupid sailed past me on a dolphin the day before and shot one of his arrows into my heart? It would make sense of this unexpected madness that had descended on me. This inspiring woman, who dreamed of being bum-raped by some men, was turning my thoughts to the poetry of life. It was strange to be looking at the artefacts and the home of people long dead while feeling so alive. It put things into perspective, making me want to let these feelings overtake me while I was still capable of experiencing them.

Life is so short and so random and we should make the most of it while we can. I started to become interested not so much in the mosaics, as great as they were, but in the areas of damage that occurred to them while hidden underground in the hundreds of years since the palace was burned to the ground. There was a burial (still in situ) in the middle of one floor, and another mosaic had been ruined by a tree's roots growing bang in the centre of it. A couple of the floors had the scar of a medieval plough coursing through them and then at the far end was a more regular trench caused by a digger in 1960, which is significant as it was actually this work that led to the discovery of the palace. The unspoiled Cupid mosaic is right in the middle of several areas of damage, preserved by chance. If the family of the skeleton had buried their relative ten feet to the west then Cupid would have been obliterated. If the acorn that the tree grew from had landed five feet to the east, the dolphin would never have been seen. If the man operating the digger had not been as observant as he was, or had just thought, oh, fuck it!, the only eyes that would have seen these wonders would have melted into the dirt over a thousand years before. Indeed, the people building the houses and the roads to the south obviously totally failed to notice the other end of the palace and who knows what amazing treasures were lost by their observational paucity?

Life is full of crazy chance. Had I not fired off an overly keen email a few weeks before, or happened to step outside that pub at the moment I did, or if that Indian café had had longer tablecloths, then I might have had a girlfriend already. But life's tree roots and medieval ploughs and graves had destroyed those particular mosaics. That Cupid on his dolphin might still survive.

Ignoring the facts that Catherine already had a boyfriend and might have no interest in me.

But I was oddly confident that everything would work out fine.

My attempts to be cool and wait to get in touch with her were overwhelmed by the desperation in my enchanted brain. And pretty much as soon as I was in my hotel that afternoon (at 3.50pm as it happens) I sent Catherine a message via Facebook (you can date the various stages of this relationship by which social networking site was cool at the time), asking if she wanted to meet up for a drink the next time she was in London, ostensibly to discuss comedy, but I hoped she might spot my ulterior motive.

This is what I wrote:

Hey Catherine

Really nice to see you again yesterday and glad you empathised a bit with what I had to say.

If you're ever up in London and fancy a drink or a coffee or whatever then do let me know. It would be cool to spend some time with you as I sense we'd have some stuff to talk about, but we've always been a bit surrounded thus far. But anyway...

I hope you will be doing more gigs soon as I think you could be a really great stand-up.

I've been laughing at you saying 'I want to be bum-raped' all day. I hope you remember saying it or that is going to appear odd.

OK. I am going now. Yes.

RK Herring

Yeah, that was pretty subtle.

Had I been too keen to get in touch straight away again? And was this just another crazy and fanciful obsession? I tried to keep it cool and not check for a reply every five minutes, but I was anxious about what might arrive in my inbox and more anxious about what might not.

It took her four hours and 40 minutes to respond. It's not that I was timing it: the messages are timed and dated. But I was also timing it. This is what she said:

Hello,

It was really nice to see you again too. I would love to meet up for a drink or a coffee and talk some more, sometime when I am in London. I think I will be around at some point in early (ish) December, so I will let you know.

Thank you for your kind words, saying I could be a great stand-up.

I'm relieved you found it funny when I said 'I want to be bum-raped'. I did remember saying it, but wasn't entirely sure I'd come off that well in doing so.

Hope I see you soon,

Catherine

It was positive that she had replied so quickly or at all and also that she was keen to meet up, but impossible to tell if she had taken my (actually at least partly genuine) offer of help at face value, or if she was feeling as heady and confused as me. Of course it would have been foolish to be anything but neutral at this stage.

I managed to patiently wait for all of 47 minutes before responding:

Cool.
I hope we can work something out.
The bum rape was all in the delivery.
Please don't use that out of context.
I hope I see you soon too.
Xxx

It was two and a half weeks later that Catherine came to London. We had messaged each other a fair amount and I had made it pretty clear how I felt about her, but she was keeping her cards close to her chest, obscuring both her cards and her chest. A lose-lose situation.

I had been trying to keep things in perspective and aware that I was in all probability behaving like a love-sick loon whose feelings were unrequited and who was heading for a fall. I hadn't put my life on hold, aware that Catherine was spoken for and that the chances of us being together were small, even if I had a strange inner confidence that it would all work out. But even though I'd been on dates with other women, I had ended up talking to them about how I was besotted with someone I had barely met and how I thought I might be mentally ill. Which believe me is not the best chat-up routine of all time.

I met up with her in Islington and after a fortnight of day-dreaming about her it was strange and almost unsettling to see her in the flesh. Would she live up to the possible fantasy version of herself that I had created in my mind?

Though I was nervous and she was rather shy and quiet, when I was with her the world made sense.

I had a gig that night and she came to watch. Downstairs in the pub afterwards we had a drink and I finally stopped beating around the bush. 'You have been occupying my thoughts so completely for the last few weeks. I don't understand it. It's a bit mad. But I think you're amazing and I'm just worried that these feelings are completely one-sided…'

She looked a bit uncomfortable and meekly replied, 'They are just one-sided.'

My heart felt like it had fallen through a trap door on to a hard concrete floor, where it was now being kicked around like a football by some love-hating thugs. This blast of reality after the days of fantasy made my head drop. Of course it was all just one-sided, of course she didn't feel the same way. Why would she? She didn't know me. It was just another dating disaster to add to all the ones that had gone before.

'But I felt so sure that there was something there,' I told her. 'I really felt a connection between us. I can't believe I got it wrong.'

She looked awkward and contrite. 'Well, you're not exactly wrong. Maybe it isn't one-sided. But there's nothing I can do about it. I've got a boyfriend.'

My heart leapt. I wasn't crazy. Or not crazy in the way I had thought, at least.

Admittedly it wasn't all good news and there still seemed a long way to go, but there was hope. She felt an obligation to someone she'd been with for many years, but from things I'd heard and things she'd said, it was clear that they had run their course. I just hoped that she would realise it now rather than five years down the line.

She had to go and get the train back home, and I accompanied her as far as Bank station, where I had to change for the Central Line. We sat next to each other under the harsh lighting of the tube carriage. I could see our reflections, warped in the curved glass of the window opposite. Even with a stretched head and bulbous middle she looked amazing. As the train came to a halt, I leaned over to her and kissed her goodbye, just long enough to overstep the boundary between friends and something more than friends. Only by mere milliseconds, but we both knew what it meant. It was right, it was wrong, it was beautiful and left me smiling all the way down the Central Line to Shepherd's Bush.

She wouldn't be back in London until the New Year. We had some time to think.

Joe A, Joe B, Joe C, Joe D, Joey!
Acon, Beacon, Ceacon, Deacon!

CHAPTER 13
NOT YET DISABLED

We were sitting in the green room going over last-minute script changes at the next radio recording, but I couldn't keep it in.

'I've done it.'

'Done what?' asked Emma.

'What we were talking about last time.'

'What we were talking about what?'

'The threesome. I did it. I finally did it.'

'In the last three weeks?' asked Steve.

'Yup!'

'You and two girls?' asked 'two guys and one girl' Dave (as I now called him).

'Uh-huh!'

'You bastard!'

'Ha ha!' laughed Emma. 'And was it all right or not as good as you thought?'

'Both of those things.'

'So how do you feel about it now?'

'I think it's been good for me. But better still, I think I'm in love.'

'With one of the threesome girls?' asked Emma.

'No!'

'With both of the threesome girls?' asked the increasingly pissed-off Dave.

'No, no. Not with them. I met someone else.'

'In the last three weeks?' asked Steve.

'Yes.'

'You've been busy, Richard Keith,' chuckled Emma. 'Is she in love with you too?'

'Yes... well, maybe. I don't know. The problem is, she's got a boyfriend.'

'And she wants you to have a threesome with him?' asked Dave.

'No, no. I'm done with threesomes. And I'm not interested in having a threesome with another bloke like you are.'

'You can't ever just take the easy option, can you, Rich?' Emma interjected with some pity.

'I think this might be it this time. I know you've heard that before. But if I can only get her to leave her boyfriend and fall for me and go out with me, then I think everything will be fine.'

'Come on, we've got a show to do,' said Elizabeth. 'And your next new love is probably waiting out there in the audience!'

My hedonistic life had not come to an end since I'd met Catherine. I continued as the single man that I undoubtedly was, carrying on with the drinking and socialising, which with the proximity of Christmas was only on the increase. And how happy Jesus must be that his birth is such a cause of gluttony and drunkenness, which as I understand it was mainly what he was about.[2]

I was getting no work done, but at the back of my mind was writing off December, planning (as I always did at this time of year) to turn my life around with a raft of draconian New Year's resolutions. I was getting sick of my lifestyle, fed up with the drinking and the debauchery, yearning for something and someone more special. Unable to bear the fact that my heart might get squashed again.

---

3. Indeed, according to Matthew 11:19 his enemies called Jesus 'a man gluttonous, and a winebibber, a friend of publicans and sinners'. He sounds right up my street.

Three days after my kiss on the underground, my alarm woke me at the ungodly hour of 9am (surely not another human being was awake at such a time). I had the all-too-familiar sensation of a throbbing hangover. I turned over and went back to sleep.

Half an hour later I woke with a start, remembering that today was the day I had promised to head to West Sussex to see a school play and that my train was leaving Victoria in about an hour. I got up, hurriedly showered and dressed and ran for the tube.

Clearly, being childless, none of the kids at the school were mine, but nor were they the children of anyone I actually knew. I wasn't going there to act as Father Christmas, though I certainly had the belly for it. If you had seen a fat, unshaven, sweaty, childless single man in his forties rushing desperately to attend a school concert that he had no seeming connection to, then you might jump to the wrong conclusion.

But I had every right to be going there. The school was run by Scope, a charity that works on behalf of people with cerebral palsy and is running an admirable campaign (Time To Get Equal) to try and achieve equal rights for disabled people.

Like Heather Mills, I hate to discuss my charity work, but like Heather Mills I am going to anyway.

I had been supporting Scope for about four years. When I say supporting all I really mean is that I had been doing a collection for them at some of my gigs and had performed at a couple of their events. Why had I been doing that? Because I am an excellent bloke? Not quite.

My relationship with Scope started by accident. I had had my first midlife crisis early, at the age of 35, when I had broken up with Steph, the girlfriend that I had bought my house to live with, and was struggling to come to terms with my career being in the doldrums. I had been looking for something to give my life some meaning and because I went jogging every now and again a few people had suggested I run the London Marathon. A friend of mine was doing it and told me that if I raised money for a charity they would guarantee my entry to the event. He was doing it for Scope. So I did it for them too. If he'd been doing it to raise funds to put more landmines in third world countries, then I would have as well. It was self-interest and laziness that fostered this connection.

I had no massive personal connection to the cause – my friend, the brilliant comedian Francesca Martinez, has cerebral palsy and another friend has a daughter who is very slightly affected by the condition. I had spent most of my schooldays doing hilarious impressions of people with cerebral palsy or calling my friends 'Spaz' or 'Joey',[3] so perhaps had some sins to atone for – but in all honesty I didn't care about who I would be raising money for. I just wanted a place in the race and the fundraising was something I had to do to get it.

The marathon became one of a dozen improbable feats that I attempted that year, and the story of those endeavours became my live show for that year, 'The Twelve Tasks of Hercules Terrace'. I decided to produce a programme for the show, which I would give out free in return for donations to a charity (mainly because it turned out to be unprofitable and too much of an effort to try and charge people for it), and it seemed to make sense that given the show's connection with Scope they should be the beneficiaries. The costs would be covered by advertisers and then all the money collected would go to what was once, but thankfully is no more, called the Spastics Society. Though I didn't like it when Opal Fruits, Marathon and Mr Dog changed their names, I think the people at Scope have done the right thing, branding-wise.

It was cool to be raising some cash and awareness for a good cause, but I was getting something out of it too. I got to produce and give out a free bit of self-promoting merchandise. I even joked in the show about how much I hated the dispossessed and that I'd have more sympathy with the cause if the kids I was raising money for came round and did something for me – like maybe washing my car. 'But no,' I complained. 'It's all take, take, take with these people!'

---

4. Joey Deacon was the man who *Blue Peter* focused on when they were trying to raise awareness of disabled issues in the 1970s, but for most of the kids they were trying to educate this merely gave rise to an additional insult.

I also claimed I was hoping that in return for my support the charity might see their way clear to giving me one of those blue disabled parking badges or at least some special pass that would allow me to use any disabled toilet at any time I wanted.

Perhaps I wasn't quite that cynical, but it's certainly true that I was getting as much if not more out of all this as I was putting in.

The scheme worked well and Scope have since been involved in the production of all my subsequent show programmes and I (or rather the people kind enough to donate at gigs or to have their names mentioned in the brochure) have raised a lot of money for them. But I confess, I had never really thought too much about where the coins I was grudgingly having to count up and bag up on my dining room table were going.

On this day in December 2007 I had been invited to visit one of the schools that I was raising money for, Ingfield Manor School. It was way out in the middle of nowhere, quite a long way away from my house in Shepherd's Bush, and on this headachy, furry-mouthed, blurry-visioned morning I was resentful of that fact. I was actually wishing that I hadn't agreed to go. It would have been much better if I could just have stayed in bed. Didn't these bastards think that me raising money for them was enough? I had to go and watch their stupid Christmas show as well?

I didn't think I was going to get to Victoria in time and when my tube stopped in the tunnel for a good five minutes I was convinced I'd screwed my whole day up. Though I was frustrated by the hold-up and anxious about missing the train, there was a part of me thinking that maybe that might be a good thing. Maybe I could just ring up the people at Scope and let them know that thanks to the inefficiency of London Underground and despite my best efforts to get to the school on time, I wasn't going to be able to make it. Maybe next year.

A part of me, though, thought that it would be an awful travesty if I had got up this early and done all this dashing around if I didn't even get to show my face. I'd just have to get up early another time. Best to get it over with.

The tube started moving again and I got to the station with seconds to spare, sprinted to the platform, no time to get a ticket, through a ticket barrier that for some reason was jammed open and got on the train about fifteen seconds before it pulled away.

Unfit, out of breath and with my heart pounding out through my sweaty shirt like a cartoon character's, I thought to myself, this better be the best Christmas show of all time...

As it turned out, it might have been the best show of any kind of all time. If that ticket barrier had been closed as it should have been then I would have missed out on the most moving, amazing and life-affirming experience.

Have you seen that film *Sliding Doors*?

It's a load of fucking shit, isn't it? Just awful.

It felt strange going to the Christmas show of a school to which I had no actual personal connection. I felt out of place and uncomfortable upon my arrival and I suppose at the back of my mind was also concerned about how I would interact with the kids. I knew that many of the kids had quite severe disabilities. Would I be able to stop myself looking shocked? Or worse, would I overcompensate and try and act like all this was super-normal and be over-effusive and touchy-feely and patronising, like a desperate celebrity on a telethon show, with a rictus grin, trying to demonstrate just how unfazed they are by kids in wheelchairs, but accidentally revealing the exact opposite?

I wished I wasn't so hungover.

I had been met off the train by Scope executive Vivian Elliot and her team. Vivian is a no-nonsense Canadian matriarch, devoted to raising funds for this excellent charity and for the kids she clearly loves but treats (as she does with everyone) with an admirable matter-of-factness. Wise and shrewd, she subtly eased my unspoken concerns, completely aware that I would have misgivings at this point in the day but be bowled over by the end of it. She'd seen the effect that this experience had on people before and she knew that this depraved, unhealthy comedian would be no different.

She also primed me for the minefield (if that's not an inappropriate metaphor given the disabilities one can cause) that is appropriate vocabulary for discussing disabled people. 'Handicapped' is now considered offensive, as, of course, thanks to the efforts of me and a million other schoolchildren, is 'spastic.' 'Differently abled' has also thankfully been seen as patronising and meaningless (we are all, of course, differently abled). The word that was guaranteed to cause no offence in 2007 was 'disabled' (though I suspect with time, this also might change). I had slight issues with this as a descriptive term, mainly because I wasn't sure what it said about people who weren't disabled. Were they supposed to be 'abled'? Because in my opinion many weren't. Or should they be called 'not disabled'? That seemed just as heavy-handed and wrong. One of the disabled people I had met at a previous Scope event had put me straight. 'We call you the "not yet disabled"!'

That seemed to sum up the issue beautifully and if more 'not yet disabled' people thought of themselves in those terms, then they might have more concerns about wheelchair issues and the shameful lack of toilet facilities for people with disabilities in many pubs and nightclubs. As well as the lack of parking permits for comedians who raise large amounts of money for them. All right, maybe not. It's worth a try.

Ingfield is an impressive and large old manor house, set in extensive grounds and surrounded by woods. It was bequeathed to Scope by a generous supporter and has been painstakingly and expensively converted to provide all the amenities that these children require. Work was still going on on a new wing, and we were taken on a tour of it by the headmaster, Alistair Bruce. Vivian would lob in a well-timed comment every now and again about how outrageously expensive some vital piece of kit was. But I didn't need convincing now that the limited fundraising I was involved with was helping towards something fantastic.

Then we went into the classrooms to meet the children.

There are 36 pupils at the school, most of whom also board there, and about 40 members of staff. Many of the kids need one-to-one tuition and care. They were all a little bit preoccupied, preparing for the upcoming theatrics, so I just stood slightly awkwardly in the corner, smiling and waving while most of them ignored this strange interloper in their classroom. I must admit that I found it hard to imagine how many of these children would be capable of performing in a play. Cerebral palsy affects people in a whole host of different ways, affecting movement, speech and coordination in varying degrees. Could a child who couldn't walk or speak be capable of any kind of meaningful performance? I hated myself for allowing such prejudiced views to come to the surface, but surely this was just common sense. You can be as well meaning as you like, but if someone can't talk or move, surely they can't perform on stage.

I was then taken through to the hall to find a seat for the performance. I was feeling out of place and alone and no less hungover, anticipating the worst, practising my fixed grin.

Finally it all began. To start with, inevitably I suppose, it was hard not to feel a mixture of pity and shock that a child is disabled and unable to do all the things other kids take for granted. Some of the kids couldn't hold up their heads, which to begin with made them look heartbreakingly sad. Instinctively when you see a child like this you want to comfort and hug them, but when I saw the faces of these tykes, I realised they weren't unhappy at all. Quite the opposite. They were all getting so much out of what they were doing that it was impossible not to be carried along with their joy.

Indeed, despite my unimaginative prejudices, every single child was able to play a meaningful role. With the assistance of the staff, the less mobile could move around and with the help of Stephen Hawking-style voice synthesisers those who couldn't speak could deliver their lines.

It didn't take long before I forgot about their disabilities and my engrained attitudes and realised that like much so-called 'common sense', my previous ideas had come from a place of ignorance.

These students, regardless of their disabilities, were just children like any others. Certainly life would never be easy for them, but through their dedication and commitment to these shows they demonstrated that in some ways they will get more from life than others who take basic attributes such as speech and movement for granted.

There were many moving and inspiring moments, but the one that will stay with me for ever was the scene where three kids of around eight years old, dressed as Christmas trees, with vastly varying degrees of mobility, all danced to the Toploader song 'Dancing In The Moonlight'. It isn't a song that I particularly like and nor, I imagine, did the writer of the piece envisage that the people doing the dancing would be eight years old, have cerebral palsy or be dressed as Christmas trees, but the effort and joy that these kids put into the piece was an inspiration to me both as a performer and a human being. It turned a catchy though slightly vacuous pop song into something very deep and meaningful and made me look at Toploader in a totally different way. I wished that I had had some part in the creation of their version of 'Dancing In The Moonlight' because it had made this wondrous moment. Before, when I heard this song, I would have thought of young women, dancing around in revealing party clothes, drinking, taking drugs, about to commit lewd acts with the Toploader band members, and I would have felt slightly soiled. But from now on I will think of these three tiny Christmas trees and remember what it actually means to be human.

Ultimately I was just enchanted to be at a school's Christmas show. It was funny and fun and human and something I have missed out on due to choices I have made in my life. I wished I had had someone special to share this day with. In fact, there was someone special I specifically wished was there. I wanted Catherine to be at my side, right now, seeing what I was seeing, feeling what I was feeling, holding my hand. This, more than anything, made me realise this wasn't like the infatuations or sexual obsessions I had experienced in the previous few months. There was much, much more to this woman and the emotions she had awakened in me.

So the tinge of tragedy that I felt within me at the start of the day had transformed into an overwhelming state of triumph by the time I boarded the train back home. I was shattered yet uplifted and sat in silence not because of the hangover that had hung over me on the outward journey but because I was thinking about everything I'd seen and felt.

While it might be a wonderful world if no child was born with disabilities, the fact is that that is not the world we live in, and while some idiots might feel the disabled should be hidden away (or worse), in truth, with assistance, they can live lives with more meaning than some people who never even think about how lucky they are to have functioning bodies.

And this in turn made me reconsider some choices I was making and influenced my decision to change them. Certainly something like this puts one's own problems into some kind of perspective. We all have things we are unable to do and aren't very good at and most of us choose to not do those things at all. But having the balls to do something difficult to the best of your abilities is as good as being the best at it, in my opinion. Watching children who had to struggle to form a word, delivering sentences of dialogue, had been a lesson for both my chosen profession and my life.

'Did you enjoy that?' asked Vivian with the slyest of smiles on her face.

'Yes. Yes I did,' I replied.

She nodded sagely. Everything had transpired as she knew it would.

I think the fact that when the train pulled back into Victoria station I was wishing I had kids of my own is as much of a testament as I can give. The world seemed a better place than it had before. Even stinky, boisterous London seemed beautiful now I stopped to look at it. I felt inspired to try and be a better person and make more of my own abilities which I sometimes squander.

If that isn't great art then I don't know what is.

The magic carried on for the rest of the day. That evening I was telling some stories in a little trendy bar near Hoxton, where a couple of bands would also be performing.

When I got off the tube I walked quickly towards the steps out of the station. A stranger, a pretty young woman, was walking beside me. Apropos of nothing she turned to me and said, 'I'll race you up the stairs!' I like to run up the steps at the tube station, so it was odd that she should ask this without knowing me, but I took her up on her challenge and we hurried up the dozen or so steps, reaching the top in a dead heat. She clearly couldn't quite believe that this fat man had equalled her speed.

'Balls!' she exclaimed.

But she didn't know that I had run a marathon, so a few stairs were nothing to me. It had been fun to race a stranger. Then we came to the escalators. There were two and they were quite long; one was moving upwards and the other was static. We looked at each other and I said, 'Let's do it! I'll give you a chance,' and I took the non-moving side. Although she had to negotiate other commuters she quickly took the lead and beat me by about eight steps – though without the advantage, who knows? We shook hands at the top and went on with our lives. It was a charming, enchanting and exhausting interaction with someone I didn't know and would never see again. We were embracing life and winning and losing were not important. Taking part was once again the key. But then I lost, so I would say that.

It did remind me that I was very out of shape. I'd have to do something about that.

The gig was also amazing: it was taking place in a little club that was more like someone's lounge and there was a smallish but appreciative audience and free mulled wine. The opening band were terrific, and the highlight of their set was when one of the musicians started playing a saw. And making beautiful music with it. I then read some stories that I haven't done on stage before and though they were rather more charming and less offensive than my usual fare, they went down well with the trendy crowd.

It just felt like such a special day: I'd seen three children with CP dancing in the moonlight, I'd had a race up an escalator with a stranger and I'd watched a woman turn a saw into a violin. Life doesn't get any better than that.

*

Perhaps everything that I'd experienced in the last few months had been leading towards this time, towards me making a change, but this two weeks which had started with depravity and ended with nativity, with a blinding epiphany in between, made me sure that after all those false starts and delayed new beginnings it was time to clean up my life, properly this time (if not my act, which the comedy gods seemed to be telling me should remain as puerile and dirty as ever). It hadn't been a single moment of truth exactly; it had taken three smacks in the face from the fact fairy to make me see the error of my ways. But maybe Ben Folds had been wrong. Maybe I could change. Maybe I didn't have to learn to live with what I was.

It was 10 December 2007, roughly halfway through my 41st year. I had had enough of the hangovers, enough of the shortness of breath and lethargy, enough of my fat stomach and enough sex with people I had only just met. I was going to give up drinking, moderate my eating, start exercising and stop sleeping around. I wanted happiness and meaning in my life and if that couldn't be with Catherine then I would find someone else. I was going to stop moaning about my lucky life and start enjoying my dream job in the way that the Ingfield kids had shown me. I was going to act if not exactly my age then something closer to it.

And I was going to do it straight away...

Once Christmas and New Year were over.

And to protect my poor heart I couldn't pin all my hopes on Catherine just yet, though she wouldn't leave my thoughts. We were exchanging messages daily on Facebook and really getting to know each other. I had discovered that one of her unfulfilled ambitions was to build a pyramid of Ferrero Rocher chocolates on a silver tray, like the one in the famous ambassador's reception advert. I liked the fact she hadn't done this even though it was quite an easy thing to arrange. It made me love her more. By now I was really opening up to her. This message goes some way to describing my emotional confusion:

I am excited and terrified by you. My gut tells me you are someone potentially very special. I have some massive visceral connection with you that I can't begin to understand. My gut says it's fine and you're going to come along with it and all will be good, in spite of the contrary evidence and the fact I don't know you at all beyond these messages. My heart is more cautious and yet characteristically optimistic. My heart prefers my gut to my brain. Personally I think my brain is the best thing about me, but the rest of my body rebels against it. My brain is bamboozled by you. It thinks I am (and thus it is) crazy. Yet every day some tiny vestige of hope seeps through, that I am not on my own here. That some of the yearning is mutual.

I am drunk and shouldn't say too much...

Oh dear.

And my new life started one day earlier than planned. Back in London after a Cheddar Christmas, I absented myself from New Year celebrations and stayed in on my own drinking camomile tea on New Year's Eve. This was incredibly liberating.

It felt wonderful to be in a little island of calm, while I imagined all the chaos and unpleasantness and desperation going on in the outside world.

Being alone as midnight approached should have felt wrong, but it was a novelty to be sober and meant I could think back over the year and look forward to the new one with some kind of clarity. '*I am hopeful,*' I wrote in my diary, '*that I might leave behind the sloth and fuggy-mindedness of 2007 and get on with pushing forwards. And it's good to have a 2008 full of possibilities, but not really knowing where I will be this time next year, nor indeed what I will be doing. Will I have another Edinburgh show under my belt? Will I have fathered my first child? (Will really have to get a move on with that one.) Will I be lying mouldering in my grave?*

'*Will I be on my own listening to the next-door neighbours constantly blowing little party trumpets, as if trying to convince themselves that that is actually fun, while I try to convince myself that being alone at New Year isn't ultimately tragic?'*

The plan was to get up early in the morning, go to the gym, see how many other people manage to get down there on the morning of 1 January, write a book proposal and start work on a new sitcom script. I'd already managed one day without drinking before the year had even begun.

Midnight came. I raised my cup of tea to myself, feeling genuinely optimistic.

I wanted my first action of 2008 to be to text Catherine and wish her all the best for a year that I hoped I might be playing rather a large part in. But I was conscious she was with someone else and didn't want to create a problem. So I just thought about it instead and tried to send the text telepathically.

I don't think it got through. But then New Year's Eve is a busy time for telepathic texts.

I had, though, messaged her earlier in the day and said:

Have a lovely new year's eve.

I think I am going to spend it alone. But am quite happy with that.

Next year, though, we'll be on holiday together somewhere exotic.

Well, you never know...

It was at least something to aim for.

If fat is a feminist issue, then where did that leave Bernard Manning?

CHAPTER 14
HAPPY NEW YEAR

The world was suspiciously quiet the next morning. I wasn't up THAT early, leaving the house at about 10.30am, but there was hardly anyone about. It was like the reverse of a normal day when everyone else is at work and I am in bed. Like a slacker version of *Freaky Friday*. Was I in the right body?

I was, almost certainly, the least hungover I have been on any 1 January morning since probably about 1980 and my resolve paid dividends as I sat in a café and wrote my book proposal. It was done by lunchtime. Twelve hours into the new year and I had already achieved something.

I then headed down to the gym, determined to get my new healthy regime off to a good and sweaty start. But I was disappointed to discover that the gym was closed. On New Year's Day? That's like closing a suicide booth on Valentine's Day. Surely this would be their busiest potential day, where loads of people, sickened by their debauchery, would be knocking at the door, at least wanting to sign up to join? But I suppose that only idiots want to come to the gym on 1 January. Everyone else would be in bed. Or maybe not even yet in bed and still out celebrating. How the new me pitied those shallow fools.

And I wasn't going to let the rest of the world's laziness stop me. I went home for a healthy lunch of fish and salad, before heading out for a three-mile run. My body was a bit confused by what was going on, but it thanked me for the break from the alcohol-based punishment I have been giving it, even if it slightly objected having to utilise muscles that, escalator-racing and running for trains excepted, it had not had to use for months.

I stayed in alone for the second night in a row. I couldn't remember the last time that had happened. I wasn't climbing up the walls with frustration either. I read a little, feeling good about my healthy and productive day.

As I went to bed I experienced another long-forgotten sensation: my stomach was growling, because it was, for once, not stretched to capacity with food. In the last six months I had eaten when I felt the slightest pang of hunger and often when I didn't. But as of today I was keeping a food diary, detailing calories consumed and calories burned and trying to keep the aggregate at less than 2000. I hadn't gone for a faddy scheme where I only ate bananas or protein or had a shake for breakfast and a shake for lunch (though, believe me, I've tried everything in the past). I had come up with an astonishing diet of my own, that surely no one else could ever have thought of. I was going to consume less calories and do more exercise and see how that worked out for me.

Like many overweight people I had kidded myself that my propensity to chub up was down to my genes or my metabolism, but even if there was any truth in this (and in my case there wasn't), these were just excuses. Weight loss is so simple that it's incredible that so many people and companies manage to make millions of pounds by complicating it. Though you perhaps need to address the psychological reasons why you feel the need to eat too much or why you subconsciously might wish to be fat to fulfil a role in your social group, once you have made the decision to get things in control there is only one way of doing it. You need to work out how many calories a day your body needs to operate (and there are many websites that can help you with this – I used www.fitday.com), then accept that there is simple mathematics at play. If you consume more calories than your daily allowance and fail to burn them off then you will put on weight and if you consume less calories than that or exercise enough to negate the excess then you will lose weight. That is all you need to know. If this was a diet book I would try and stretch that out to 200 pages, but I am giving you the info for free in the middle of another book. If it's still too complicated for you, here's the Herring Diet (which is probably a confusing name for it and might have been taken already) in four words: eat less, exercise more.

I estimated I needed 2500 calories a day to operate, so decided to try and set myself a limit of 2000 calories a day for the moment, meaning I should gradually lose weight. If I ran for 30 minutes, as I had on the 1 January, then I would have burned up 300 calories, which meant I could eat 2300 calories and still hit my 2000 aggregate.

If I splurged out a bit and consumed 2500 calories one day then that wouldn't really matter as I wouldn't actually put any weight on. If I ate 3500 calories, then as long as I came in at around the 2000 mark for the rest of the week I'd still lose weight. Or I could go to the gym for an hour and that would burn up 700 or so calories and put me back on track.

The weight loss might not be immediate (and the mistake many people make, including myself on many occasions, is to want instant results and then to lose heart if they don't come), but science dictated that, as long as I was honest, it had to work. I hoped I could sustain it for ever. Once I'd hit my target weight I just had to keep my intake to 2500 calories and I shouldn't put any weight back on.

Good theory.

Once I become aware of the calorific values of the stuff I was eating it was obvious why I was getting fat. I, for example, would regularly eat a large piece of malt loaf thinking that was a healthy snack, but now discovered that it would account for about a fifth of my daily food allowance.

Of course this diet did not entail giving up any specific kind of food, but once I understood that a bar of chocolate would take me half an hour to run off, it did make me consider the value of eating it. If you looked at it one way, not eating the bar of chocolate was the equivalent of doing 30 minutes in the gym. I kept a chunky KitKat in my fridge, refusing to eat it, concluding that every time

I looked at it I had done the equivalent of a minor workout! If I looked at it 100 times a day, according to my logic, I should weigh a negative amount by the end of the week. Brilliant!

Similarly, once I was at the gym I would be thinking what extra food I could eat if I did an extra ten minutes on a machine. It appealed to the obsessive-compulsive element within me and pushed me onwards to do more exercise. I also realised that if I just used my bike to get around or walked for an hour a day that I was putting myself further into calorie credit. It was, to begin with at least, incredibly easy and addictive.

Though I could have chosen to eat eight bars of chocolate or twenty Flumpses a day (though that might shorten my lifespan), in reality I avoided fatty, sugary and high-calorie foods and instead sought out stuff that was filling and healthy. I was actually astonished by the quantity of food I could eat. Sometimes, in fact, I couldn't even manage to get to 2000 calories.

The fact that I had stopped drinking, of course, helped. A night on the piss could easily clock up 1000 calories and then also make me lose self-control and send me running to Chicken Cottage for an extra dinner and another 1000 calories. And then I would sleep badly, not feel like exercising and attempt to fight my hangover with fried food or some hair of the dog the next night.

But now I was waking up feeling well rested and full of energy, more than happy to start the day with a bowl of porridge filled with fruit. All I needed was to renounce my atheism and welcome Jesus into my heart and my transformation would be complete.

The first thing that struck me was just how slowly time was passing, proving the old adage that you don't live longer if you don't drink, it just feels like it. Suddenly I seemed to have several extra hours in my day and industriously filled them with exercise and work. I started writing the sitcom that I'd been dragging my heels on and ideas were coming in thick and fast. I was even finding it hard to sleep at night; without the comforting knock-out effect of being trolleyed, my unfuddled brain was racing every time I went to bed. This was how it had been when I was in my early twenties and excited by my job and ambitious to succeed.

Had I finally realised how lucky I was to have this brilliant way of making a living?

I was experiencing a rather alien sensation in my chest. What was it? Was it contentment? Could it be that simple that just a few days of healthy living and application could turn things around that much? I felt so evangelical that I began considering keeping up with this experiment and not drinking for a whole year and actually making good on that idea of writing about my experiences (or lack of them – my life was surely more eventful when I was drunk), but I worried about the repercussions on my social life. Would I stop going out altogether (I had barely spoken to another human being for four days)? Had I got so used to being drunk when I was out that I needed booze as a social crutch? And would I be able to go out on dates if I was sober? Wouldn't potential partners think I was weird? Would I be so boring that they would quickly lose interest?

Surely I was entertaining enough to have a social and dating life without being pissed... wasn't I? I was enjoying the novelty now but would I soon start craving human company? And I was thinking that it would be nice to have sex at some point during the year and you have to be drunk to do that, don't you? I couldn't remember the last time I'd had totally sober sex. Certainly not with someone who wasn't a long-time partner. It was technically possible to have sex with a drunk woman when one wasn't drunk oneself, but that seemed creepy and wrong somehow. Interestingly, more wrong than both of you being too out of it to know what you were doing.

For the moment I was more concerned about what Catherine would make of the new clean-living me. If it wasn't for booze then I doubt I would have opened up to her so much in my messages. What if I clammed up and she realised how dull I actually was? Being blind drunk for the first month or so of seeing someone can help you overcome the embarrassment of all the horrendous things you are supposed to go through together.

She was moving to London on the third and had agreed to come out for dinner with me on the fifth. Which seemed positive.

I was desperate to see her again after three weeks apart and hoped that she might be too. Or was I heading for another fall that would see me spiralling out of control once again and reaching for the whisky bottle that sat provocatively on my kitchen windowsill? Would I discover that I had built her up over all this time and that she couldn't match my expectations?

I was taking her to a swanky Indian restaurant in Westminster. Catherine didn't seem fazed by my not drinking, though it certainly didn't stop her indulging herself, which I was glad of, because I didn't want to impose my new resolution on anyone else. So while I had a ginger ale, she had a champagne cocktail.

And though I felt initially self-conscious, I soon forgot about my sobriety. She was even more beautiful than I had remembered and as she sat opposite me I felt that same calmness and certainty that I had felt as she walked silently by my side just before we talked about bum rape. When I was with her everything felt right and my delirious mind needed no alcohol to provide further intoxication. I was more smitten and certain than ever.

After the meal we went to the bar downstairs for another drink. At last we could sit next to each other without a table between us and it felt even more right to have her beside me. We were close together and the magnetic attraction was pulling us further inwards.

'Can I kiss you?' I asked, but she shook her head and pulled away, though clearly conflicted. Yet here she was, out for dinner with me and clearly liking me as much as I had hoped. Were the same forces at work inside her? Did she feel the same as me? If so, it would take an iron will to resist these burgeoning emotions.

We talked intensely. 'I can't tell you how good it feels to be with you,' I emoted. 'And that's enough for now. I can wait. This is enough.'

She smiled shyly, looking confused and concerned. She was in a difficult position and though determined to do the right thing, something inside her was causing her resolve to waver. Having spoken to her about her circumstances, it seemed clearer than ever to me that her current relationship had already failed and that she and her boyfriend were bound together only by a sense of loyalty.

Later we looked at each other in silence, the tension as obvious as the unspoken feelings between us. 'What do you want to do now?' she asked and I leaned forward and answered her with a kiss. A kiss that this time clearly overstepped the friendship line, a kiss that she returned, if only briefly, before remembering herself.

I apologised, but it was an empty apology. I could not have held out any longer.

We walked through the cold January night, crossing the river at Westminster Bridge and walked up to the Oxo Tower and headed up to the rooftop bar for cocktails. Or rather for cocktail. I held firm on my resolve and had some water.

And without alcohol clouding my brain I knew that all the things I was feeling were genuine and real. Or at least created by the hormones and pheromones in our bodies. Of course she was pissed on champagne cocktails, so I couldn't be sure about her.

Eight floors up I kissed her again, a passionate and reciprocated and spectacular kiss. I had never experienced anything like it. There was actual genuine heat. I felt like my lips were on fire. Perhaps it was the curry or the ginger ale, but I think it was more than that. It was so incredible that it actually made me fearful: fearful that I would never be able to let her go, fearful that if every kiss we had was so much better than the last, forming some kind of exponential curve, that very soon I would explode. But most fearful that it would never happen again. That I had finally found the woman who could do this to me and she'd walk out and sober up and tell me she couldn't see me again.

I have kissed way too many people, some of whom I was in love with, and yet I'd honestly never experienced a kiss like this one. It was intoxicating and incredible, but it was a bit of a jolt too, like being slapped awake from the daydream I'd been living in, with someone shouting at me, 'See, that's what it's about, you cock!'

I wondered if it was as profound for her as it was for me.

I had gone weak at the knees and that had only happened to me once before in my life because of a woman, when I had passed

Jenny Agutter, the woman of my teenage dreams (and let's be honest, of my teenage wanks – hence the poor quality of my *American Werewolf in London* video), in the BBC canteen. Overwhelmed by the surprise of seeing her and her breathtaking beauty, I had buckled as I walked by.

But now it had happened again, with someone who wasn't just a fantasy figure, with someone I was holding in my arms, someone who felt right and who smelled right. That was almost the most astonishing thing about her. I held her head in my hands and smelled her hair and it smelled so perfect that I felt we might merge and become just a single vapour.

It struck me that so far each kiss we'd had had been higher than the last: the first on the tube, the second in the basement bar and now this one high above the Thames. Would I have to hire a hot-air balloon before we kissed again? There seemed something poetic and apt about heading upwards as we kissed; that she was pulling me out of the ground where Morlock-like I had been skulking.

Earlier, as I had tried to make sense of the feelings that I was having for her and where they had come from, I had expressed my worry that I had become fixated with her, as perhaps I had with some of the other girls I'd met recently, because I knew in my heart that I couldn't have her, so I'd be able to carry on with my irresponsible life alone, feeling sorry for myself that love had treated me so harshly once again.

But while I didn't know how or why my gut had felt so sure that she was the one, I could see now that that snap decision had been entirely right. I wanted her and I needed her and would be devastated if she couldn't be mine.

I walked her back to her bus stop. The streets were quiet and a mist hung around the buildings and it genuinely felt like the whole city had been built just for us and that we were the only people in it.

CHAPTER 15
I SEE DRUNK PEOPLE

'You've done well to give up the sauce so easily,' my mum said when she phoned me in the second week of the year. 'At least it proves you're not an alcoholic.'

'I'm not an alcoholic, Mum,' I told her.

'I know,' she replied unconvincingly. 'I'm just saying.'

'It won't last, Richy boy. Richard the Lionheart! Rich Tea Biscuit!' buffooned Dad. 'I give you another three days, tops!'

'Shut up, Keith.'

'Come on, son. Have a drink! Go on, you know you want to.'

'Shut up, you silly old man. It's good he's not drinking. Don't listen to him, Richard. You're doing the right thing.'

My mum worries about everything, though perhaps with some reason in this case, as one of her grandfathers had been an aggressive drunk. One of my dad's grandfathers was a Methodist minister who was at the forefront of the Temperance Movement, so maybe that explained my internal struggle on this issue – two opposing ideals programmed into my genes. I could go, it seemed, one way or the other, but found it difficult to occupy the middle ground.

Ironically, the grandson of the Methodist wanted me to drink and the granddaughter of the boozehound wanted me to be sober.

I began daydreaming that I had an angel on one shoulder and a devil on the other – the angel looking suspiciously like my mum and the devil having something of my father about him (with a bit of Bono thrown in for good measure).

'Keep it up,' the angel was saying. 'Jesus would be proud of your abstinence.'

'What are you talking about, you winged buffoon?' retorted the devil. 'Jesus loved a drink more than anyone. Why do you think he had to turn the water into wine? Cos he'd drunk all the actual booze at the wedding. And if you believe the Catholics, his blood is actually made of the stuff.'

The angel was blustering. She was flustered. Had she inadvertently had a go at the boss's son? She retorted, 'Jesus tasted the wine, but he never swallowed it. Anyway, didn't he say, "Do as I say, not as I do"? It was something like that.'

The pantomime demon was laughing away, knowing he was winning. 'There's some vodka in the fridge, Rich. You don't have to do any work today – you're self-employed.'

'I'm not sure. I've said I've given up.'

'Who would even know? Drink it! DRINK it. If you drink alone in the daytime then you don't have to worry about embarrassing yourself in front of other people. So you'll keep your self-respect.'

'But I need to write a stand-up routine about cocks.'

'Write it drunk. You're much funnier when you're drunk anyway. Everyone says so.'

It was a very persuasive argument. I do FEEL funnier when I'm pissed.

'No, wait, you're trying to trick me too, Satan,' I resisted. 'How unlike you. I'm very disappointed in you.' The devil looked a little shamefaced, but he had a bit of a grin on his face too. He's such a lovable rogue. You can't stay mad at him for long.

'I knew you'd see sense,' said the angel sanctimoniously. 'That's right. Don't drink, work hard on your routine about cocks... Oh hold on. I'm not sure how Jesus would feel about that. Why not write a routine about parsimony instead?'

'Parsimony?'

'Yeah, I don't really know what it is either. It was the first thing that came into my head and it sounds really holy.'

'You can both shut up. You're as bad as each other. Leave me be!'

That's the problem with shoulder angels and devils: they're both so extreme.

*

But I wasn't going to crumble just yet. I was enjoying the benefits of feeling healthy and full of life. Even so, my subconscious was unhappy with my new puritan lifestyle. I was having some horrific and vivid nightmares, perhaps a rebellion of my brain, aware that if it didn't get booze soon it would no longer have the excuse for the abnegation of responsibility. So like the caretaker in a *Scooby-Doo* show, it is creating nightmarish ghouls to try and frighten me off this healthy course and back into the bar.

Yet not only were my brain and my skin clearer, I also lost an astonishing half a stone in the first fortnight of my new regime. I felt like I was a snake that had shed a skin, or a Russian doll that had busted out of its bigger, fatter sister. In love and high from all the exercising, I was in an annoyingly happy mood.

Now I wasn't drinking it was a bit alarming how much I was noticing the booze casualties in the everyday world who I would otherwise have ignored. I saw old, lonely men with gnarled, beetroot-coloured faces and sad eyes walking down the street towards me. I wondered if I was looking into my own future and then I speculated about how much older than me these guys really were. Everywhere I looked I saw drunks.

One day I was on a bus at about 7pm and there was a woman of about 30 sleeping across two or three pull-down seats near the front. She was snorting and snoring and pissed off her face, with a not insubstantial beer gut peeking out from under her T-shirt. I wondered, in fact, if she might be pregnant, but one would hope not given the state of her. There were damp patches around the crotch of her tracksuit bottoms. In a packed bus it was massively unpleasant for everyone else to have to stand and be near her, and also very sad. She didn't look like she was homeless and nor did she appear to be an office worker who had overdone it after knocking off early on a Friday afternoon. But when you get into this kind of state, then clearly alcohol is a problem.

I knew I was being sanctimonious and hypocritical, because although things have never got that bad for me, I have done plenty to be ashamed of when plastered. But I wasn't really judging the drunks, just worrying about the possibility that I could join them. I always assume I am never going to be one of the purple-faced men with a W. C. Fields nose and nothing in my life but a can of beer and some urine-soaked sweatpants, but it wouldn't take much to push me into drinking enough for that to happen. I already spend my evenings shouting swear words in the faces of respectable people, but luckily I get paid for doing that and have a home. If I didn't have that home, I'd be homeless and not just in the most obvious sense.

The more I didn't drink, the more drunks I saw, like sobriety turned me into Haley Joel Osment in a dipsomaniac version of *The Sixth Sense*: 'I see drunk people... Walking around like regular people, only slightly less steadily. They don't see each other. They only see what they want to see... They don't know they're drunk.'

But the army of zombie pissheads even started haunting me at work, holding a mirror up to how I might once have been. A few days later I was doing a gig that was almost scuppered by a persistent and drunken heckler. It had been a lovely evening up to then, with some newer acts all doing interesting and funny stuff to a small but appreciative audience in one of London's many tiny clubs. People think it must get more nerve-wracking and difficult the bigger the crowd, but, in fact, smaller audiences are a greater challenge. Not only can you see every face, but it's harder for them to lose themselves in the moment and no one wants to be the only person laughing. Also, if ten per cent of people in a room with 2000 people are laughing, that's still a big noise. If you just get two people enjoying themselves out of twenty, it feels like an eggy failure.

Tonight, though, the crowd were all laughing and up for more experimental acts, understanding that if something didn't quite work that there'd be something amusing along in a minute. Everyone was having fun. I sat at the back, watching, laughing and looking forward to taking the stage.

But in the interval someone had found a girl crying in the toilets, complaining that she'd had the worst day of her life and the compere kindly, if unwisely, asked her if she wanted to come into the gig for free to see if that would cheer her up.

She repaid his generosity by heckling him the minute he stepped on to the stage. He was wearing a pork pie hat and she leered, 'Hey, did you steal your hat from Pete Doherty?' and laughed raucously and alone. You could actually hear the rest of the small crowd bristling.

This, unbelievably, would be the funniest thing she would say all night. She became increasingly rude to him, labouring under the delusion that the audience was finding her remarks more amusing than the charming host's act. In fact, it made everyone immediately aware that a great evening was in danger of being ruined. She sucked the atmosphere out of the room in less than 30 seconds, like a ghost that fed on happiness. Her misery had spread like a virus.

As I had fully expected, she didn't shut up when I came on stage, but kept up her constant unamusing commentary, mistiming her remarks so that they crashed into punchlines. Had I also been drunk, as I might well have been if this had happened just a month earlier, I might have lost my temper, gone for her too brutally, used a sledgehammer to crack this nut, and then once she was down carried on hitting her till her head was a mess of squashed brain and bone splinter. But my mind was clear and I had no doubt that she was David and I was Goliath, but that she was so pissed that she'd forgotten her slingshot. So I dealt with her calmly and with measured steadiness, totally unfazed by her ruining my jokes, resolving to change the performance so it would incorporate her.

'You're not funny!' she shouted.

'Perhaps it would be fairer to actually let me get a joke out before you make that judgement,' I told her. 'I mean, you might well be right, but I am not sure how you would know, unless you're psychic. And if you're psychic then I would expect you to have prepared better responses to these put-downs.'

'Yeah... well... you say that, but... you're rubbish.'

'I think we have just proven that this young lady is not psychic, ladies and gentlemen.'

'No, it's all right. Ignore me. You're funny,' she shouted with no apparent sarcasm or awareness of this complete turnaround in her assessment of my performance.

'Thanks. And I'm going to cut you a bit of slack because you're in a bit of a state and a little bit tiddly... though something about you tells me that you might be as much of a nightmare when you're sober.'

The rest of the audience laughed rather heartily, detecting the truth in this remark, but she didn't really understand what I was saying. Drunks are like tiny children and if you talk fast enough and use a few complicated words they can't make sense of what's being said.

If this was a duel then I was armed with an ornate pistol which always shot true and clear and she in turn had a runny blancmange, which she was cupping in her hands and which if she tried to throw at me was just going to fly back into her face.

Yet with the natural instinct of the drunk she was managing to hone in on all my insecurities.

'Who ate all the pies?'

'Are you insinuating I am fat?' I asked. 'Because I have actually lost over half a stone this year, so imagine how much funnier that heckle would have been if you had got it in a fortnight ago. I'm not that fat. I don't think I've eaten *all* the pies. I think I've only eaten about four of the pies, leaving plenty of pies in the fridge for the proper fatties to have a go at.'

I was pleased with that off the top of my head, but nothing was going to make this woman be quiet and she seemed to feel that the fact that she had had a bad day was enough of an excuse to ruin everyone else's.

Her babbling taunts continued unabated. In her head she was matching me blow for blow.

'Quieten down,' I told her. 'You're too talkative. You're loquacious. It's annoying. You're the one woman in the world that a bloke would put Rohypnol in your drink and leave you in the pub.'

She was flabbergasted. Drunk, pretty, young women seem to be the most persistent hecklers because no one has ever told them to shut up in their lives and they are especially affronted when it finally happens. Most men, however pissed, will back down once they've been humiliated.

'Is that a waste of Rohypnol?' I asked myself. 'It's quite expensive.' 'No, no,' I replied. 'It's the right thing to do. Tonight I think I'll just go home and have a wank.'

The audience, united in hatred for this party-pooper, lapped up my remarks despite their cruelty. They knew they weren't getting the act that they would have had if she had not been there, but were getting something different and improvised and a little exciting. We all have to deal with arseholes at work every now and again and they pitied and empathised with me and yet envied me for the fact that, unlike them, I was able to tell the arsehole that they were an arsehole. There was a catharsis for us all.

But I was most impressed with how I remained in control and how I didn't lose my temper, which I have often done in such circumstances.

'At times like these,' I said with an exasperated expression on my face, 'when you get a heckler who is never going to shut up and is ruining the gig for all the people who have paid to see some comedy, I sometimes wonder if we could get away with a *Murder on the Orient Express* style scenario. What if we all stabbed her once each and then when the police came tell them that a masked man ran into the gig and stabbed her twenty times? As long as we all stuck to the story we'd get away with murder!'

I think if I had pressed the point, I might actually have been able to make it happen, so deep was the hatred for this awful harpy.[4]

'What's your proper job?' shouted the woman, in a further attempt to undermine me.

'How do you mean?' I asked, feigning misunderstanding.

'Well, you're not funny enough to do this professionally, are you?'

---

5. To see me dealing with another drunk along the same lines, put Richard Herring + heckler into YouTube.

'I seem to be doing OK.'

'Yeah, but if you were successful you wouldn't be playing this tiny room to twenty people, would you?'

And this was it. This was the moment I'd been unknowingly waiting for ever since I'd turned 40. Six months ago I may have crumpled, sat on the floor, sobbing, 'Yes, yes, you're right! Why aren't I more successful? Why am I playing this little club which isn't even full? What happened? I used to be on telly!'

But now, standing on stage, stone-cold sober and my brain clear and focused, I knew she was wrong. Instead of crushing me, she only reminded me of my immense good fortune. I could see how these smaller gigs are in many ways preferable to the massive ones. Because the audience is more up for experimentation, because anything could happen, because I really had to prove myself, because I was doing a brilliant, childish, stupid job and had been doing it for twenty years and hopefully would do it for twenty more. Maybe the venues would get bigger (they couldn't be much smaller than tonight's), maybe they wouldn't, but as long as I was out there doing it, making a living and making people laugh, then that was all that mattered. If I kept working at it one day I might be as funny as Billy Connolly is just standing in a lift.

In this most unlikely of circumstances I felt at one with myself, comfortable with who I was and what I was doing. I had learned to live with what I was. I had grown up enough to know that it wasn't a cause for concern that I had such a childish occupation.

Bit by bit I was getting things into perspective. It took someone with no perspective to help me on the way.

I wrote in my diary that night, '*I love my job.*'

Things were progressing rapidly with Catherine too. We'd met up a couple more times and walked and talked and kissed a little without immolating. I would accompany her back to her bus stop at the end of the night, hope that the bus wouldn't arrive too soon and then kiss her when it did, not wanting to let her go. Yet aside from stealing kisses I made no further overtures and did not try to persuade her to come back to mine or let me come back to hers, as the more desperate 2007 Richard Herring might have done. I wanted to do it all properly and I wanted her to be ready and free. It was becoming clearer and clearer that these feelings were mutual and, despite her current unavailability, that eventually we would be together. The instinctive forces at play were too powerful and too strong to overcome. She was doing an admirable job of resisting them but eventually she would have to succumb. We had more chance of controlling the wind and making it do our bidding than we did of stopping our love taking its course.

It felt like this had been going on for weeks, but the year wasn't even two weeks old when we went on our third date. We agreed we'd go to the cinema, but hadn't decided what we wanted to see and so spent some time trawling the cinemas of the West End, not finding anything that appealed. Finally, when indecision was in danger of stranding us out on the cold January streets, we settled on *Dan in Real Life* simply because it had the bloke from the American version of *The Office* in it. We were still in high spirits despite all the walking around and were finding the whole shambles charming and amusing in a way that you can only do at the start of a romance.

The cinema we ended up in, in the heart of London's entertainment centre, seemed to be set up to suck as much fun out of the experience of movie-going as was possible. The staff were miserable, the lighting in the foyer harsh and unforgiving and a sense of gloom hung in the air. We bought our tickets from a surly youth at the counter and then headed up to the screen. We were a little early, but when we attempted to get on to the escalator a middle-aged female employee of the cinema barged into our path and barked at us, 'The screen is not open yet!' It was ludicrously abrupt. From my memory there was a bar on the next level, but we were not allowed to go up. It hadn't been a polite rebuff, we had been made to feel that we had done something terribly wrong, like being yelled at by a bulldoggish deputy headmistress.

We laughed it off and stood by a window and looked out on to Shaftesbury Avenue. Catherine seemed more relaxed about physical contact tonight and we kissed and held each other. As we enjoyed this private moment, the yelping woman interrupted us. 'You can go up now!' she hollered. When we did not immediately move, still in an embrace, she shouted again, 'Excuse me! You can go up!'

We had been shouted at for daring to want to ascend the stairs a few seconds before the cinema was ready and now we were being condemned for dawdling. Another person might have thought to leave these happy lovers to their fripperies, but she had a job to do and there was no place for anyone having fun tonight.

Luckily for her, given our choice of film, that was going to be unlikely. Both of us quickly tired of the mawkish movie, but I wasn't complaining as it allowed us to behave like the teenagers that we certainly weren't and make out on the back row. Halfway through the film Catherine leaned across to me. I thought she wanted more kissing – and who can blame her, she's only human – but instead she whispered, 'I've split up with my boyfriend.'

It was the news I wanted to hear, though I couldn't be too delighted about it because I knew how tough that must have been for her and especially for him. It wasn't nice to know that my actions would have caused this turmoil, especially given the circumstances of how this had all begun. But it's a rare occasion when two people meet and fall in love when they are both totally free from commitment. As wonderful as these feelings are for the couple involved, there are always likely to be others for whom it will bring nothing but pain. I have been the casualty enough times in the past.

That night, as usual, I walked Catherine back to her bus stop – there was no question of this being the right time for us to spend the night together, as much as I wanted to wake up with her. I held her and kissed her and reluctantly let her go when her bus arrived all too soon.

I knew now that she would be mine.

My gut was rather smug. It had known long before the rest of me.

Sex is an act of aggression between two people who hate each other.

CHAPTER 16
FIRST-NIGHT NERVES

'Who are you and what have you done with the real Richard Herring?' Emma asked as she pulled at the skin on my face, presumably hoping to unmask the impostor or cyborg beneath.

'I am the real one,' I protested.

'No, you're not. You're an impressive doppelgänger, I will give you that. You've got so much right.' She circled me as she ticked things off on an imaginary clipboard. 'The stupid hairstyle, the ridiculously short legs. The voice, I have to say, is excellent as is the unusual smell – that must have taken you many long weeks to duplicate in the laboratory and the zoo. But I'm on to you. You're not Richard Keith Herring.'

'All right, what gave me away?'

'I first realised something was amiss when you were at the bar and, thinking I wasn't listening, ordered yourself –' she referred to an invisible notepad '– a pint of lime and soda! Oh dear. Oh deary deary me. The real Richard Herring might have ordered many drinks, a Guinness, a lager beer, even on occasions a glass of white wine, but lime and soda? If only you'd asked for vodka in it you would have been fine. Lime and soda? I should coco!'

'I've given up drinking, Emma. I've done that before.'

'All right, possibly, but look over there – two attractive young women in their early twenties, one displaying an enticing proportion of bosomage, another with rather shapely legs. You, evil robot Richard Herring, did not even give them a second look. And thus you are unmasked.'

'That is, admittedly, strange, but I only have eyes for one woman now.'

'Is it me?' asked Emma, possibly with the merest hint of sarcasm.

'No. It definitely isn't, you hideous slattern.'

'That is the kind of thing Richard Herring would say. Your research is excellent. But the worst mistake you made was here…' She prodded my stomach and then my jowls. 'Nowhere near enough padding, mate. I can appreciate that there's only so much cotton wool in the world, but you're way too slim. But if I'm honest with you, I much prefer you to the genuine article, so if you don't tell anyone, then I won't.'

'All right, all right. And I would have gotten away with it too…'

Emma joined in, laughing. 'If it wasn't for you pesky, meddling kids!'

'Ooooh Shraggy!' Emma added, doing a perfect impression of yet another cartoon character.

This was a rare night out for me. Apart from my dates with Catherine I'd been keeping myself to myself, staying at home, reading, eating stir-fries, drinking liquorice tea. And what was remarkable was how comfortable I was with this new lifestyle. A few weeks before I would have felt bereft and alone and like a tragic failure, but I was happy being on my own with my thoughts now. Mainly because those thoughts were lighter and happier and less self-critical. If I looked at the moon now I didn't want to howl at it, but it made me feel full of romance. That the moon is worshipped by both lovers and the insane is perhaps not just a coincidence.

'I can't believe how well the diet is going,' I told Emma. 'And I'm so full of energy it's a bit frightening.'

'Yeah, that's because you've got a demanding 27-year-old woman putting you through your paces.'

'No, not really. We haven't actually had sex yet…'

'What?! Wait. You know I was joking about you not being you, but now I'm wondering if I was right. You're dating a girl, exclusively, and not having sex with her, or anyone else? What's happened to you? I mean, not that that it isn't good. It just isn't you!'

'I know it's a bit crazy, Em, and I'm not saying my life has totally changed for ever. I am well aware that I've given up drinking before, only to fall spectacularly off the wagon, and I've lost weight before, only to then stuff my face with more chocolate than Augustus Gloop managed when he fell into Willy Wonka's river…'

'Oompah loompah didgerdoo…' Emma sang.

'Shut up. And I know I've been in love before, only to have my heart crushed into the dust, or to crush someone else's heart when I've got itchy feet after seven or eight months…'

'I can't believe you didn't let me sing the Oompah Loompah song,' pouted Emma.

'And I know this evangelical me is as much of a midlife crisis as the degenerate, libidinous, crapulous, oafishness I was displaying the last time I saw you, but…' I drifted off.

'But what?' said Emma.

'I just really, really hope it will all work out this time. I just think that maybe I'm growing up.'

Emma blew a small raspberry.

'I don't mean getting all serious and humourless and wearing a suit and tie… though I did wear one for a gig last week and it felt really cool…' Emma groaned. 'Just maybe leaving behind some of the stupid old habits that were making me unhappy.'

'That's all well and good,' Emma agreed, 'but don't let the pendulum swing too far. It's good that you're calming down a bit, but don't become boring. You can grow up a bit without becoming a dull and grumpy old man.'

'Not much danger of that,' I said. 'Your round. I'll have another lime and soda, but can you ask him to put a bit less lime in than last time. It was a little bit strong for my tastes.'

I got a deserved slap in the head.

*

Perhaps my mature approach to life was having an effect on my outlook. I seemed to be getting more concerned by poor etiquette of my fellow human beings. Earlier that day I had stopped to fill up my car with petrol, and the passenger in the car parked in front of me opened his door and dropped out his paper coffee cup right on to the forecourt. He was less than a metre from a bin and the car was stationary. Such flagrant disrespect for other people and general flippant laziness made me tut like an old lady. I was not so foolish as to openly chastise him, for fear of being knifed in the eye, but maybe I should have said something. Instead I waited until he had gone and then picked up and binned the cup myself. Which is exactly what my dad would have done. Was that a good thing?

And when I was at the gym (as I regularly was now) the self-ishness of some other users was also making me fume. I was amazed by how few people clean up after themselves, leaving their dirty towels on the benches by the lockers. It seemed such a simple matter to pick up your wet towel and place it in the bins provided, but that is too much trouble for some people. Presumably they feel they are paying to be a member of the gym and there are people paid to clean the changing rooms, so why shouldn't they just leave it for them? But why make that shitty job worse and what about the other gym users whose space is being filled with dirty, stinky towels? As another young man walked away from his soggy, soiled towel on the bench I wanted to shout after him, 'Excuse me, mate, I don't think your mum works here. You have to tidy up after yourself.' But he was big and muscly and pumped up after a session on the weights and I thought he might hit me. Or knowing my luck, he'd turn and say, 'Actually she does.' And then a tiny old lady would come round the corner, pick up his towel for him, while staring lasciviously at the bare bottoms of the other gym users.

Again I chose to clear the towels up myself.

I was also becoming quite obsessive about plastic bags. It comes from a good place – I was trying to cut down my plastic bag consumption (I don't eat them and anyone who says I do is lying) and so was attempting to remember to take my 'bag for life' bags out with me at all times when I was going shopping and also reuse old regular shopping bags as bin-liners and so on. I loved my 'bags for life', which was another sea change. To the old me even a 'bag for life' would have been too much of a commitment. What if I wanted to use another bag in the future? I couldn't have taken the chance.

But my obsessions, once knowing and comic, were now getting crotchety and geriatric. I got quite annoyed when my friends arrived for poker bringing drinks and crisps in carrier bags and thus adding another five or six bags to my drawer of bags. I knew this was faintly ridiculous (although I do feel that people's reticence to be concerned about this issue pretty much demonstrates that the environment is fucked – if we can't even carry a plastic bag with us then what hope do we have on the big stuff), but was aware I was only a matter of years away from being one of those angry old people, obsessed with trivia and furious when their routine is disturbed. I fear mental illness because my job involves skirting round the edge of it, like a child playing at seeing how close to the fire he can get. I know one day I could fall into the flames.

I got annoyed with myself on one supermarket trip, when I took four 'bags for life' with me, but decided I would also recycle a few of my non-'bag for life' bags to try and help the world. I took about eight of them with me and stuffed them into the small and packed receptacle that Sainsbury's put aside for recycled bags. I felt a bit bad that some of the bags I was recycling were perfectly good for reuse and knew in an optimum world I should have run them into the ground before recycling, but at least I was being better than nearly everyone else in the shop.

Feeling smug and superior, I filled my trolley with a month's worth of shopping. While I'm at the big supermarket I like to stock up on cleaning fluids and toilet paper and other non-perishable goods. I got to the checkout and started bagging it all up, then realised with horror that I was not going to have quite enough bags for all the groceries I had bought.

'I don't believe it,' I complained to the man at the till. 'I actually brought some perfectly usable bags with me but I recycled them when I got here. Now I need to take two more bags from you so I can get all my shopping home. How annoying is that?'

He shrugged as if it wasn't all that annoying or important.

'Don't you see? I could have reused the bags I had recycled, but instead I have not only not reused them, I have added two extra bags to the plague of plastic bags out there in the world.'

'Ah well, it's just two bags,' he offered.

'If everyone thought like that do you know how many bags would be out there?'

He shook his head and awaited an answer. I realised I didn't know.

'A lot more, that's how many. Still, I'm not going to beat myself up about it. I'm still six bags up as I have recycled eight and taken away only two. But why didn't I wait till I'd finished shopping until I recycled the bags? What an idiot. Anyway, goodbye.'

The only way I could have looked more like a mental old person was to have had one of those little shopping bags on wheels to pull away behind me as I left.

Actually, maybe I should get one of those. Think of the bags I'll save.

Was Emma right to express concern? Was I going too far the other way with my new lifestyle? Did I need to find a balance? I wasn't 21, but I wasn't 61 either.

And I could fight against the ageing process as much as I liked, but it wouldn't make me any younger. As I was looking for my membership card at the gym one day, I accidentally pulled out my organ donor card. I had had it in various wallets since 8 November 1994 and, to be honest, it looked like it. It was so worn down that it was not immediately recognisable as a donor card. In fact, only the 'nor' of donor was still properly legible and the 'card' bit had worn away completely.

Over the years it had got all furry at the edges, slightly ripped and only scarcely functional – much like the organs it promised to donate. Back then I was 27 and relatively fit and my organs might have been of some use to somebody, had I been unlucky enough to die. Now, I was not sure that even the most organ-needy person in the world would really want to have any of my organs deep inside them.

Even though my liver must have been in slightly better shape than it was three weeks ago, if I was unfortunate enough to be waiting for an untimely death to save my life, I'd really be wanting someone with a newer and less fucked-up donor card. Mine seemed to work as a sort of metaphorical endoscope, showing the state of my insides by its own appearance. There is something both comforting and deeply upsetting about that. I sensed some kind of 'Donor Card of Dorian Gray' style short story forming in my head.

I am sure some unfortunate soul might still find my old and battered organs are better than their own, so I decided to keep the card in my wallet and hope it is recognised for what it is by any doctor declaring me dead and not just thrown away as a piece of mouldy and unpleasant card. Just in case, I also signed up to the NHS Organ Donor Register (https://www.uktransplant.org.uk/), which would hopefully clear up any confusion. That presumably won't degrade, though I think it would be a nice touch if it included cartoon drawings of your organs alongside your details, and they slowly shrivelled and turned green as you got older. It would help doctors in selecting the best donor out of two pos-sible choices, I suppose.

Fogeyism aside, my new lifestyle was leading to a contentment that I hadn't had before. Not that I hadn't enjoyed my years of shallow debauchery, because in many ways it had been phenomenal to be so out of control, but if I carried on that way then I probably wouldn't live to see my 50th birthday. As brilliant as it would be to die in a hotel room snorting cocaine off the breasts of two hookers (or in my case, eating Flumpses with them), I kind of wanted to stick around for a bit longer than that. And my new career plan was to try and stay alive as long as possible, keep working and gain a level of notoriety just through my persistence and perspicacity. So people would say, 'God, he's still going, is he? Well, you have to admire him for that at least.' Plus if I could outlive the other comics then I would be able to write the history of our times and give myself a much bigger role than I actually had.

I was conscious that the turnaround in my life might not be a totally positive thing. It is always tempting as a human to think that when things aren't right you should just do the opposite and that will make you happy. So the miserable drunk will seek an epiphany in being teetotal, the soulless shagger will decide monogamy is his salvation, the priggish Christian will think that maybe Satanism might bring more personal satisfaction (though alas it more usually happens the other way round). Because if something is making you unhappy, our logic runs, then the opposite will obviously make you happy.

It doesn't work like that, of course. Just because something is opposite in one sense doesn't mean it will be the opposite in every other way as well. And being sober or monogamous might just make me miserable in a different way to being drunk and promiscuous.

But it's not a bad thing to take some time out from what you're doing and consider whether it's a good idea. Drinking wasn't really making me totally unhappy. But if I had kept it up then things might have started to suffer. And in the short term I was appreciating the change, even though I knew it would be better to find some kind of balance rather than veering from extreme to extreme.

I was at least showing that it was possible for me to operate without alcohol. I was still funny and still capable of social interaction. I had proven not that I wasn't an alcoholic, but that I didn't need booze to have fun or more pertinently to have a successful date. If anything, being sober meant that I had enjoyed Catherine's company more and been a more entertaining companion myself and more likely to do the right thing.

On our next date we went to my local snooker hall to shoot a few frames of pool. This was the first time Catherine had come to Shepherd's Bush and we were both aware that this might be the first night where I didn't walk her to the bus stop and bid her goodbye. We weren't just playing pool, this was an intricate dance of love around the green baize, invested with all kinds of symbolism: the phallic cue, the masturbatory cue action, the spherical and colourful orbs and the balls dropping into the pocket (though if in lovemaking your balls drop into the pocket, you're doing it wrong).

It was sexy and fun to be competing, however frivolously, and although it's not a contact sport there are plenty of opportunities to brush against one another seductively. Better still, if I won a frame Catherine would give me a kiss and if she won, I would give her a kiss. I was a winner even when I was a loser.

The first few frames were close, neither of us proving to be particularly adept at the game, but as she downed lager and I downed water, the advantage fell to me. She was silly and giddy and I was sober, though also a little giddy. I really felt that she was a free agent for the first time, and so did she, and we were able to enjoy ourselves unfettered by other commitments.

I had already decided that I wanted to be with her and her alone, but tonight I attempted to express it.

'I want you to be my girl,' I told her.

She looked confused and thrown by this, though she had also had three pints of lager. 'What does that involve?' she asked.

That wasn't quite the response I had been anticipating from my romantic entreaty. 'Isn't it obvious what that would involve? Surely everyone in the world knows what that involves. It's pretty clear.'

'I'm honestly not sure what you mean.'

Although she was smart and funny, Catherine seemed to have occasional gaps in her knowledge, both of popular culture and sometimes social convention, which had roused my suspicions a little bit. There was really only one possible reason for this.

'Are you an alien?' I asked, not entirely joking. 'Because if you are then that's still cool, I'm still interested in seeing you, and if I am honest I am quite into the idea of intergalactic, interspecies relations. I'll happily impregnate you to provide the first hybrid baby from our two different worlds. But you need to tell me if you are. You can trust me.'

'I'm not an alien,' she insisted. 'I just don't know what you mean by me being your girl or what you're expecting of me.'

'I mean I want you to be my girlfriend. I want to be your boyfriend,' I told her. 'I know it's early days and we haven't known each other all that long, though I have to say it really feels like we've known each other for ever… I want us to be together. In an exclusive relationship.'

Catherine, alien or not, now seemed to get it. 'Oh right,' she replied. 'It's just I've only just split up with my boyfriend and… I really like you… but I don't know if I want to get into something like that straight away.'

'No, no, of course not. But look, you can obviously do whatever you want, but I know that I want to be with you and I'm not going to be with anyone else but you.'

There was a bit of a pause.

'It's your shot,' said Catherine, like an alien who didn't understand human conventions. But she is shy and self-conscious and perhaps she was just a bit flummoxed by my candour and didn't know how to respond. I wasn't sure how things would work out either – of course we never can be – but I knew that here and now she was all that I needed and wanted.

Midnight had passed by the time we got bored of the game. Catherine had carried on drinking and her already limited pool skills had fallen to pieces. 'Do you want to come back to mine for another drink?' I asked.

She smiled coyly, not quite wanting to make eye contact. 'OK,' she meekly agreed.

The wonder of booze is that it acts as a kind of magic carpet or time machine which transports anyone who has drunk enough of it from the bar to home in what feels like seconds. So usually when I have propositioned someone, from my perspective at least, we have pretty much teleported immediately to bed. Catherine was well aboard that fantastical ride, but I was three weeks sober and had to live every nervous second of the ten-minute walk to my house. And I was alarmingly anxious about everything, simply because Catherine meant so much to me. When filled with booze and nonchalance, the path from bar to bed is an easy one, but tonight I needed everything to be right, to not let

Catherine down, to be everything she needed me to be. Suddenly I realised why sleeping with someone on the first date can be a blessing, because at least it gets it out of the way. There had been so much anticipation and so much of a battle to win this woman's heart and I felt under almost impossible pressure.

On top of that, I realised that she was rather more than tipsy now. 'Are you sure you want to do this?' I asked as our footsteps echoed on the rain-sodden paving stones around Shepherd's Bush Green.

'Yes, I am,' she slurred, with a big smile on her beautiful mouth. 'Don't you?'

'God, yes, of course I do. I just don't want to take advantage.'

She laughed. 'You're really not taking advantage.'

'It's just that I haven't drunk anything and you're just a tinsy bit drunk and...'

'I'm not drunk!' came the indignant response.

'You've had four or five pints. I think you might be.'

'I know when I'm drunk and I'm not drunk,' she proclaimed. Charmingly she walked into a bollard at that exact moment. She covered her blushing face. 'Oh, I can't believe I did that. How embarrassing. I'm not drunk though. I just didn't see that stupid bollard there.'

I laughed and hugged her, but still felt a little uncomfortable about this imbalance.

Everything had happened much quicker than I had anticipated. A week ago I was sure it would take months to convince her to leave her boyfriend, yet here we were now, heading home together, about to spend the night together. If I had been more drunk then it wouldn't have bothered me, no doubt, but I was in control and compos mentis and it was hard to let go.

Back home, in my lounge, we kissed on the sofa and I had a crisis of conscience, not only because she was pickled and I was not. Were we doing the right thing? I wondered if this was like the bit at the end of *The Graduate*, when Dustin Hoffman has persuaded Katharine Ross to leave her fiancé at the altar and run off with him. They are exhilarated and happy and caught up in the crazy romance and then they sit on the back of the bus and their faces drop as they consider the reality of what they've done.

What if all this really had been about the difficulty of the conquest? What if I had subconsciously stolen her away from her boyfriend just to prove that I could? Were my friends right to be sceptical about my claims to have fallen in love? Now I had won her, would I lose interest? For just a second I felt that I had got carried away with a dream and that I was possibly the biggest shit on the planet earth.

Here I was kissing her and all of a sudden I was terrified that I would let this woman down.

But that in itself was a positive thing: the fact that I feared that. Such trepidation and nervousness was very unusual for me and I knew I was only having these paranoid thoughts because I cared about her and really wanted this to work. Of course, as with any relationship, there is every chance it will go wrong. But I didn't want this one to go wrong. I wanted everything to be right.

It was only a momentary wobble. I wanted to impress her and was also concerned that she was too drunk to know what she was doing, or to remember it. I wanted our first time together to be meaningful and considered and so, with my sensible new mature head on, I took her to bed, and though I wasn't exactly the perfect gentleman, I insisted that we waited until the morning before we made love, just so she was sure this was really what she wanted.

Was I growing up?

In the morning, with balance restored, there were no more wobbles (or at least only the kind that you would hope for in the circumstances) and Catherine was mine and I was hers.

On Valentine's Day I gave her a single Ferrero Rocher chocolate, promising to give her another the next year and another the next, until finally she had enough for the pyramid.

Alcohol, the cause of, and solution to, all life's problems.
Homer Simpson

CHAPTER 17
OH DEAR, WHAT CAN THE MATTER BE?

'I think that's Chris Martin,' I whispered to Catherine.

'Who?' she said.

'What planet are you from? You must know who Chris Martin is. The lead singer of Coldplay.'

'I know who Chris Martin is, I just didn't hear what you said.' Although of course that would be what her alien superiors would have told her to say in such circumstances.

'And those other blokes with him, they're probably the other men in the band. It's impossible to know. No one knows what any of them look like.'

'One of them is holding a guitar.'

'He's probably... the guitar one.' There wasn't a person on earth who would know his name. Including him.

'That's pretty cool, don't you think?' I commented. 'That they're just waiting for their bags like everyone else? You'd think most internationally famous pop stars – though not galactically famous, clearly – would be off to sit in the jacuzzi in their limo, leaving their roadies to do the waiting and lifting. Look at them, pretending to be just regular people.'

We had just arrived in Catania airport in Sicily for a week's holiday. It was 7 April, Catherine and I were about three months into our relationship and she was now officially my girl and I was her boy (well, old man). We were still high on our new love and very much looking forward to spending seven days and nights together, with no other distractions. I had been away on tour and had missed her terribly.

Even more remarkably, today was my 99th consecutive day without a drink of alcohol. Unbelievably I made it through my entire tour without stumbling. I had always thought that a couple of glasses of wine were a necessary part of the post-gig winding-down process and that I wouldn't sleep without them, but it was actually much more relaxing to get away from the venues, now not even thinking about seeing if I could pull a woman from the audience, and watch DVDs or read back in my hotel. As often as not I would drive home, to save myself some money and to give me a chance to spend some time with my amazing girlfriend. I enjoyed the tour more than any other I had done; certainly it was a massive improvement on the one of the previous year, with all its tears and tantrums and ineffectual fisticuffs.

I had also managed to complete my sit-com script while on the road and had started work on my new stand-up show. Being boring seemed to be paying off. And though my new routines were no longer of fighting and fucking, but gym towels and plastic bags, I was still making people laugh in spite of my sobriety.

I was also about as slim as I have ever been in my adult life. Despite inevitably putting on a bit of weight while out on the road, when it's sometimes hard to get healthy food, I was still almost two stone lighter than I had been at Christmas. When I was packing for the holiday I had tried on some trousers that I hadn't worn for over ten years and they were a comfortable fit. I realised I had a whole new wardrobe of old clothes to take with me. I felt ecstatic.

I was feeling so incredibly healthy that I was wondering if I would ever drink again. And yet it seemed a little unfair on Catherine. She had been patient and understanding through this long and dull experiment and very supportive. After one night out, she'd come back to mine and I'd poured her a glass of wine while I made myself a bowl of Weetabix for supper. Self-consciously I said, 'God, you must think I'm a strange old man, obsessed with Weetabix.'

She simply replied, 'There are no rules!'

I laughed and said, 'You're very cool. I like you a lot.'

But I was starting to feel like a bit of a party-pooper, guilty for insisting she drink alone. And here we were, on a romantic week away. It seemed a shame not to have a Peroni or an occasional glass of wine while I was there.

And yet the compulsive part of my brain knew that there was no way I could get this far and not take it to triple figures. I would get to 100 days without booze and then make a decision about whether I was going to carry on with it, or try and ease myself back into a life of (hopefully) moderate drinking. If I carried on past the 100-day mark then surely I was pretty much bound to go for the year. It sent a bit of a chill down my spine. While I wasn't missing the alcohol, I was concerned I might never be interesting again.

'I'm sure it's him, you know,' I said as Catherine watched the suitcases, that typically did not yet include ours, travelling round the conveyor belt like giant and unpalatable sushi dishes. 'But you'd think he'd be being mobbed if it was.'

Just on cue a young man approached the possible Chris Martin and asked if he could have a photo. Possible Chris Martin smiled and nodded and then when the fan tried to take it himself said, 'What's the point if you're not in it?' and asked a woman who looked like she might be a PA or a record company executive to operate the camera. It was low-key and friendly and he genuinely seemed delighted to be doing it. I was impressed by his humility.

'It's him,' I said with triumph. 'I wonder if I should go and say hello.'

'What, cos you're both "celebrities"?' Catherine joked sarcastically.

'No,' I replied with mock affront. 'And I *am* a celebrity, actually. I played the voice of a spider on a school's TV programme in 1993. But the tape went wrong and they had to rerecord it and they got a different actor in, but still…'

Catherine laughed.

'In actual fact, I am acquainted with Chris, as I call him… Well, I've met him a couple of times before. Years ago, before he was a superstar. He's friends with Al Murray and I was at a couple of parties with him. In fact one of my few remaining claims to fame is that I have played Trivial Pursuit with Chris Martin.'

'It's an impressive claim.'

'And it was funny, because every time his pie-slice container was on a History question, Al and me would say, "He's landed on Yellll-ooo-oow!"'

Catherine shook her head at my childishness.

'I'd quite like to play him again now, because he's released more songs. And if he landed on green I could sing, "Questions of science, science and nature!"'

I stared wistfully at Chris Martin.

'You should go and say hello if you know him,' Catherine observed.

'No, no, I don't want to bother him and he might not remember who I am.'

'Oh, I am sure you and your Trivial Pursuit antics are etched on his memory. I should think he wakes in a cold sweat most mornings having recurring nightmares about it.'

'I could go off you,' I lied.

I was actually in a bit of a quandary. I didn't want to impose myself on him, but also worried that he might recognise me, and see me blanking him and feel I was being rude. But ultimately I knew my place and remained in fitting awe at his celebrity and left him to it, preferring to observe from a distance and see what a charming, genuine, unaffected, normal person he clearly is. You know, when he isn't drawing stuff on his hands, marrying movie stars and naming his children after fruit.

Funnily enough, I had crossed paths with Al Murray just a week or so before the holiday. I was being healthy and fit and eschewing public transport to walk back home from central London after coffee with a friend. I had a carrier bag with my dinner in it, microwaveable low-calorie sausage and mash. I was really looking forward to it. I was just crossing the Shepherd's Bush roundabout when I heard a voice shouting my name. It was Al Murray passing in a chauffeured, executive BMW. He offered me a lift and even though I was nearly home by now and I had to run a good couple of hundred metres to get to a point where the car could stop, I accepted. Al was on his way home from a rehearsal for his TV show.

'How's your tour going?' he asked.

'It's been really great fun this year. Numbers are gradually moving upwards and the show went down well. I wasn't miserable at all. Which is a bit of achievement. How's your chat show going? I saw the one with Lembit Opik. What a twat!'

'Yeah, it's been going really well. People seem to really like it, but there's no way of knowing if the channel will recommission it.' I could see the worry etched on his face and remembered that even when your career is flying high, there are, if anything, more things to fret about. It's hard to get to a place where you feel happy and satisfied.

Our relative levels of success were bound to jar a little. Al is now an instantly recognisable, proper TV star, while I can walk down the road from Holland Park with a low-calorie ready meal in a plastic bag without anyone bothering me (apart from Al Murray). What is cool is that I think both of us are happy with our different lots. Neither of us would swap places with the other (though Al does like sausage and mash), but it's weird the way fortunes rise and fall. Five years before I might have been envious or angry at my relative lack of success, but I had things in proportion now. I am also man enough to be happy when my friends are successful. It's not a competition. There are ups and downs in our chosen profession and I had learned that you must enjoy the successes while you have them and just ride out the lows. As long as I can afford sausages and mash then I am happy.

*

Catherine and I were staying in Syracuse, a beautiful town on the south-east coast of Sicily with a rich history dating back to the ancient Greeks and the birthplace of Archimedes, the man who discovered that if you get in a bath with too much water in it, some of the water will spill out. Genius!

I'd been very grown up and booked us into a posh hotel and hired a car, though was childishly nervous about driving in a foreign country for the first time and confused by the Sicilians' unusual attitude to roundabouts and any kind of driving rules at all. It made travelling around a seat-of-the-pants exhilarating dance with death. But it's not a bad thing to be reminded of your mortality. I wasn't so scared of dying any more, resolving to live life harder in the face of its inevitability.

I got lost and flustered once we were in the town itself, finding myself driving down impossibly narrow ancient back streets, convinced I was going to scrape or dent the paintwork and incur all kinds of fiscal penalties. But finally we found the hotel and settled in.

Our hotel room had a lounge as well as a bedroom and a balcony that looked out over a secluded courtyard. Most importantly it had a big bed. It was going to be a great week.

We had a little walk around the town and found a restaurant where we ate giant cheese-laden pizzas (the diet was out of the window for a week). It was a massive struggle to resist the lure of a cheeky beer, but I held firm.

It felt like we were on our honeymoon, so happy and in love were we. The next morning at breakfast we were delighted to be offered proper and gorgeous cappuccinos, along with a vast array of delicious pastries and fruit.

While we were love's young (and not so young) dream, I was amused to watch the couple at the next table at breakfast, who were less enamoured with each other. They were both in their late forties and from their studied silence and frostiness towards one another had clearly been together for a while – familiarity breeds contempt, always remember this. They barely spoke to each other and when they did it was little more than a grunt. The man popped outside for a smoke. There was a fire door right next to their table, which closed behind him. Five minutes later he had finished his cigarette and his face appeared hopefully at the window. It was time for his wife to let him in. But even though she was no more than two steps away and could almost have reached over from her seat, she shrugged and sighed and indicated that he should go round the building and come in another door. Not surprisingly he was somewhat aggrieved by this suggestion, but who knows what slight had occurred earlier for him to deserve this treatment and he vociferously gestured for her to stop being so stupid and to let him in. She was indeed being ludicrously petty and after a couple of minutes made a big show of getting out of her seat and pushing the door for him. He entered and by now was too cross to thank her and they sat in fuming silence for the rest of the meal. It was spectacularly childish even by my standards.

Catherine and I laughed behind our napkins, though when one considers that they have to spend all their time in this battle of wills, scoring points off one another, it is actually mildly tragic. You only seem to see two types of couple on holiday, either those who have just got together or just been married who are ridiculously happy and demonstrative about their affection, or those who have been together for too long, have nothing left to say and can only derive any pleasure from tormenting their companion who is both their gaoler and their prisoner. The new couples never seem to look at the old and see a frightening vision of their inevitable future and the old couple never seem to look at the new and remember that they once felt this way too, which might rekindle some lost emotion and warm their heart (or more likely break it). Ultimately love is doomed and yet we all carry on despite the mountains of historical evidence ahead of us. You have to admire this triumph of hope over experience.

Would our love transmute over time and inevitably change from this breathtaking butterfly to a stinking, fetid grub?

We spent the day sightseeing. We had fun looking at the old cathedral (incorporating columns from the ancient Temple of

Athena), the archaeological park and the catacombs. At the entrance was a statue of a cherub weeing into a fountain. It made me giggle like a four-year- old. Though I had made some progress as an adult, I hadn't lost my puerile sense of humour. But, I wondered, does anyone not find a weeing cherub amusing? Surely even the most pretentious art critic must internally snigger when he sees such a thing, even though he would do all he could to deny such an accusation. It's funny. It was more evidence for me that a childish sense of glee is something to be prized.

We also visited the grotesque and gigantic modern cathedral, which I was less impressed with. It was built around a statue of the Virgin Mary that apparently produced tears for a week back in the 1950s. It is quite amazing to see grown-ups bowing in homage to a plaster representation of a semi-mythical character, when surely common sense dictates that this was an accident or more likely some kind of confidence trick. But then maybe the Virgin Mary likes to use her magical powers to make inanimate, tacky objects weep for a short period of time, rather than cure sick children or banish world poverty. Anything is possible.

The cathedral, designed to resemble a giant teardrop, is an edifice to ugliness as well as childish gullibility, though I think many children would question the plausibility of this story that seemingly many adults believed unquestioningly. Again I considered what it truly meant to be an adult, because I am sure the people who were venerating this place would consider themselves grown up and a man who laughed at a peeing cherub to be puerile. But in my mind they had an infantile need to deny the true nature of the universe and to escape the harsh realities of life with these reassuring and odd fantasies. And at least I didn't believe that the cherub urinated due to some magic perpetrated by some immortal virgin in the sky.

Much more moving in a religious sense, for my money, was the crypt beneath another old cathedral, which had been one of the gathering places of the first European Christians and has a first-century altar at which it is likely that St Paul preached. Now if I was a Christian, that would be the kind of thing that got my juices going, not a lachrymose statue. Indeed my historian and ex-Christian heart jumped a little in any case when I realised St Paul had probably been in the little grotto in which I was standing. He arguably had more influence on the spread and the philosophy of Christianity even than Jesus himself. He is certainly responsible for the misogyny of the religion and there shouldn't be a man alive who doesn't thank him for that! He kept the bitches in their place, whereas Jesus, the sandal-wearing hippie, clearly thought they should have equality or something. Thank goodness that sense prevailed. All women are good for is crying, preferably in statue form. That's what I and St Paul think and so I was pleased to have been in the same room that he had breathed his hateful words.

That evening was my 100th night of abstinence.

'Are you going to have a drink?' asked Catherine, a slight glint of excitement or possibly hope in her eyes, though I might have been imagining this and projecting my own wishes on to her.

'I'm not sure,' I wavered and then I released my inner pedant. 'The thing is that technically speaking I had my last drink at around midnight on 30 December, so if I were to have a drink now at 8pm, I would actually be falling four or five hours short of the full 100 days. I think, to be sure of the 100-day landmark, I should wait till tomorrow.'

'Right!' said Catherine, smirking, still finding my obsessive pedantry amusing, which was a good sign.

But we didn't need booze. It was a balmy spring evening and the moon was high in the sky and we were in love, for better, for worse.

After a day of turning a bit pink on a deserted and slightly run-down beach just out of town, we returned to our hotel, dressed up in our smartest clothes and went to the poshest restaurant we could find, down Syracuse's windy, cobbled, wing-mirror-destroying alleyways. I still wasn't sure if I should do it. What would I be unleashing? Was my calm and sober Dr Jekyll going to return to the libidinous and uncontrollable Mr Hyde? Or would I just be able to enjoy a glass of wine or two with Catherine, for the first time as a couple?

'Are you going to do it?' she asked, with as much neutrality as she could muster.

'I don't know. I worry that it was the booze that made me the way I used to be. I worry that you won't like the drunk me the way you clearly like the sober me. I'm worried that it will be a slippery slope back to my former life.'

'I know what you're like when you're drunk,' she protested. 'Your entire early courtship of me was via drunken emails. You know, it's totally up to you. It doesn't matter to me if you drink or not. But it looks to me like you'd like to.'

'The people of your planet exhibit much wisdom,' I told her. 'I hope our earth wine can match up to your space ale. And if I don't do this now I think there's a chance I might never do it again.'

And it wasn't drink that was making me unhappy before. I was drinking too much *because* I was unhappy and now life had given me something to make me happy, it was a shame to be in Italy, on holiday, with someone I loved and not make the most of it.

I ordered the second most expensive bottle of wine.

The waiter brought it over, showed me the label. 'Yes, that seems to be wine,' I remarked, a comment that is as much a part of my script as anything my dad says on the phone.

'Would you like to taste the wine, *signore*?'

I felt uncertain and strange. It felt like a long time since I'd tasted alcohol and I wasn't sure about letting it back into my life. But I took a sip. It felt odd and alien, syrupy and potent as it dribbled slowly down my throat. Catherine smiled, perhaps with relief, perhaps merely with excitement at this momentous event.

'*Bella*,' I said, slightly unconvincingly.

'How do you feel?' asked Catherine.

I contemplated. 'The old, funny me is back,' I said, cackling like the devil which had finally won the argument over the disappointed shoulder angel. She laughed.

It was actually a bit of a relief. I was part of humanity again. Nothing much had immediately changed, but I felt more comfortable with myself and was pleased to now be able to hold up a glass of cold, white wine, clink my glass with Catherine's and have a toast with the woman that I loved. I had, I think, earned a drink. I had lasted 100 days and 22 hours. Not that I was counting.

And I didn't turn into a crazy Mr Hyde. I just had half a bottle of nice wine. If I was going to carry on with this healthy lifestyle I needed to be at the point where I could have an occasional drink. Balance was required, and though I've always found that difficult, it was better than veering back and forth from one extreme to the other.

Not just in my diet. I needed balance in my maturity. To keep some of the good things about being childish and not turn into a fogey. To let the inner child out every now and again. Understand which changes I needed to make. Learn to live with who I am. To acknowledge the person I was, but to rein in his excesses. I felt slowly and steadily I was starting to get it right. Or at least less wrong.

I think that hitting 40 had made me aware of what the world expected of me and perhaps much of my unhappiness came from not having hit those imposed targets. But just because I wasn't married and didn't have kids and liked eating Flumpses and talked about cocks for money didn't make me a bad person. It wasn't essential I did those things at a certain time. Not everyone can work in a bank. Having kids is not a necessity to a fulfilling life.

The next day I didn't feel any different. There was no noticeable hangover and no side effects. We went to drink coffee and read books in the sunny main piazza. After a couple of cappuccinos and half a big bottle of water (and no beer at this point, I promise), I was quite desperate for the loo. I walked into the café but could only find the ladies and a disabled toilet. Despite all my work for Scope, I didn't think I had the right to use the disabled one, but the ladies was just a single cubicle and no one was around, so I thought it wouldn't matter if I popped in unnoticed.

So that's what I did. I'd only be a second after all. Nobody would ever know. In any case I had long hair and for once I had shaved (being possibly the only man in the world who has a full shave when I am holidaying but is stubbly the rest of the time) so I reckoned I could front it out.

I couldn't quite work out the lock on the door and though I fiddled with it a bit, and pressed the button, even tinkered with an odd bit of wire sticking out the top, nothing seemed to happen. So I just did the normal unlocked toilet thing and held on to the door with one hand and my old Jack the Dripper with the other while I went about my business. After I was done I washed my hands and, proud of having got away with the crime of the century, reached for the handle and turned it... but it wouldn't turn. I pressed the button, but it didn't do anything. I flicked at the little bit of metal, pushing it this way and then that, but the door, which ironically I thought had been unsecured, was shut fast. I was imprisoned in a small ladies' toilet in a country where I didn't speak the language and, to add insult to injury, I was a man. Surely I would be able to free myself before my shame was discovered or at least to utilise something in the sparse restroom to slowly hack off my genitalia and fashion some kind of make-shift vagina, which would pass muster on a perfunctory examination if my liberator questioned my gender.

The door was not budging and I didn't even have my phone so could not alert Catherine out in the piazza. No amount of pressing or pulling or hoping was going to help. Should I start banging and shouting and if so what was Italian for 'Help, I am stuck in the ladies, and I am a lady and will give you a flash of my vagina to prove it as long as you promise not to look too closely!'?

I had spent most of my time with the phrase book learning how to say, 'I am allergic to condoms,' which I knew I would never need to use, as I was neither allergic to condoms nor wanting to have sex with anyone who only spoke Italian. It just amused me that that was in the phrase book, presumably for amorous tourists who wanted to have an excuse not to 'bag up' with their holiday fling. It's 'Sono allergico ai preservativi' if you are that irresponsible (or actually allergic – yeah right!).

I laughed to myself at my own predicament. A comedian stuck in a lavatory. It would be a fitting hell for me to spend eternity in. A feedline and a punchline all in one. And in a women's lavatory, just in case the original premise was not amusing enough for you.

Oh dear, what can the matter be?

I noticed a small window high above the cistern and considered trying to climb up there, but I wouldn't have fitted through even at the beginning of the holiday. I was either going to have to spend a few hours in there, keeping quiet, in the hope that I would die and be saved the mortification of discovery or I was going to have to be rescued and face the disdain and shame that I deserved.

But how long would it be before I was missed? It could be days, weeks. I thought I should start drinking water out of the toilet bowl straight away just in case. Even though there was a sink in there. I don't trust that the tap water on the continent is totally hygienic. How long would Catherine leave it before she came to search for me? Would she ever think to look in the ladies for me? Or would she assume I had finally got cold feet and run off?

As I rattled the door I heard a woman's voice inquiring in Italian, presumably asking if everything was OK. '*Mi scusi*,' I started, before realising there was nowhere to go with my limited vocabulary, unless I wanted to use the condom thing. I opted instead for 'I am locked in the toilet'. My voice trailed off, but I think she got the drift. '*Una momento*,' she shouted. More than one moment later a man arrived and again I tried to explain what was going on, as if any explanation was required. The man went away and returned and soon the door opened and I saw the disapproving face of a café employee with a key in his hand. How I had managed to lock the door to that extent is beyond me. I thanked him, without looking him in the eye, and shuffled back to my table outside.

Catherine had not even been the slightest bit worried.

On our last full day on the island, we went on a lengthy drive to see the Villa Romana del Casale near Piazza Armerina, which promised the most amazing mosaics in the western world. Last time I'd viewed some Roman mosaics I was at Fishbourne Palace and feeling the first pricks of Cupid's arrows. There was something apt and satisfying about now going to see more Roman art with the woman I was falling for back then.

It was an even longer drive than I had anticipated, partly because we went the scenic route on the way there (though I have to say the non-scenic route on the return was pretty bloody scenic too – Sicily is beautiful) and partly because the main road on the scenic route was inexplicably closed to traffic so I had to use my sat nav to find an even longer and windier way around it. It was three and a half hours of driving and the kind of driving that needed intense concentration, due to the tightness of the turns and the unpredictability of Sicilian drivers. It was a stressful journey, made somewhat more bearable by the breathtaking valleys that appeared over every hill. We passed by orange groves, which had spilled fruit on to the tarmac, which I enjoyed squishing beneath my tyres.

By the time I got to the villa I was exhausted, and annoyed that, as the Lonely Planet guide had predicted, the place was full of coach trips of middle-aged and elderly Europeans, who got in our way on the narrow walkways above the mosaics. Even so, the quality of what we managed to see was almost unbelievable. It made Fishbourne Palace's previously impressive mosaics look like some bathroom tiles that had been smashed into bits and thrown into some mud by a drunken, blind monkey. The intricacy and detail was just astounding.

The parties of old people were doubly annoying when access was limited. In one room we were trapped behind some French people whose guide was giving them every possible detail about a mosaic based on the labours of Hercules (which I was especially interested in given my recent attempts to emulate him). Eventually I got bored of waiting and tried to squeeze past them so I could get out. An elderly man saw me and stood in front of me, pushing his arm in my chest, halting my progress and shouting, '*Non! Groupe. Groupe!*'

'Yeah, I know you're part of a *groupe*,' I told him as I pushed his hand away from my torso. 'That's the problem. Your *groupe* is in my way.'

He didn't seem to understand and poked me again. '*Non! Non! Interdit! Groupe.*'

'Stop saying *groupe*. I know you're in a *groupe*. But being in a *groupe* doesn't mean you own the villa.'

I think the man was worried that I was trying to listen in for free on the guided tour that he had paid for. But I am English. My French, though slightly better than my Italian (though I don't know how to discuss my pretend allergy to latex in French), is still not good enough for me to follow a detailed discussion about mosaics. In any case I was only trying to get out at this point. Yet here I was being poked in the chest by a Frenchman in his sixties. A year before I might have tried to fight him, but I just said, 'I have paid the same as you, probably more because you'll have got a discount for being in a *groupe*, and I am still allowed to look at the mosaics.' And though the Frenchman didn't understand me, he probably now realised that I wasn't French and he stopped poking me and shouting '*groupe*' at me and I got past, so that was some kind of victory. I should have pointed out that it was a Norman, King William the Bad, who had done his best to destroy this villa. So if anyone should leave, it should be the descendants of this naughty man.

Aside from this experience and the general overcrowding I loved being transported back 2000 years. Catherine seemed to be enjoying it all too or at the very least seeing me so joyous and in my element. It was much better having someone to share this all with. We took a photo of ourselves kissing each other in front of what turned out to be the ruined Roman sewers.

I was particularly impressed by one awesome 65-metre-long mosaic, which depicted an elaborate hunting scene and in which, according to my guide book, one of the figures depicted was the arrogant man who had owned this palace (probably Maximianus Herculius or maybe his son). Could he have known that his face would still be glaring out of the tessellated floor, so many centuries after his death? Did this little slice of immortality and fame even matter if he was not around to enjoy it? Was there something significant in the fact that it was luck, rather than anything impressive on his part, that had preserved this work of art? Had a mudslide not covered it all up 1500 years ago then surely all we were now seeing would have been lost.

Even though his wealth and the opulent way he displayed it was a little distasteful, I wished that I had lived in Roman times, been friends with this man and been invited around to see this villa in all its glory. I'd have loved to have gone out on one of those hunting trips or just to have stayed in and got involved in one of the bacchic feasts or depraved orgies that I imagined went on here. I love the Romans, but then I love electricity too and they didn't have that, the idiots, so maybe it's best that I live in the present day. Our modern lives are in many ways as opulent and fortunate as his was.

Being renowned and remembered is one thing, but there's no value in that once you're dead. The flesh and bones that are depicted in the mosaic have long since crumbled into dust. It was another reminder to live life to the full while blood still coursed through my veins.

Even so, I decided that once I've made my millions, I'm going to spend the lot on a gold and diamond mosaic of my own laughing face which I'll have constructed on the floor of my basement. Then with luck it'll still be there in AD 3500 and the archaeologists of the future will be forced to conclude that I was some massively important nobleman or king. Not because I am arrogant or vain, because it's just fun to dick around with people every now and again. Even if you're not around to see the payoff to the joke. And if my dad asked if I was famous I could say, 'Not yet, but you just wait a millennia and a half and then see who everyone is talking about!'

The tragedy of old age is not that one is old, but that one is young.
Oscar Wilde, *The Picture of Dorian Gray*

CHAPTER 18
HAVE A TWINKLE IN YOUR WRINKLE

I was sitting on a throne made of ice, in a room that was also fashioned from frozen water and filled with glistening crystal statues, drinking an unusual-coloured drink from an icy cube-shaped goblet. Had Catherine taken me back to her home planet? Or maybe to her secret ice palace at the North Pole, where the history of her lost alien world is kept in special energy crystals? Had she finally decided to tell me the truth about her extra-terrestrial origins?

No, we were at the Ice Bar in central London, where the whole room is essentially a freezer, in which people come to drink chilled flavoured vodka, while wearing fur-lined coats and mittens provided by the venue and basically pretend they're in an adult, boozy version of Narnia.

This was my surprise 41st birthday treat.

'It's embarrassing when you turn up at a party and find everyone else is wearing the same outfit as you, isn't it?' I joked as I sipped my vodka and ginger beer, surely the most childish drink on the menu.

Catherine somehow looked even more shimmeringly beautiful and regal in these sub-zero temperatures. Or maybe I was just getting off on imagining she was an evil Ice Queen.

'This place is amazing,' I cooed. 'I can't believe I've never heard of it before. This would have been an excellent place to bring one of my 50 dates in 50 days.'

Catherine gave me a disbelieving look and shook her head. 'And you think I don't understand human conventions. Yet it's appropriate for you to discuss your previous dates when you're out on a date with me.' Luckily she found my blundering amusing.

'I was paying you a compliment,' I defended. 'I scoured this town for 50 different things to do and never found this place. And it's just the perfect place for a date. I would definitely have pulled if I'd brought someone here!'

I looked up to check she was still laughing and luckily she was.

'And I'm telling you, sweetheart, that you've definitely pulled too. Anything you want tonight I will do. *Anything*.' I held her gaze meaningfully and then added unnecessary clarification. 'I am including anything sexual.'

Catherine had heard this joke many times before, but still laughed and played her part, 'Yes, I understood that.'

I kissed her. Another ginger-tinged kiss. But this time I didn't feel like I'd explode. I felt safe and secure and content.

'Do you ever miss it?'

'Miss what?'

'Your life before you met me. The freedom. The girls.'

I thought about how to respond. Research conducted by generations of boyfriends has concluded that the correct rejoinder here is to lie. But I decided to go against received wisdom.

'Yes, I suppose I do. Sometimes. I've had the freedom to do whatever I wanted for most of my life and in some ways that was a wonderful thing. And occasionally I wish that I had it again. I'm only human.'

Catherine's face betrayed no anger. Perhaps on her world there is no jealousy.

'But,' I added quickly, just in case on her planet, even infidelity in the mind is punishable by having your head bitten off by your furious lover's powerful mandibles, 'what I have now... what we have now... is so much better. Genuinely. I was miserable and alone most of the time back then, my life was sad and empty. Brilliant, but sad and empty.' I tipped my head to acknowledge the stupidity of my need to undercut the heartfelt with humour and then continued. 'But now I've got you and unbelievably you love me and care about me. And it's made me happy and healthy – look at me, I've lost two fucking stone. I can't tell you how much it means to me that you've gone to all this effort for my birthday. The world seems a fun place to be in when I'm with you. '

'But we've only been together six months. How do you know you'll feel the same this time next year?'

'I don't know, Catherine, not for sure. There's no way of knowing. I don't have any illusions. I've lived enough and loved enough to know something could go wrong. You might wake up one day and realise how brilliant you are and see that you're way too good for me. I know how I've been in the past, swinging between monogamy and debauchery, drunkenness and sobriety, fitness and fatness. Maybe in twelve months I'll be single and fat and be lying on the back seat of a bus having pissed myself.'

'Urgh!'

'But I hope not. I don't want to go back to that. Not that I've pissed myself on a bus, but the other stuff. I want to be with you and I hope I will be. Maybe the mosaic of our love will get smashed up by Normans or destroyed by a tree's roots or maybe it'll survive for ever, getting more beautiful and incredible with each passing year. There's no way of being totally sure. But we're happy now and that's a good start.'

'I'm not sure I entirely understood that.'

'It doesn't matter. I'm just saying I love you. You're the best thing that's ever happened to me. I can't be sure you'll be here with me on my 95th birthday, or my 65th birthday or even my 42nd birthday. I can't even be sure that I'll be here. But I really hope you are.'

'So you're not getting cold feet?' she asked.

'A little bit… but then we have been standing in a freezer for the last 30 minutes.'

*

Last year at this point I had looked back with regret, and forward with terror, but now I seemed to have my place in the grand scheme of things much more in perspective.

Had I grown up?

Shortly before my birthday I had been sitting on the bench outside WHSmith's in Hammersmith and drinking the warm bottle of Diet Coke that I had just bought from the store. 'Sorry the fridge isn't working,' said the lady at the checkout. She seemed genuinely contrite about the refrigerator malfunction. I didn't really mind. It was going to get warm in my stomach in any case. I just needed the liquid and the caffeine hit. I was feeling pretty tired. I had been working hard on my new stand-up show – a year ago it would have been a hangover that had sent me reaching for tepid carbonated beverages.

I had just done a supermarket shop. I put my bags – now more full of fruit and stir-fries than Wotsits and Curlywurlys – on the bench beside me and sipped my room-temperature beverage. I saw an old couple shuffling very slowly towards me. They were probably in their eighties, using sticks to get about, nattering away sweetly. They were assisting each other, working together to overcome their various physical deficiencies. I moved my bags on to the floor. 'Don't worry,' chirped the sweet-natured old man. 'Only one sitting down. Only room for one required.' He was a happy old man. He was infirm and, it became apparent, partially sighted, but he was enjoying his life. I hate the grumpy old men. I like the happy ones. I want to be one of the happy ones. One with a twinkle in my wrinkle.

The man was popping into Smith's to buy a paper while his wife had a rest on the bench. She was looking after the money though and got her change out of her pocket and they tried to count out the necessary two or three coins to buy their tabloid. The man couldn't really see the coins properly and the woman wasn't holding on to them too well. A couple of coins fell on to the floor.

I didn't hesitate to come to their aid, realising that neither of them were in any fit state to get down on their hands and knees.

I could not have bothered or, if I had been inclined, could just have run off with the pound I'd picked up, but that would not have made such a heart-warming denouement to this book.

I sat back down again, with the happy thanks of the oldies ringing in my ear. They joked about their clumsiness and the man said, 'Damn these useless old eyes. Cataracts, don't you know?' But he was speaking with humour and no desire for pity.

Another coin fell to the floor. A less saintly person than me might have shouted, 'Oh, for fuck's sake!' and maybe punched the old woman in the face in an attempt to teach her to be less foolish. But I was down to recover the copper and put it back in the lady's hand. I wanted to try and help them count out the right money, but they looked like they needed to do this themselves.

And sure enough after a couple of minutes the man had his money and shuffled towards the shop to pick up his paper – a paper that I presume his wife would have to read to him. I looked at his bent back and his bandy legs and I wondered how many years I had before I was similarly stricken down by age. Every simple task is like a marathon for our old folk. I felt sad and happy at the same time. He was so chirpy that it was impossible to feel too sorry for him.

He made it there eventually and got to the front of the queue and bought his red-top. He cheerfully chatted with the woman at the till for a couple of minutes. A queue was building up behind him as he bantered, passing the time of day. 'There are people behind you,' his missus chided playfully, but he couldn't hear. 'Hurry up, silly,' she shouted, clearly loving the foolish and happy old man that she had been lucky enough to end up (now almost literally) hitched to.

These were not two lonely old people who had met each other in later life. They had a familiarity and a love for each other that clearly indicated that they had been together for years. And familiarity had not bred contempt for them, just contentment. They understood and forgave each other's faults and helped with each other's physical deficiencies.

The old fella bid the Smith's cashier goodbye and came back to the bench. I was getting up to leave. 'The people behind you must have been getting cross. You were holding them up,' teased the wife. He just smiled and gently mimicked her nagging, by moving his mouth up and down like a fish. She gave him the lightest of taps and laughed.

It was genuinely lovely. And even sweeter was the fact that here were octogenarians still clearly feeling like they were teenagers and doing their best to act like it. Growing up can sometimes mean giving up. They stayed young at heart and were still smiling despite their problems. Because they had each other. Because they could see the positives in life despite their many negatives.

I walked off with my functioning though tired legs, considering what the rest of their day might involve and how long it might take for them to do whatever they were going to do. But also thinking about the rest of my life and who I might be spending it with and how the idea of having that kind of relationship now appealed. The more time you have shared, the easier, I suppose, it is to cope with the ravages of time.

They were coming to the end of their toboggan ride to oblivion, but they seemed to understand that toboggan rides are still fun. You don't have to leave your childishness behind when you're over the hill. Keep hold of your youth, even if it's just a handful of grass from the summit that's come away in your fist, even if the grass is brown and rotten and decayed. Hold on to it for ever.

You don't stop playing because you get old, you get old because you stop playing.

The new stand-up show that I was writing was about my school days and I'd been looking back at my diaries, reflecting on what the teenage me would make of the 40-something me. Would he be proud that I had such an uncomformist and childish life or ashamed that I hadn't even got married yet? His ambitions knew no boundaries, imagining that he might grow up to be like a mixture of Keats, Gandhi and Jesus. Had I let him down?

I hoped that he would be pleased and amazed that I was making my living as a writer and a comedian. I think that underneath his pretensions that was all he really wanted.

One diary entry really made me laugh. It read, '*I'm glad I'm writing this, because in a few years' time I'll be able to look back and hate myself for being immature.*'

Then the me of the past addresses the me of now. He reaches through time to leave me a message and writes, '*Well, Rich, I'd just like to point out to you. I know I'm being immature, but I enjoy it. And I don't want to grow up too fast.*'

If only he knew how long he'd keep that up for.

So had I grown up?

A little bit perhaps. But not entirely. I'd made some significant changes, but for the most part I had just learned to live with what I was. And to appreciate how fortunate I was and to stop feeling sorry for myself.

I certainly wasn't leaving my inner child behind. I was trying to shed the bad things that made one childish – the selfishness, the sulking, the greed and the tantrums – and try to retain the good – the playfulness, the wonder, the rebellion against the pretensions of the premature maturions.

You become an adult when you realise that the world doesn't revolve around you, when you understand you have responsibility to others. It seems to me that many of the people who consider themselves to be mature have not yet understood this. How many 'mature' adults still childishly want to possess everything without sharing it, even if they have more than they will ever need? How many 'mature' adults believe there is a big man in the sky watching everything they do or that when they die they will live for ever in a fairyland paradise? How many 'mature' adults try to resolve their differences not by talking things through and trying to understand both sides of an argument, but by using bullying and force to get what they want?

My most important realisation was that none of us ever actually grow up. Inside, we are all still children: stupid, gullible, terrified, puerile children. Some of us, like celebrities at a garden party pretending to be unfazed and blasé, are just better at hiding it than others. Many of us feel we have to pretend to be grown-ups because that is what is expected of us, maybe some of us even convince ourselves that we are. But somewhere in there is a child that gets scared of a bump in the dark and will laugh at a cherub weeing in a fountain and who is excited when a flying fish jumps out of the sea.

As if to illustrate this point, as I was writing this book I was on a train home after recording a panel show in Wales. Because I have just been on television I have been given first-class train tickets, paid for by the broadcaster. The basic concept of first class is to keep riff-raff like me out of the sight of the swanky businessmen who might want to do proper work while commuting. But by a twist of fate, because I get paid for being childish, here I was among them. I found myself sitting opposite a businessman who had been on the phone all morning trying to make some deals. He eyed me suspiciously when he sat down, but didn't quite have the balls to check with the conductor whether I should actually be there.

He took a business call and was being all sensible and serious and saying things like 'Their loss is our gain' with utter commitment and satisfaction and no sense of embarrassment. He described some of his competitors as being like 'blind men in a room discussing colours'. I presume he was trying to malign them with this simile, saying they had no idea what they were talking about. But to my mind I can think of little more interesting than getting a group of blind people into a room and making them discuss colours using nothing but their imagination. It would surely make for a magical and poetical happening that might tell us a lot about the human condition. But this businessman was not interested in that. He was only interested in business and closing his deals and making money.

The thing that really set him apart from me and which clearly demonstrated that there is a child within us all, which some of us choose to repress, was when whoever was on the other end of the phone suggested a possible associate for them to work with on their latest project.

'What's his name?' asked my bullish travelling companion. He blanched slightly and repeated what his colleague had just said. 'Will Lee? His name is Will Lee?' For a second he looked like he might revert back to the six-year-old boy that is surely hidden somewhere inside the recesses of everyone's brain and openly snigger. After all, the man who he was being asked to work with was called Will Lee. Which sounds like 'willy'. You'd think if your name was Will Lee you might insist on being called William.

There was a definite pause as the businessman tried to keep his composure and remember he was in the middle of an important call possibly worth millions to him and his company and that shrieking, 'Will Lee? That sounds like willy!' might ruin everything and destroy the facade.

I would definitely have done that if I was him, which is why I will never hold down a real job. But I know that he was having to resist the temptation to mock that bloody idiot, Will Lee. Might he get away with a risqué, 'Well, he sounds like a cock!' Best not risk it. Maturity and adult expectations meant that instead he said, 'Is he the kind of fella we can work with?' (which I suppose might have been a very tangential masturbation reference, but I don't think so) and carried on with his serious yet ultimate entirely phoney business chat. Like a desperate contestant on *The Apprentice*, he was projecting a persona of seriousness and professionalism that he thought was expected of him and maybe he'd been doing it for so long that he actually believed this is what he was like. But when a man doesn't openly snigger on discovering that someone is called Will Lee or I. P. Freely or Stewart Wee then something inside him has died.

POSTSCRIPT

GRENADA? NO, SHE WENT OF HER OWN ACCORD

'Happy Christmas, Mum!' I instinctively bellowed into my phone, even though the line was unbelievably clear.

'Rich! It's Richard!' she shrieked to the assembled throng.

'Richy. Richelieu. Richmond Park!' bellowed my father.

'Are you having a good day?' Mum squealed excitedly.

'Well, the sun is hot, I'm standing on a white sandy beach, looking at the green waves crashing on the shore and I'm drinking a piña colada. But apart from that it's fine. How's Cheddar?'

'Cold!' laughed Mum. 'You're a jammy beggar!'

'You should be here,' shouted my nephew Andy from the periphery. He was cross with me for missing the big day, but I couldn't feel too guilty.

'Maybe if you bought me better presents I'd be there, you little scrotum. Farting slippers, I ask you!' I retorted.

'Richard!' chided Mum. 'Is Catherine OK?'

'She's brilliant.'

'And you're having a good time?'

'The best.'

'So you're happy?' Mum asked.

I chuckled and a slight tear welled in my eye as I was able to say with complete honesty, 'Yes, Mum, I'm happy.'

'He says he's happy, everyone,' Mum relayed and an ironic cheer went up.

'I should bloody well hope so!' my sister grouched.

'That's all very well,' said Dad, 'but is he famous yet?'

I allowed myself a laugh for once. After all, it was Christmas.

*

I had kept my last Christmas's promise to Catherine. Now a year into our relationship, we were spending Christmas and New Year 2008 together on a tropical island – as it turned out it was Grenada. We'd booked into a small hotel right on the beach in the middle of a secluded bay and scarcely left the place for the entire two weeks, preferring to move in a triangle between our room, the beach and the restaurant. It had been a hectic year and it was wonderful to just rest and eat and drink and spend time together.

When New Year arrived it turned out to be a little different than the last one. Then I'd been alone in Shepherd's Bush, drinking camomile tea, planning a new regime of sobriety and hard work, wondering whether I'd lose weight (check), whether I'd have another Edinburgh show under my belt (check), whether I would win Catherine's heart (check), whether I'd have fathered a child (nope). Not that I know of anyway!!! Ha ha ha. Actually, for once in my life I could be certain that I hadn't done that... well, along with the first nineteen years of my existence, when it would have been pretty remarkable too.

Now I was with my girlfriend in the Caribbean, drinking wine and feeling rather content with my lot in life.

We'd been keeping ourselves to ourselves and enjoying each other's company, without really trying to make any new friends. A couple of our fellow guests had invited us to join them that night when they were heading into town to celebrate in a bar and watch a fireworks display, but we resolved to have a quiet time together, eat some nice food and see the New Year in with a bottle of wine on the beach.

I ate lobster tail followed by banana flambé and drank coconut and rum cocktails. If the gods had any sense they'd chuck out the ambrosia and nectar and go for what I had. It was divine. Then as midnight approached we headed to the beach. No one was there but us.

The night sky was clear and the view of the heavens was breathtaking. These days it is very hard to find anywhere in the world where you can get a clear look at the starscape without having most of it blotted out by light pollution. But this night there were thousands and thousands of stars, bright and clear and actually twinkling in the black sky. In my memory there used to be nights like this in the UK in my childhood, but you don't get them any more. It was majestic and awesome and now it felt like the universe had been created for us, for this one moment.

Though I was grown up enough to know that it hadn't, which took the pressure off, to be honest.

And there was Catherine beside me, more wonderful than creation itself. It was all I had hoped and dreamed of a year before and somehow my dreams had come true. I knew it was still early days and I didn't want to get carried away with it all, but I had had the best of times with her and was hopeful of many more to come.

We were alone on the beach, the waves crashing in on to the shore, searching out our toes. Just us and nature and a bottle of rosé. Then one of the hotel cats came down to see what we were up to. And you know what curiosity did to the cat.

Nothing in this instance.

I think he thought we were crazy. He sat with his back to the waves and to the sky, refusing to acknowledge the coming event, apparently unconcerned by the approaching waves – my head forwards, his back, like some kind of Sphinxy Janus (except with the head of a cat and the body of a man).

I couldn't think of a more perfect place to see in the New Year or a more perfect person to be with – certainly a lot better than being on my own in my lounge in Shepherd's Bush, listening to other people's party poppers. Rather diametrically opposed book-ends to the year 2008.

Looking at the stars, we were observing the distant past, stand-ing on the beach with the warm breeze on our faces and the sand beneath our toes we were firmly fixed in the present, and some-where in front of us, the first wave of 2009 was already heading towards us, unstoppable, inevitable – the future. Then behind it the next wave, the future ticking onwards in roughly six-second intervals and there was nothing we could do to stop it. Somewhere out there was the wave that would hit the shore as we left the beach for the last time. Somewhere the wave that would break as I turned 42 in July. Somewhere (hopefully thousands of miles over the horizon) was the wave that would strike as I breathed my last breath. Waves would be hitting that beach in 100 years' time when everyone I knew would be gone and in 10,000 years when pretty much everything I had witnessed would have dissolved.

But it made me feel good to understand my insignificance, to know that I was there right now, in this moment. Seeing the wave that was hitting the shore now. Feeling fortunate to have been the sperm who made it through against those odds.

Life was not a hill and I was not over it. The T-shirts have it right – Life's a beach. And we're standing on it, powerless, a load of stupid Cnuts, as the waves crash against the shore and the wind blows in our faces and the planet and the stars spin ever onwards. The longer we stand here the more weathered we become, but the more we get to see, the more we understand our insignificance in the grand scheme of things, the more we appreciate our fortune at being here at all. The more waves we see.

And sometimes there are flying fish.

I wasn't old. Not compared to the sea or the sand or the stars. I was nothing but a baby gawping in wonder and awe.

Midnight came with a kiss and with wine, two things missing from the picture last year, and the fireworks created a dim glow in the distance over the hill. But we'd made the right choice. Fireworks seemed tawdry compared to what nature was giving for free. As if to emphasise that point, a shooting star blazed through the sky. A bit more impressive than a bottle rocket.

I can't imagine I will experience a better new year's arrival in my life and it's certainly the best of (admittedly quite a miserable selection) the 42 new years I'd been around to see.

Then we went back to our room and watched a film called *Wanted* and if anything can snap you back into the mundanity and misery of existence then it is that (if you want to see a movie that is a cross between *Fight Club* and *The Matrix*, but much,

much worse than either of them, then this is a film for you). We lay beside each other, my arm around her waist, watching the preposterous movie, laughing and merrily pointing out its inadequacies and inconsistencies. Mere mortals gleefully frittering away a few more precious minutes of our lives.

But for a few moments, out on that beach, we had been gods with our fingers touching the seams of creation.

CONVERSATION 3

Barney, age seven and three-quarters

In the spring of 2009 I was touring the country again and staying with my friends Jeremy and Deborah in Newcastle. They have two young kids, a seven-year-old boy, Barney, and his shy younger sister, Nell. She wasn't quite sure about me. At breakfast she made herself a small hide out of cereal boxes which blocked me out or her in depending on which way you look at it. She would occasionally suspiciously peep over the top, but mainly remained hidden, though the silliness of such a construct made us both giggle, so we still shared something. Laughter is a wonderful thing and though it can't bring down barriers, it can go over them and still be a mutual experience.

After breakfast I asked Barney, 'What's your favourite subject at school?'

'History!' he immediately responded.

'History? Really? I studied history at Oxford University, the poshest university in the world and thus know every single historical fact that there has ever been!'

'Wow!' he remarked, believing me unquestioningly. Which was lucky for me as the most minimal research on his part would reveal that I had wasted my three years of higher education eating crisps, performing comedy and learning next to nothing.

'Wow is right,' I brazenly continued. 'Go on, ask me any question about anything in history and I'll be able to tell you the answer.'

'OK,' he replied, excited by the challenge, creasing his forehead as he thought of a suitably hard query. 'What year was Guy Fawkes born in?'

'Ha ha, easy!' I bluffed. I knew the Gunpowder Plot was in 1605 and guessed that he had been around about 30 at the time, so confidently delivered my complete guess. 'Guy Fawkes was born in 1574!'

'Oh!' he replied, accepting that as definitive fact, nodding with interest. I had thought he might have asked me something he had known, to test my claims, but he was just interested in finding out something unknown.

His trust was endearing, but I decided I should give him the real answer, just in case he believed me his whole life and then ended up on Who Wants To Be a Millionaire and that was his question and he then blamed me for getting it wrong.

Thanks to Wikipedia we have instant access to every fact in the world (and I trust it implicitly like a seven-year-old). It revealed that Guy Fawkes was born in 1570, so I had been close. I knew some facts about Fawkes, not from university, of course, but from a comedy history sketch show that I wrote.

'Did you know, Barney, that when Guy Fawkes was discovered in the cellars of the Houses of Parliament and challenged, he said his name was John Johnson? How pathetic and unimaginative is that? "I'm John... er... Johnson." I bet you could come up with a better pseudonym than that. Go on, I'll be the guard and you be Guy Fawkes, OK?'

'Yes.'

'What are you doing down here with those barrels of gunpowder?' I bellowed in Barney's laughing face.

'Nothing!' he innocently replied.

'What's your name?'

'It's er... Mike Thompson,' he improvised.

'Brilliant!' I told him. 'Much more believable that John Johnson. If Guy Fawkes had been as sharp as you he would probably have gotten away with it!'

Looking through Wikipedia, I discovered something I didn't know – that Fawkes had cheated the hangman by jumping off the scaffold before he could be hanged, thus breaking his own neck.

'That wasn't much of an escape though, was it?' remarked Barney. 'He avoided being killed by killing himself.'

'At least he had taken his fate into his own gunpowder-encrusted hands, though. And look,' I said, pointing at the computer screen, 'he also managed to avoid the rather gruesome

*fate of being drawn and quartered. Can I tell Barney what that
means? It's pretty horrible,' I asked his dad.*

Jeremy said it was OK.

*'Right, well, they drag you to the place of execution on a
wooden frame, hang you by the neck until you are nearly dead!'*

Barney gave out an amused but disgusted little gasp.

*'Then they disembowel you, cut out all your insides and emas-
culate you, which is… something a bit worse and… oh God…
burn all your guts in front of your eyes. Sick!'*

*Barney was chuckling along, enjoying how gruesome it was in
a way that only kids can.*

*'Then the body is divided into four parts, then beheaded.
Which is just unnecessarily nasty if you ask me.'*

'Yes, it is,' Jeremy noted, perhaps regretting his permission.

*But Barney took it quite matter-of-factly, merely satisfying his
historical curiosity. At that age, I suppose, a story is just a story.
The more ghastly the better.*

*'Do you think it's right to kill someone like that?' Jeremy
asked Barney.*

'Yes, because he had done a bad thing.'

*'But if you hurt and kill someone, doesn't that make you just
as bad as the person you're killing?'*

*'And,' I added, 'Guy Fawkes didn't even kill anyone. Even
though he wanted to.'*

*Barney thought about it. 'Yes, I think they should just be
locked up in a dungeon, not hunged, drawn and quartered.'*

*I was impressed that it was possible to have a discussion about
morality with someone so young and Barney spoke a lot more
sense than many adults on this issue as well as showing an
admirable ability to consider the facts and change his mind.*

*'Having your head chopped off wouldn't be so bad, would it?'
I said, but Barney disagreed.*

*'It would be really bad. You'd have no head. How would
you eat?'*

*'That's a good point and well made, but don't dismiss it out
of hand. If someone chopped off your head your mum and dad*

could put it on the wall, like they used to in the olden days with stags.'

Barney shrieked with laughter. 'Imagine coming into a room to see someone had stuck your head on the wall!' he said.

'Well, you wouldn't be able to see it, if your head was on the wall.'

'No, you'd have no head. You'd be walking in and bumping into things, saying, "Where's my head? Give me back my head!"'

Barney got up and blundered around as if he was headless.

'And your head would be on the wall,' I continued. 'Saying, "Hey stupid, I'm over here. On the wall. Why can't you see me? I can see you."'

We were both laughing now at this stupid idea.

'You're pretty funny, Barney,' I said. 'You and me should write comedy together. We're on about the same level. You're a bit more mature perhaps, but I could raise my game.'

Finally I truly understood that having the mind of a seven-year-old was a compliment, not a slur. Barney was unfettered and imaginative and his ideas were silly and wonderful, but he was sharp as a tack too.

'You're not like the other grown-ups,' he observed with incredible insight. 'You're silly, like a kid.'

'How do you know I'm not a kid?'

'Because you're too big!' exclaimed Barney.

'I just ate a lot of Flumpses.'

'And you've got a beard and kids don't have beards. But you act like a kid.'

'It's weird, isn't it?'

'Maybe you look like an adult on the outside, but inside there's a kid like me, operating you, like a robot.'

'That is probably the most perceptive thing anyone has ever said about me. That would explain a lot.'

'Have you got kids?' asked Barney.

'No, have you?'

'No,' he chortled, 'I'm too young. Why haven't you got kids?'

'I just never quite got round to it, but I'm thinking about

having one. So what I'm doing is talking to as many kids as possible so I can find out what they're like, so I can tell if I want one.'

'Good idea,' he said.

'I had worried that children were annoying,' I told him, 'but you don't seem annoying at all. You're a pretty good advert for the whole children idea.'

'Thanks. But be careful, not all kids are like me. A lot of children are annoying,' he warned.

'What if I got an annoying one?' I asked.

'That'd be bad.'

We agreed that it was maybe too big a risk to take.

'In any case,' I told him, 'we've really got to think about the polar bears.'

He nodded sagely and then did a perfect double take.

'Huh?'

ACKNOWLEDGEMENTS

I would like to give especial thanks to my editor Jake Lingwood who not only realised there was a book to be written about this ridiculous year, but also gave invaluable advice on how the story should be told.

But respect is also due to Ali Nightingale and everyone at Ebury, James Taylor, Jon Thoday, Alice Russell and the rest of the staff at my evil management, Avalon, Rob Sedgebeer for running my website (www.richardherring.com), C.W., Emma Kennedy, Al Murray, Stewart Lee, Vivian Eliot and the good folk at SCOPE and Ingfield school and everyone who gave me permission to write about them, especially Buster, Scarlett and Barney. And let's not forget the people who didn't give me permission to write about them – cheers for making my 41st year so memorable and apologies for being a bit of a prick. Recognition is also due to Andrew Collins, though his only input was to suggest the title 'Immature, Cheddar' which we immediately discounted, but still. Thanks to my mum and dad who I have unfairly lampooned in this book and to all my family, who I love very much (even my dad, there, happy now?), particularly my wonderful grandma, Doris Hannan, who is just the best.

Happy 99th birthday.